Central America

CENTRAL AMERICA
Crisis and Adaptation

Edited by
Steve C. Ropp
and
James A. Morris

University of New Mexico Press
Albuquerque

**IUPUI
UNIVERSITY LIBRARIES**
COLUMBUS CENTER
COLUMBUS, IN 47201

Library of Congress Cataloging in Publication Data

Main entry under title:

Central America: crisis and adaptation.

  Bibliography: p.
  Includes index.
  1. Central America—Politics and government—1979—
—Addresses, essays, lectures. 2. Central America—
History—Addresses, essays, lectures. I. Ropp, Steve C.
II. Morris, James A., 1938–
F1439.5.C454 1984   972.8   84–2273
ISBN 0-8263-0745-0
ISBN 0-8263-0746-9 (pbk.)

© 1984 by the University of New Mexico Press.
All rights reserved.
Manufactured in the United States of America.
Library of Congress Catalog Card Number 84-2273.
International Standard Book Number
0-8263-0745-0 (cloth).
0-8263-0746-9 (paper).
Second paperback printing 1985

To
Jo-Carol Ropp
and
Yvonne Garcia

Contents

Tables, Figures, and Maps   xi
Preface   xiii
Introduction   xv

1. The Setting   1
    Land and Peoples
    Historical Background
        Colonial Period: 1500–1800
        Independence: 1808–1839
        Liberal Reformism: 1870–1930
        Dictatorship and Political Order: 1930–1945
        The Postwar Period: 1945–present

2. Social Change and Political Revolution: The Case of Nicaragua
    Stephen M. Gorman   33
    Man, Land, and Politics in Nicaragua
    The Evolution of Nicaraguan Dependency
    Rising Social Mobilization after 1950
    Government and Opposition: 1967–1978
    Revolution and Consolidation
    Conclusion

3. El Salvador: The Roots of Revolution
    Tommie Sue Montgomery   67
    The Oligarchy
    The Military
    The Church

The Revolutionary Organizations
   The October Coup, or The Regime's Last Chance
   Influence from Outside: The United States
   The Future of the Regime

4. Origins of the Crisis of the Established Order in
   Guatemala
   Julio Castellanos Cambranes   119
   Colonial Legacies
   Independence
   Coffee Culture and Land
   The Liberals and Barrios
   Frustrated Reforms, 1940s
   Prelude to Rebellion
   Unstable Order

5. Representative Constitutional Democracy in Costa
   Rica: Adaptation to Crisis in the Turbulent 1980s
   John A. Booth   153
   Introduction: Democracy, Stability, and Political Culture
   The History of Costa Rica's Constitutional Democracy
   Political Culture
      Mass and Elite Values and Behaviors
      Political Resources and Constraints
      State and Economy
      Political Parties
      Pressure Groups and Demand-Making
   Policy Problems Facing Costa Rica in the 1980s
      Economic Problems
      Political Problems
   Conclusion

6. Honduras: The Burden of Survival in Central
   America
   James A. Morris   189
   The Setting
   Political History
   Nature of the Crisis
      Political Aspects
      Economic Aspects
      External Aspects

Adaptation and Survival
      Political Aspects of Adaptation
      External Aid and Adaptation
      Adaptation within the Context of the Regional Crisis
   Conclusions

7. Leadership and Political Transformation in Panama:
   Two Levels of Regime Crisis
   Steve C. Ropp   227
      Introduction
      The Country and Its People
      Historical Perspective on Political Crises in Panama
      Structural Conditions and Crisis: Panama Compared with
         Other Central American Countries
      The 1968 Coup and the Structure of the Resulting Regime
      Leadership and Regime Crisis
      External Influences on Crisis and Adaptation
      Conclusions

8. Conclusions   257

Notes on Bibliography   273
Selected Bibliography on Central America   281
Note on Editors and Contributors   297
Index   299

Tables, Figures, and Maps

Tables

Table 1.1	Central America Land and Population Data	6
Table 1.2	Contribution of Five Primary Products to Total Value of Merchandise Exports	22
Table 1.3	Central American Intraregional Trade	23
Table 1.4	External Public Debt Outstanding	24
Table 1.5	Distribution of Agricultural Land Holdings	26
Table 1.6	Population and Urban Population	27
Table 3.1	Structure of the Salvadoran Left	91
Table 4.1	Electoral Results in Guatemala	136
Table 4.2	Agricultural Census in Guatemala	137
Table 5.1	Characteristics of Costa Rican Presidencies	160
Table 5.2	Election Participation in Costa Rica	162
Table 5.3	Political Activities of Costa Rican Family Heads	166
Table 5.4	Selected Social Indicators for Costa Rica	171
Table 6.1	National Elections in Honduras	200
Table 6.2	Chief Executives and Changes of Government in Honduras	202
Table 6.3	U.S. Aid to Honduras	211
Table 7.1	Primary Export Products in the Total Value of Merchandise Exports in Panama	239

Table 7.2 Inflation and Economic Growth Indices in
          Panama   240
Table 8.1 Factors Associated with Adaptation   265

Figures

Figure 6.1 U.S. Aid to Honduras   218
Figure 7.1 Gross Domestic Product at Market Prices
            in Panama   244

Maps

Caribbean Basin and Central America   2
Nicaragua   34
El Salvador   68
Guatemala   120
Costa Rica   154
Honduras   190
Panama   228

Preface

Where the idea began is difficult to say—but for some time a book on Central America has been needed that would attempt to explain the crisis of the 1980s, that would explore the manner in which those embattled countries have adapted, or have failed to adapt, to internal and external pressures; a book that might contribute to a greater and more appreciative understanding of Central America by North Americans, whether they be students, scholars, policymakers, or concerned citizens.

The editors' paths first crossed in 1974 through a mutual interest in the region and through work that each had done on Honduran politics. During a year when both of us were teaching at New Mexico State University, the relationship broadened into one characterized by collegiality, friendship, and mutual respect. In the wake of the 1978 Nicaraguan crisis that eventually led to the overthrow of Anastasio Somoza Debayle, we organized a small Central American Working Group in Las Cruces, which drew upon the talents and perspectives of colleagues such as José García, Gene Mueller, and Ray Sadler. A workshop was sponsored in December 1978 and another during the following year, relying on generous support from the College of Arts and Sciences at New Mexico State University, El Paso Community College, and the University of Texas at El Paso. By 1981, the central ideas shaping this book had taken form, and initial versions of the chapters were presented in 1982 at the annual meeting of the Rocky Mountain Council on Latin American Studies.

Along the path toward completion of this book, there has been a note of regret—the death of our colleague Stephen M. Gorman.

Steve was a young scholar who had already established his reputation as an expert on Peruvian politics when he turned his attention to Central America. His energies, creativeness, and scholarly achievements will be missed by us all. While his chapter on Nicaragua is surely not the last of his works that will eventually appear in print (he had almost completed an edited book on leftist opposition movements), we would like to present his essay as a lasting memorial to his scholarship.

In addition to our chapter authors, many other individuals have contributed in various ways toward making this book possible. We wish to thank the outside readers for their astute and supportive criticisms. Thomas Walker, the nation's foremost expert on Nicaraguan politics, was particularly helpful in this regard. Steve Chilton of New Mexico State University suggested ways in which to clarify both theme development and policy perspectives. We owe an eternal debt of gratitude to David O. Wise of Texas Women's University for his expertise and willingness to translate the chapter on Guatemala.

Editor David Holtby of the University of New Mexico Press guided us through the complicated phases of editorial decision making and production. He was receptive to the idea when it was initially presented in 1981, and he stuck with us through thick and thin over the following three years. Finally, our deepest thanks go to Jo-Carol Ropp and Yvonne García, to whom this volume is dedicated. Their love, coupled with a willingness to tolerate our outrageously high phone bills, helped make this volume possible.

Introduction

> Blood of Abel. The war trumpets
> Fraternal struggles; noise, horrors;
> the standards wave, the grapeshot kills,
> and the emperors wear purple.
>
> (Rubén Darío, "Song of the Blood")

During the past half-decade, Central America has moved from the extreme periphery of the global conflict arena toward a more central position. Tensions between classes and races that existed for centuries have been released in an orgy of violence that does full justice to Nicaraguan poet Rubén Darío's description of fraternal conflict. As the violence has intensified and expanded regionally, armies have been mobilized by both the forces that oppose drastic socioeconomic change and those who welcome it. The clash of these armies has led in turn to the creation of a vast pool of refugees who have fled not only into neighboring Central American countries to escape the fighting but to more distant lands such as Mexico and the United States.

In Nicaragua, a ruthless dictator is overthrown in 1979 and replaced by a government identified with the left. Neighboring El Salvador is rent by a civil war that pits right-wing death squads and the military against a growing army of guerrillas. To the north, another guerrilla army composed increasingly of Indian peasants challenges the authority of the existing regime. Even those countries that have attempted to avoid being drawn into the conflict have become deeply involved. Thousands of people from El Salvador and Nicaragua seek refuge in Honduras, and increased right- and left-wing activities there threaten the country's fragile democratic regime. Refugees also pour by the thousands into Costa Rica, exacerbating political and economic conditions there. Meanwhile, a nervous group of military and civilian leaders in Panama conduct maneuvers along the Costa Rican border to warn against further regional expansion of the conflict arena.

As the conflict spreads and intensifies, it becomes internationalized. Global and hemispheric powers pressure Central American leaders to bolster their commitment to the "right" cause. At the same time, Central Americans pressure these powers to defend their regional interests. The result is a rapid proliferation of military and economic activities aimed at shoring up existing regimes of both right- and left-wing proclivity. Cubans enter Nicaragua in substantial numbers to work on a wide variety of economic and military projects. The United States sends military advisers to Honduras and conducts major maneuvers there, in part to insure that the existing government survives. Throughout the region, the superpowers and their hemispheric allies seek a clearer definition of regime loyalties. The result is polarization and a hardening of regional battle lines, a political stance that led to the dispatch of U.S. troops to the tiny Caribbean country of Grenada in October 1983.

Until recently, Central America remained a series of footnotes within the broader narrative of U.S. diplomatic history, rarely arousing the attention of policy makers, and even more rarely capturing the fancy of the North American public. Only during periods of upheaval or overt crisis have Central American events penetrated the public consciousness. In each instance, these events have been perceived as a bothersome irritant within the U.S. sphere of strategic interests. Revolutionary changes occurring in Guatemala were effectively reversed through covert action in 1954. In 1969, a military conflict between El Salvador and Honduras, which disrupted commercial relations in the region, was brought to an end. Friction over the status of the Panama Canal led to increasing tension between the United States and Panama, which subsided after ratification of the new treaty in 1978.

Crisis conditions exist objectively and also, just as importantly, when we believe them to exist.[1] While many of the historical conditions affecting Central America can and have been described in crisis terms, it was not until the early 1980s that a consensus began to develop concerning the magnitude and importance of developments in the area. In the United States, the view that a regional crisis existed resulted from increasing violence and political tension that culminated in the emergence of a new left-wing government (Nicaragua's) and strengthened guerrilla movements in El Salvador and Guatemala. These developments were perceived, particularly by high officials in the Reagan administration, as directly affecting U.S. security interests.

In the series of events that encouraged the general perception that a regional crisis existed, none was more important than the overthrow of the government of Anastasio "Tachito" Somoza in Nicaragua. The beginning of the end for the Somoza dynasty came in January 1978, when Pedro Joaquín Chamorro, the internationally known editor of a major opposition newspaper, was assassinated in the streets of Managua. It was widely assumed that Somoza was responsible for the assassination, and this event touched off a number of mass demonstrations and strikes.

Somoza's refusal to step down from the presidency before the end of his term in 1981 led to a further series of violent confrontations in the late summer and fall of 1978. On August 22, members of the Sandinista Liberation Front seized the National Palace and held some fifteen hundred legislators and government bureaucrats hostage. Somoza was forced to make a number of highly embarrassing concessions to the guerrillas that demonstrated the regime's vulnerability. This successful guerrilla operation triggered, in turn, a series of mass uprisings in major Nicaraguan cities. The brutality with which the National Guard treated the urban insurgents fueled the fire of domestic and international contempt for the regime.

During the fall of 1978, the struggle became international in scope with enemies of the Somoza dictatorship such as the governments of Cuba, Panama, and Venezuela supplying arms to the Sandinista guerrillas and the United States attempting to play a mediating role. International opposition to the dynasty was broadened to include a cross section of the population. Bloody battles followed in which an estimated fifty thousand Nicaraguans lost their lives. It all ended on July 19, 1979, when the victorious Sandinistas marched into Managua and took control of the national government.

The importance of the fall of Somoza cannot be overestimated in setting a crisis tone throughout the region. The dynasty had endured for forty-four years. In 1936, Anastasio "Tacho" Somoza had used the National Guard (which had been established with the help of the U.S. Marines) to overthrow the elected government of Juan Sacasa. Because of the historical backing of the United States, which included large amounts of military aid and training for the Guard, the dynasty was widely believed to be a permanent Central American fixture. Its collapse led to the perception on the part of U.S. policy makers that the collapse of other regional governments closely tied to the United States might not be out of the question. And from the standpoint of the Central American left, it demonstrated that the latent social and economic crisis conditions that they had pointed to for so long were at last beginning to manifest themselves in overt political struggle.

Compounding this perception of crisis were events in El Salvador that followed closely on the heels of Somoza's fall. Although the roots of the Salvadoran crisis run deep, and numerous manifestations of its existence can be found in previous decades, it was in the fall of 1978 that events there began to receive sustained international attention. On October 15, the government of General Carlos Humberto Romero was overthrown by a group of young army officers who promised to address the country's serious social and economic problems.

The cabinet established by the new military *junta* contained a broad cross section of civilian and military figures who represented middle-of-the-road positions. Yet they were perceived as "radicals" in the context of El Salvador's historically repressive political system. The government's efforts to terminate official terrorism, to institute an agrarian reform program, and to restore democratic institutions were met by incredulity and opposition by groups on both the far right and left. Under the pressure of escalating violence, this government collapsed on January 3, 1980, and was replaced by a more conservative junta in which the Christian Democratic Party played a larger role.

The new junta was no more successful than the old in establishing a middle ground of economic and social policies around which a national political consensus could be erected. Although the United States began to devote serious attention to the attempt to bolster the position of the junta and succeeded in lobbying for a new agrarian reform law, the violence escalated. Official terror continued and a number of moderate political leaders were assassinated, including Archbishop Oscar Arnulfo Romero.

During 1981 guerrilla activities increased, and the violence reached levels comparable to those in Nicaragua. The conflict became internationalized with outside powers such as the United States, West Germany, France, Mexico, Cuba, and Venezuela attempting to sway the course of events. United States efforts to encourage a "moderate" solution took a turn for the worse in March 1982, when national elections resulted in the ascension to power of a new government dominated by right-wing groups. While the Falkland Islands conflict and other global events briefly eclipsed the Salvadoran crisis, the political situation there remained polarized and continued to deteriorate.

The ongoing conflict in El Salvador had the effect of further encouraging the view on the part of both Central Americans and outside observers that the crisis was indeed regional and enduring. Events in Nicaragua might have been interpreted as short term and relatively unique had not violence in El Salvador escalated. The serious difficulties experienced by a second long-lived Central American regime tended to confirm the broader perspective. After all, the structure of Salvadoran politics had not significantly changed since the early 1930s, when the military led by Maximiliano Hernández Martínez overthrew a progressive civilian government.

The overthrow of Somoza in 1979 and the rapidly escalating violence in El Salvador were the two primary catalytic events encouraging a broadly held perspective that the region was in crisis. It was through the lens of these two events that observers began to minutely examine developments in surrounding countries. Was Costa Rican democracy as stable as recent history would suggest, or was the country experiencing a latent structural crisis which would soon manifest itself in escalating violence? Was Honduras the "oasis of peace" that outside observers and local boosters claimed it to be and, if so, what unique features contributed to the Honduran ability to avoid crises? How did the origins of the escalating violence in Guatemala compare with their roots in Nicaragua and El Salvador? What specific conditions had so far allowed Panama to preserve a certain measure of domestic tranquillity?

Although these catalytic events have heightened U.S. public awareness of developments in Central America, confusion and uncertainty characterize the national debate. The leftist drift of the Nicaraguan government, the rapidly disintegrating Salvadoran regime, the ominous trend toward violence in Guatemala, the death of Panamanian strongman Omar Torrijos, coupled with less visible but nonetheless significant deterioration of the Costa Rican and Honduran economies have raised the specter of further violence, drastic social change, and the potential undermining of U.S. influence within the Caribbean basin. Yet the public is far from united in its belief that such social change, even if brought about through violent means, is undesirable or that it threatens vital national interests. Perhaps the clearest indication of this lack of consensus at both the public and governmental levels was President Reagan's appointment of a twelve-member National Bipartisan Commission on Central America headed by Henry Kissinger in July 1983.

There is need for better understanding of this Central American crisis that can inform public debate as to the course we should pursue in the region. However, much of the existing literature that might serve such a purpose lacks sufficient breadth. It tends to be narrow in both a temporal and spatial sense, concentrating on recent developments in Nicaragua and El Salvador, while largely ignoring less dramatic crisis-related events in countries such as Costa Rica and Panama. This book places the contemporary crisis in long-term historical perspective and presents analyses by specialists that cover all of the Central American countries with the exception of Belize.[2]

The background of the crisis is discussed in Chapter 1. Primarily historical-descriptive, it deals with developments during the colonial and subsequent periods that may have contributed to recent crisis conditions and interpretations. Six subsequent chapters discuss the origins and evolution of crisis conditions in the individual countries of the region.

The order of chapters reflects the chronological sequence in which the crises in these countries have become dramatically visible at the global level. Each author was asked to address the following set of questions:

1) What is the general nature of the crisis in this particular country?

2) Has the current political regime successfully dealt with the crisis, and if so, how?

3) What historical and contemporary factors best explain the regime's ability to adapt to existing crisis conditions? If the regime has failed to adapt, why has this been the case?

Two of the six country chapters were contributed by the editors, and the other four were written by other country specialists. We sought to find experts with a wide range of theoretical and ideological perspectives in order to achieve some overall balance in the analysis. The final chapter summarizes the country findings, discusses similarities and differences related to the crisis and adaptive process, and suggests some implications of these findings for thinking about the role of the United States in Central America.

Notes

1. Political crises have been defined by Sidney Verba as "situations in which the basic institutional patterns of the political system are challenged and routine response is inadequate." We define adaptation as the political system's ability to develop new institutional means (that fall short of revolution) for handling society's problems. There is an extensive body of literature on crises as they occur in developing societies. Two of the best-known works resulted from the activity in the 1960s of the Social Sciences Research Council. They are Lucian Pye, *Aspects of Political Development* (Boston: Little, Brown and Co., 1966); and Leonard Binder, et al., *Crises and Sequences in Political Development* (Princeton, N.J.: Princeton University Press, 1971), which contains Sidney Verba's definition of political crises (p. 302).

2. The unique historical origin of Belize is outlined in Chapter 1. Belize has not been included in our analysis because of its "enclave" status within the region as a traditional British rather than Spanish cultural and economic dependency. The British settlers established active (though frequently illegal) trading patterns with the Kingdom of Guatemala during the seventeenth and eighteenth centuries. After completion of the Panama railroad in the 1850s, trade plummeted and Belize became isolated from the rest of the region. With a small white colonial aristocracy and underclass of Black immigrants from the West

Indies, its historical, social, and economic evolution set it almost completely apart from the area's Hispanic population. See Ralph Lee Woodward, *Central America: A Nation Divided* (New York: Oxford University Press, 1976), pp. 51–52 and 146–47; and Wayne M. Clegern, *British Honduras: Colonial Dead End* (Baton Rouge: Louisiana State University Press, 1967), pp. 163–64.

1

The Setting

Land and Peoples

Central America extends eighteen hundred kilometers from the southern frontiers of Mexico to the jungles of Colombia on the northern edge of South America. The narrow isthmus winds in a southeasterly direction, separating the Caribbean and Atlantic Ocean on the north from the Pacific Ocean to the west and south. It lies predominantly within subtropical and tropical climatic zones and includes a variety of land forms, differing ecologies, and diverse climatic patterns.

Central America is predominantly mountainous, with a rugged topography dominated by canyons and gorges carved by the twisting course of rivers and streams. A central mountain chain is intersected by several east-west ranges. On either side of the isthmus, the land drops toward the hot, humid lowlands that line the Pacific and Atlantic coasts.

The "spine" of the isthmus is crystalline rock interspersed with volcanic peaks (many still active). Closer to the Pacific than to the Atlantic, this volcanic spine stretches for nearly thirteen hundred kilometers from Guatemala into Panama. The highest peaks are in northern Guatemala, with Mount Tajumulco rising 4,145 meters above sea level. The spine is lower in El Salvador and Nicaragua, and it all but misses Honduras. Only the tops of the mountain chain remain as islands in the Gulf of Fonseca. The richness of soils in Guatemala, El Salvador, Nicaragua, and Costa Rica derives mainly from layers of volcanic ash laid down over the centuries, and the lack of large volumes

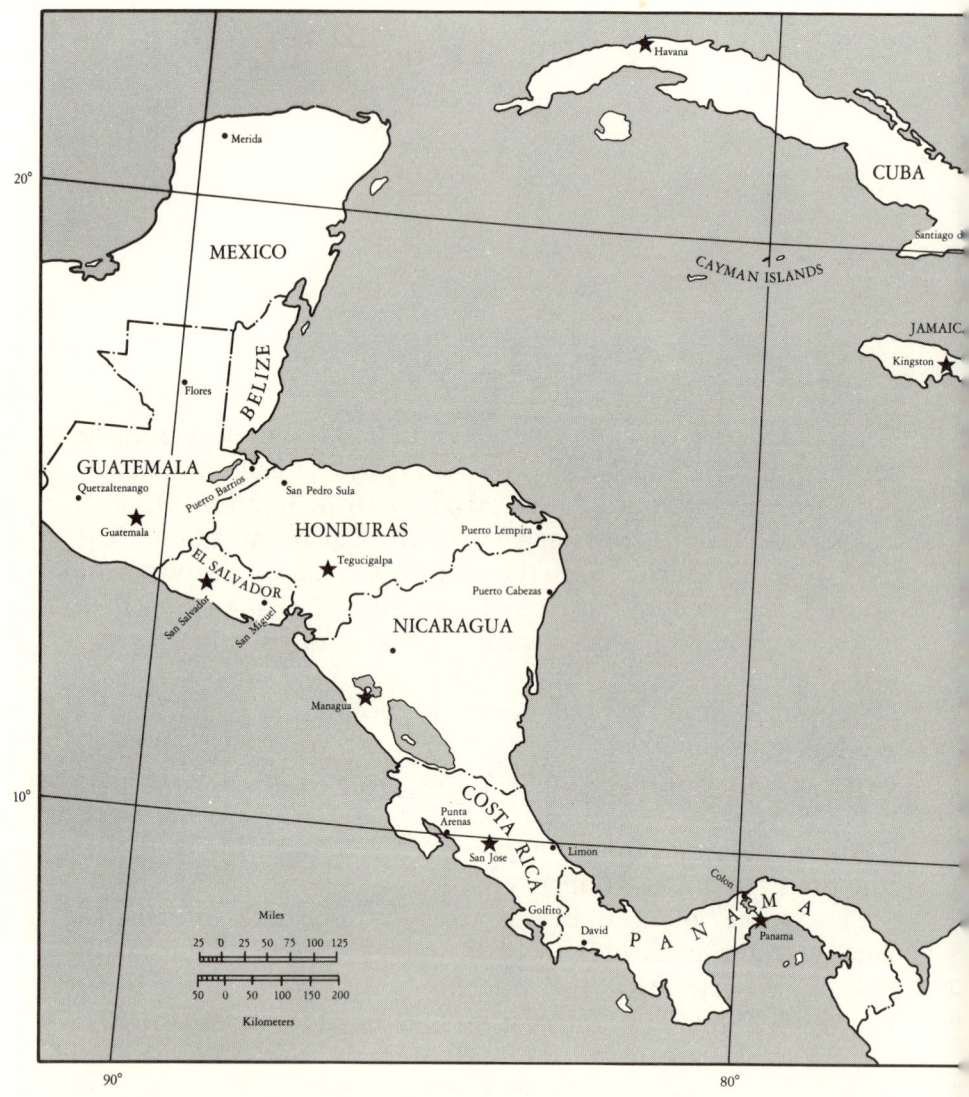

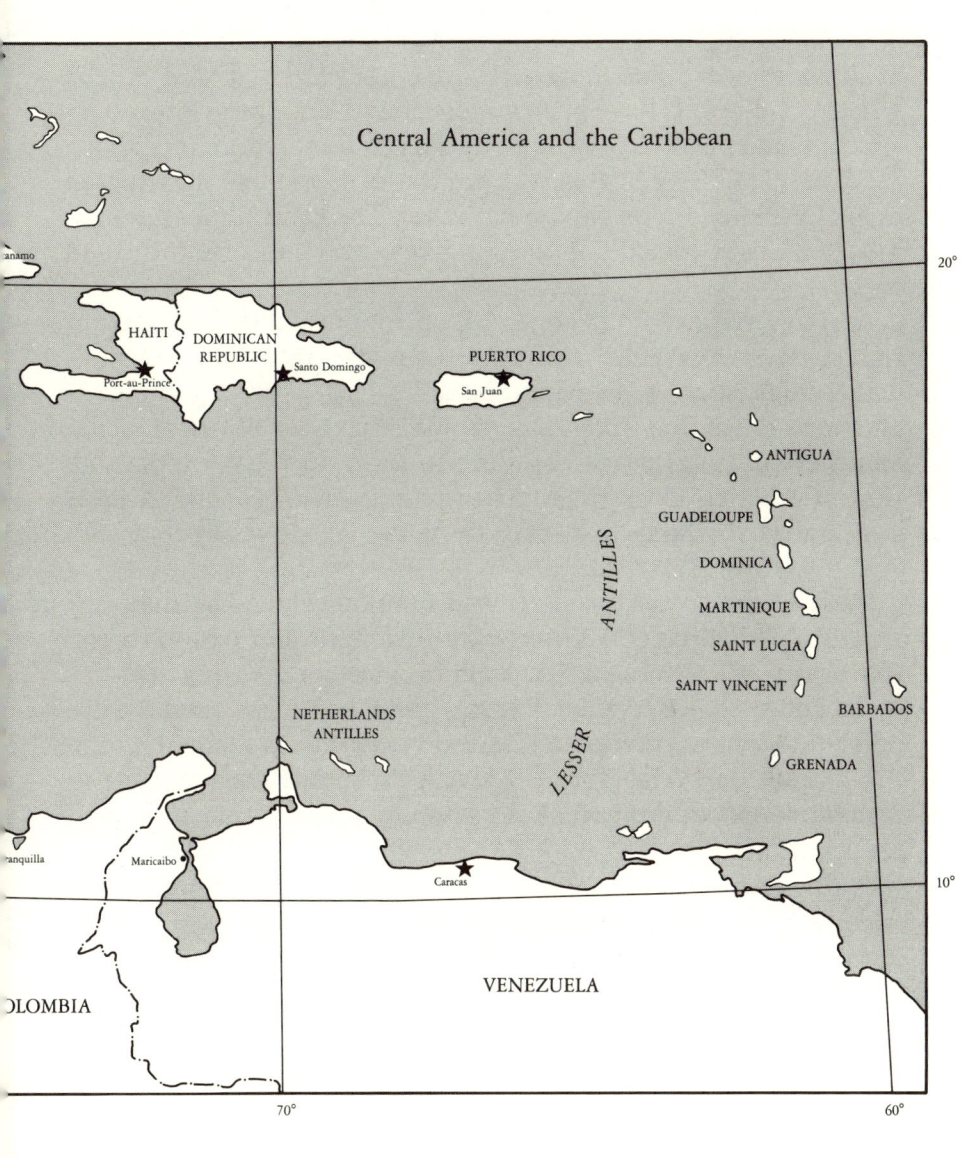

of such ash accounts for the generally less fertile terrain in Honduras and in Panama.

Central America's mountainous interior lacks a coherent form. Some of the higher mountain ranges are capped with rain forests at altitudes near 2,700 meters. There are several highland valleys where populations have been concentrated since pre-Columbian times. Guatemala City lies nearly fifteen hundred meters above sea level, and Tegucigalpa, the capital of Honduras, is situated at nine hundred meters above sea level. The central mesa, where most of Costa Rica's population lives, averages one thousand meters.

Among crisscrossing ranges, steep mountain slopes, and intermontane valleys lie a number of distinctive transisthmian depressions, such as the Motagua River Valley in Guatemala. In Honduras, the Ulúa River, Lake Yojoa, the valley of Comayagua, and the Gulf of Fonseca combine to form a transverse passage from the North Coast region to the gulf on the Pacific Coast. Nicaragua's lowlands and lakes form a wide rift valley that cuts across Central America.

Most of the rivers are short and nonnavigable. The majority range from 160 to 600 kilometers in length and exit into the Caribbean. The Motagua River dominates southeastern Guatemala, and the Ulúa, Aguán, Patuca, and Coco rivers traverse the northern coast of Honduras. Central Nicaragua is drained by the Río Grande de Matagalpa. El Salvador's Lempa and the Choluteca in Honduras are two of the few major rivers that flow into the Pacific.

Central America contains a number of lakes, some of which have become tourist centers. Amatitlán and Atitlán are located in the Guatemala highlands, and Yojoa is in Honduras. The largest enclosed bodies of water are Nicaragua's Lake Managua and Lake Nicaragua, situated in the rift valley. Although there are several major Pacific and Caribbean ports, there are few large coastal indentations. The most significant of such indentations is the Gulf of Fonseca, which touches the shores of three countries—El Salvador, Honduras, and Nicaragua. Also important on the Pacific side are Punta Arenas and Golfito in Costa Rica. Most Caribbean ports have little natural protection from tropical storms and require wharves or lighter loading and unloading facilities because of shallow water. A major exception is the Bocas del Toro area of Panama.

Despite Central America's location within lower latitudes, there are widely diverse climatic patterns. Cooler climates prevail at high elevations. Tropical lowlands along the coasts, savanna plains, low mountains, and interior basins below eight hundred meters are characteristically hot and humid. Temperate climates prevail on mountain slopes and in highland valleys between eight hundred and eighteen hundred meters.[1]

Terrain affects patterns of precipitation; and rainfall, in turn, affects temperature. Generally, the Caribbean coasts receive the most rainfall (brought by the northeastern tradewinds) with totals from two hundred to three hundred centimeters per year. During the May to October rainy season, the interior valleys and leeside mountain slopes are drier. A rainshadow is found in some Pacific coastal zones. Hurricanes frequently batter the Caribbean side with high winds and heavy precipitation. Crop damage and flooding are often the result, endangering lives and presenting massive problems of cleanup and economic recovery.

In all the countries of Central America there are isolated regions, difficult to reach even in the late twentieth century. Because of unhealthy climate, impenetrable forests, or poor communications, these regions have never attracted numerous settlers. The department of Petén in northern Guatemala is a flat lowland and tropical forest. Though scarcely populated today (an estimated two inhabitants per square kilometer), the area was once part of the thriving Mayan civilization. Another isolated region is the Mosquito Coast located on the northeastern bulge of the isthmus. The "Mosquitia" includes the departments of Gracias a Dios in Honduras and the northernmost portion of Zelaya province in Nicaragua. Population density is low, ranging from 1.5 to 2.5 persons per square kilometer. The Honduran department of Olancho, just west of Gracias a Dios, has yet to be fully explored, and it contains only eight people per square kilometer.

For most of Costa Rica's history, the Caribbean coast has remained isolated from major population centers, economically stagnant, and politically weak. The establishment of banana plantations there in the late nineteenth century did stimulate the construction of transportation links to the heavily populated

Table 1.1. Central American land and population data

Country	Population, 1983 (thousands)	Area (km²)	Pop. Density 1983/km²	% Arable 1977[a]
Costa Rica	2,600	50,900	51	40
El Salvador	4,685	21,041	222	63
Guatemala	7,714	108,889	71	25
Honduras	4,100	112,088	36	26
Nicaragua	2,812	140,746	20	37
Panama	2,059	77,080	27	22
Region	23,970	510,744	47	31

[a] Category includes permanent cultivations and permanent pasture lands.

Sources: United Nations, Economic Commission for Latin America, *Statistical Yearbook for Latin America, 1979*, pp. 364–65; Inter-American Development Bank, *Economic and Social Progress in Latin America, 1980–1981* (Washington, D.C., 1981); Secretaría Permanente del Tratado General de Integración Económica Centroamericana (SIECA), *VII Compendio estadístico centroamericano* (Guatemala, 1981), pp. 3–27; and Central Intelligence Agency, *The World Factbook, 1983* (Washington, D.C.: U.S. Government Printing Office, 1983).

central mesa. A highway and railroad traverse the central cordillera through the valley of the Río Reventazón. Heredia and Limón provinces, situated along the Caribbean littoral, average between seven and nine persons per square kilometer compared with a national average of forty-five. Panama's western province of Bocas del Toro accounts for less than 4 percent of the national population (only six people per square kilometer). Darién province at the eastern end of the country has less than two people per square kilometer. This region is all but impenetrable tropical forest with no all-weather road as yet extending into Colombia.

Were it not for the rich volcanic and alluvial soils, Central America's difficult terrain and hostile climatic regions would have seriously inhibited the establishment and growth of today's agrarian economies. The active geology of the area has contributed to high land fertility through centuries of volcanic eruptions. Arable lands comprise about 30 percent of the region's total area (see Table 1). El Salvador's agricultural lands are proportionately the greatest. This is because the volcanic mountain chain traverses the entire country, and there are few large isolated and nonarable sections such as Guatemala's Petén.

Mesoamerican influence reached from Mexico into Guatemala, El Salvador, and northwestern Honduras—the limits of the Mayan empire. Concentrated in the highlands of Nicaragua are the remnants of isolated Indian tribes. South American influence (Chibchan) reached into Panama and into portions of eastern Costa Rica and Nicaragua. Caribbean cultures had easy access to the coastal lowlands. Lowland Indian populations were more easily influenced by external forces than were people living in the mountainous interior. Today, Euro-Indian cultures predominate in the highlands and Euro-African cultures in the lowland coastal zones.[2] This pattern varies within each country and in the region as a whole.

With modernization and the growth of urban population centers, "advanced" world cultural styles have been introduced in Central America. Yet the region remains mostly rural, and it is in these areas that pre-Columbian cultural traits are still reflected in daily patterns of life. Family structure, division of labor, housing, agricultural methods, landholding patterns, and political relations, though often assuming a superficially modern guise, have retained their centuries-old flavor. Although the Spaniards used traditional Indian social structures to incorporate the Indians into their colonial system, the agricultural base of these societies and the Spanish emphasis on urban living left them on the margin of the Spanish empire.

With the possible exception of Guatemala, it is the Spanish or European imprint that overlies other cultures in Central America. However, external influence was progressively modified through the centuries as European migrants mixed and intermarried with Indians, Negroes, and the descendants of both races. The *mestizo*, or "mixed race," is the most populous group. Predominant Spanish influence can be discerned in the fact that Spanish, in addition to being the most widespread language, remains the official language of all countries. Catholicism is the dominant religion.

The black populations, a distinct minority, tend to be concentrated along the Caribbean shores. Blacks either migrated from Caribbean islands or were imported directly from Africa as slaves.

Toward the end of the nineteenth century, blacks came from Jamaica, the Cayman Islands, and the lesser Antilles to work on the banana plantations. Large numbers were also brought to Panama by France and the United States to construct the canal. Antillean blacks remain heavily influenced by British and American culture, retaining the English language and the Protestant religion.

Ethnically, the most "European" society in Central America is Costa Rica, where more than 90 percent of the population is considered to be Caucasian. Since the original settlers found few if any indigenous peoples, miscegenation was never a major factor in Costa Rica's social evolution. In contrast, Guatemala is primarily an Indian society with approximately half the population considered indigenous. The Indian population consists of between twenty-five and thirty distinct cultural language groups. Guatemala's next most prominent ethnic-cultural group is called *ladinos* (those persons who have not retained Indian customs and who speak Spanish).[3] Ladinos may be of pure Indian blood or racially and ethnically mixed because the classification relates to cultural attributes such as dress, speech, and mode of daily living.

Old-line families in all Central American countries have carefully retained their "pure" Spanish-European racial and ethnic heritage. These families are the descendants of the original colonists, many of whom abandoned Central America in favor of living better elsewhere, once their wealth had been acquired. Though not necessarily the wealthier classes today, lineage and longevity continue to provide these families with high social status.[4]

Historical Background

The Colonial Period: 1500–1800

Christopher Columbus touched the Caribbean shores of Honduras on his fourth voyage to the New World in 1502. The Spanish reached Panama in 1509, and by 1513 Vasco Núñez de Balboa had crossed the isthmus and sighted the Great South Sea. In 1519, Panama City was founded—the same year that Hernán

Cortés reached Tenochtitlán in Mexico. During the early 1520s, explorers traveled through Central America from bases in Mexico and Panama. Hernández de Córdoba bypassed the highlands of Costa Rica and established the cities of Granada and León in the Pacific lowlands of present-day Nicaragua. Pedro de Alvarado traveled to Guatemala and El Salvador. Cortés directed seafaring expeditions toward the northern coast of Honduras, and indeed he almost lost his life on an expedition to the newly founded port city of Trujillo. Honduras became in 1525 the first province to be recognized by Spain.

Central America was a disappointment to the early explorers and colonists. Wealth was not easily acquired, and its sources were not immediately apparent. Once stories of the extensive riches existing in Mexico and Peru reached the isthmus, it was rapidly abandoned by the less dedicated settlers. Besides the lack of wealth, there were relatively few native inhabitants in the region. As Spain's colonial trade routes developed with Mexico and Peru, Central America became further isolated within the Spanish empire. Colonial authority was established relatively late due to competition among the vice-royalties of Santo Domingo, Mexico, and Peru. During the 1530s, Panama, Guatemala, Honduras, Nicaragua, and Chiapas functioned under separate royal decrees.[5]

In 1543, the Captaincy General of Guatemala was created to administer the Central American region. This jurisdiction included provinces from Chiapas in the north to Panama in the south. Panama eventually became part of the vice-royalty of Peru. Santiago de Guatemala, founded in 1526, was declared the capital city in 1548, and it became the seat of the *audiencia*, or circuit court. While not entirely ignoring Guatemala, the attentions of the Spanish crown were often diverted by more pressing needs and lucrative prospects in Mexico and Peru. Spain's ties with the region were weak. In part, this was because only fragile trade and communication links existed, except for those across the isthmus of Panama. These links were further weakened by increasing French, Dutch, and English raids along the Caribbean coast.

The Hapsburgs (1516–1700) were willing to exercise rather loose control over the colonies in return for revenue and continued loyalty to the crown. They recognized the limits of royal authority, the diversity of economic interests in Central America, and the necessity for a certain measure of local autonomy. Hapsburg flexibility reinforced certain decentralizing tendencies in the region that reappeared with renewed vigor later on. Colonial authorities during this period were unable to enforce uniformly the laws and dictates of the realm. The only institution that maintained positive relations with most social and economic groups was the Catholic church. Thus, it came to be viewed by the Hapsburgs as a partner in the colonial enterprise.[6]

When the power of the crown shifted to the Bourbons after 1700, perspectives on the administration of the colonies changed. Hapsburg flexibility was replaced with tighter control and centralization. The Bourbons sought to impose the royal will upon Central America according to the principles of French absolutism and in order to defend the region from increasingly frequent foreign incursions. These Bourbon policies altered government institutions, moved the economy toward cash-crop production, and spawned new social classes. The net effect of the Bourbon reforms was to dilute that measure of provincial loyalty to Spain which had been created during the previous 150 years.

The Indian inhabitants of the region, located principally in the highlands of Guatemala, El Salvador, and northwestern Honduras, came to be dominated by the Spanish who used feudal aspects of native cultures to consolidate their conquest.[7] Disease, forced labor, enslavement, and involuntary migration decimated the Indian population and reduced the available supply of workers in the region. Spanish settlers were sometimes forced to work the land themselves or abandon it. This was especially true for those who settled Costa Rica's central mesa.

The physical isolation of Central America and its limited mineral resources left the region on the outermost fringes of the Spanish colonial empire. Panama was an exception since it was a major crossing point on the isthmus and one of the handful of routes within the empire along which goods were allowed to flow to and from Peru. But Panama lost its port monopoly during the eighteenth century, and from that point, it was forced to compete for business.

Because of such isolation, local administrative jurisdictions were left to their own devices. Colonial legislation, particularly under the Hapsburgs, was interpreted and enforced in accordance with local needs. After 1700, latent rivalry between the region and the crown became more apparent as the Bourbon monarchs sought to impose greater central authority upon local government units. Additionally, intraregional rivalries developed. Local bureaucrats, merchants, and estate owners increasingly resented the distant power of officials, creditors, and middlemen in Guatemala.[8] In part, this resentment stemmed from the separation of wealth from political control. Government positions were filled by Spanish *peninsulares* while most of the landowners were American-born Creoles. Thus, provincial aristocracies evolved with interests not only antithetical to the Spanish crown but to interests in other neighboring "city states."

Although colonial Central America lacked the wealth and mineral resources that attracted the Spanish to Mexico and Peru, it nonetheless possessed certain attributes that made it minimally attractive for settlers. Most important in this regard was the region's rich volcanic soil. As a consequence of agrarian activities, the Spanish population gradually increased, and the area was slowly integrated through mercantilist policies and contraband trade into the global economy. The economic changes which took place in Central America between 1500 and 1800 were extensive, and eventually these changes created regional distinctions that came to underlie the above-mentioned tensions between crown and local inhabitants and between the inhabitants themselves.

During the sixteenth and seventeenth centuries, the Central American economy was quite eclectic with no single avenue (as in Peru) to the achievement of wealth. In Panama and Nicaragua, commercial interests grew up around their respective transisthmian routes linking the region to the mother country and to Peru. In other areas, Spaniards looked primarily to the land as a potential source of profits. Livestock were introduced to the north coast of Honduras from Jamaica, and to Guatemala from Cuba and Veracruz. The Spanish brought with them cattle, horses, hogs, sheep, and goats, which were quickly adopted by the Indians who had no large domestic animals of their own. Stock-raising consequently became a dominant activity in the highland valleys of Guatemala and Honduras, while lowland areas in El Salvador and elsewhere were used to grow food and cash crops.

Central America has sometimes been popularly characterized

as an area historically dominated by extensive haciendas where Indians provided a limitless supply of manual labor. The actual pattern of regional economic activity was a good deal more complex with numerous variations depending on the area and particular point in time. Supplying local Indian slaves for work in the mines of Peru was an early source of wealth. Later, African slaves were traded legally or illegally with Peru across routes running from British-controlled Jamaica through Panama and Nicaragua. During the sixteenth and seventeenth centuries, large estates were relatively uncommon. Wealth was available to those who could control the local labor supply (through a system known as *repartimiento*) rather than to those who held great amounts of land. One of the primary characteristics of the early colonial economy was the constantly shifting economic base around which local elites attempted to consolidate their political power.

Although no single economic activity dominated Central America during the colonial period, there was a trend in the growth of agricultural commodity exports, particularly from Guatemala and El Salvador. Cacao flourished during the sixteenth century and was gradually replaced by indigo as the market for this dye product grew in the textile manufacturing areas of western Europe. Cochineal, a source of crimson dye, was produced in the highland areas, and tobacco was gradually commercialized. As the demand for these agricultural commodities increased, their expanded production in countries such as Guatemala and El Salvador led to the need to import foodstuffs to support the local work force. Other regional provinces, such as Nicaragua and Honduras, were gradually and indirectly linked to the global economy as they began to supply these markets with beef and other foodstuffs.

With this gradual development of export agriculture, Guatemala became not only a colonial administrative center but also a trade center. Local elites in Guatemala City came to control the economic pulse of Central America (except for the extensive contraband trade), and regional elites resented the fact. During the late eighteenth century, the indigo market collapsed due to a war between Britain and Spain, increases in British tariffs, and the development of alternative sources of indigo supplies. As a consequence, regional elites outside Guatemala City suffered severe economic losses and even lost some landholdings to Guatemalan creditors. The result was an underlying economic tension that perhaps doomed the subsequent attempt at regional political unity to ultimate failure.

Independence: 1808–1839

The centrifugal force of localism carried over into the early decades of the nineteenth century, when Central America gained its independence. Unlike the nations of Argentina, Chile, and Mexico, there were no great military campaigns to liberate the isthmian provinces from Spanish rule and to tie them potentially together. Central Americans found themselves alone, surrounded by the remnants of the collapsed Spanish empire and caught in the midst of an economic depression.

The suddenness with which Central America achieved independence left regional leaders politically and economically unprepared for effective self-government. Lacking a base for a broad "national" coalition, due to the absence of a sustained independence movement, Central Americans were carried along by developments in Mexico. Many Creole provincial leaders were disposed to ally themselves with their neighbor to the north in the hope that Guatemala's political and economic influence might be diffused. However, the alliance with Mexico lasted only two years and was marked by explosive rivalries among the region's local city governments (*cabildos*). A major point of disagreement was the extent to which government structures and policies should be centralized. The Conservatives argued for such centralization, while the Liberals generally felt that some type of federation would more effectively counter Guatemalan monopolies on political power, commerce, and education.[9]

Two years after Central America gained independence in 1821, the region's association with Mexico was dissolved, and a constitution was approved that provided for a loose confederation of states. The new government faced rising debts, due to the inability to raise tax revenues, and felt threatened by a potential invasion by Spain. Divisions persisted between Conservatives and Liberals, with the latter remaining unwilling to exchange Spanish colonial rule for that of Guatemala. These differences resulted in a series of civil wars between 1826 and 1829, which exacerbated the post-independence economic crisis.[10]

This first attempt at union had completely failed by 1840, when all of the Central American provinces declared their independence. Intense rivalries divided the new republics despite continued efforts to promote regional unity. Nicaragua, Honduras, and El Salvador joined forces in the Pact of Chinandega in 1842. Two years later, regional unity was briefly restored with the establishment of the United Provinces of Central America. Between 1821 and 1975, twenty-five attempts were made to create some form of confederated government or association of states.[11] Provincial distrust, boundary disputes, and intervention by one country in the affairs of another prevented the reestablishment of such a broader regional government. Costa Ricans preferred their isolation, refusing to become involved in the civil disarray that afflicted the other states.

Post-independence civil conflict helped to institutionalize the practice of "*caudillo* politics" in Central America. Regional political bosses and landowners supported by bands of loyal followers jealously guarded family-based wealth and political power from outside encroachment.[12] Control of the governments of the newly created republics became an objective of some regional caudillos, serving them as a means of extending their personal influence and of rewarding their followers. The problem of regional instability stemmed partly from the lack of conformity between historical socioeconomic structures and imported legal and institutional forms.[13] Political leaders in Central America had little or no experience with the principles and institutions associated with the French and American revolutions—individual liberties, republicanism, and federation. Bargaining, compromise, and public debate were not common during the period of colonial authoritarianism. The only political institution to survive after independence was the *municipio*, the most common unit of local government. However, despite the tradition of self-government embodied in the municipio, this tradition was not extended to the national or regional level.

Brute force became an accepted means of resolving internal disputes. Caudillo leaders would frequently appeal to their neighbors in other parts of Central America for assistance and support. Fragmented patterns of domestic politics encouraged such intervention by outside forces, particulary in the affairs of Honduras, El Salvador, and Nicaragua. However, the numerous revolts and civil wars seldom involved large segments of the population. An "army" of one hundred men was often sufficient to topple a government, which was usually, to begin with, of uncertain legitimacy.

Guatemala experienced less instability than its neighbors because, as the seat of Spanish colonial authority, it had a tradition of administering local institutions more directly. In addition, Guatemalan elites emphasized order and consensus because they were faced with a large mass of potentially rebellious Indian peasants. Political factionalism in Costa Rica and El Salvador gradually decreased, possibly because the wealthy classes in those countries recognized the economic value of stability. Coffee had been introduced in Costa Rica during the 1830s and had spread to El Salvador by the 1860s. Dana Munro observed in 1918 that "the wealthier classes have become very prosperous through the production and exportation of coffee, but Honduras and Nicaragua, because of almost continuous fighting between rival factions, are today but little better off than in 1821."[14] It could also be argued, of course, that it was not the elite's recognition of the value of stability that allowed coffee to be produced, but rather it was coffee revenues that served as an economic base for such elite consensus.

Political disorder and national weakness also invited intervention by extraregional powers. The lightly populated frontiers along the Caribbean coast, where the colonial presence was minimal, had long been vulnerable to French, Dutch, and English pirates who regularly preyed on shipping routes and coastal settlements. Great Britain's presence grew after the seizure of Jamaica in 1655, and it became a major Caribbean power with outposts in British Honduras (Belize) and on the Bay Islands just off the northern coast of Honduras. The Nicaraguan province of Zelaya (part of the Mosquito coast) remained a British protectorate until 1860.[15]

Britain's economic interests were restricted to regional trade and the extraction of dyewoods and lumber. Very few people became permanent settlers. However, as a result of this extended period of British influence, present-day populations along Central America's Caribbean littoral retain elements of English language and culture. The Bay Islands of Honduras provide one example: here, English is still spoken more widely in most communities than is Spanish. Another example of lingering English influence is the small country of Belize, where the British acquired trade and settlement rights under treaties signed in 1783 and 1786.

The struggle for extraregional influence in Central America intensified shortly after the end of the war between Mexico and the United States in 1846. The discovery of gold in California (1848) led the United States to fear British efforts to consolidate their position in Central America and to control isthmian transit points. Diplomatic maneuvering led in 1850 to the signing of the Clayton-Bulwer Treaty, whereby Great Britain and the United States agreed not to fortify unilaterally or to control any future canal built on the isthmus.

Liberal Reformism: 1870–1930

The triumph of Liberal over Conservative factions during the 1870s opened the economies and political systems of the Central American republics to greater external influence from the world capitalist system. The divided Liberals had been chafing under the policies of Conservative governments since independence, and they had suffered economically as commodity prices continued to fluctuate during the first half of the nineteenth century. With rapid industrial expansion occurring in Europe and the United States by mid-century, Liberals rode to power on the tide of rising commodity prices (particularly coffee).[16] The Liberal vision was supported philosophically by Comtean positivism. Economic progress would be achieved only through strong and active governments. Social order and stability would be emphasized over democracy until such time as culturally backward indigenous peoples had reached a sufficient degree of "maturity."

With the overthrow of several Conservative governments during the 1870s, radically new policies were introduced. Traditional values and institutions were rejected, with attacks upon the Catholic church eroding one potential base of indigenous nationalism.[17] However, even with Conservatives defeated in Guatemala, El Salvador, Honduras, and Costa Rica, the Liberals were still not unified at the regional level. Strains of personalism and a hunger for the spoils of office persisted. Factionalism, intrigue, and instability continued to affect political life.

The era of Liberal reforms greatly increased the economic role of central governments. Investment conditions were liberalized for foreign capital, and local taxes were reduced in order to attract international investment. Concessions were given to mining companies and to corporations interested in establishing export-oriented agribusiness enterprises. Export crops and commodities were encouraged to earn foreign exchange and to help finance imports and national development.

Liberal governments also passed laws that made it easier for individuals to acquire private landholdings. Public lands were offered for sale, and *ejidal* (communal) lands were reduced gradually as they were appropriated by private owners. Land concentration was accelerated, with the expansion of large estates and the creation of new ones. To provide adequate manpower for labor-intensive agricultural activities, legislation was passed which permitted forced labor—directly in the form of debt peonage, or indirectly through the reduction of the availability of small parcels of land. Relations between those who now owned land and those recently dispossessed were drastically altered because of the social and economic gap that separated them.

The Liberals had difficulties in persuading the peasants to accept these new policies, and thus they had to resort to force.[18] New military and police organizations were created to solve the problem of peasant recalcitrance. Not only were the lower classes dispossessed of their land, but the burden of direct taxes fell increasingly on their shoulders. At the same time, politicians associated with the expanding Liberal governments became wealthy through their involvement with foreign investors. For example, Honduran president Marco Aurelio Soto (1876–83) was one of several partners in a mining venture headed by the U.S.-based Rosario Mining Company.

The Liberal reforms did aid Central America in breaking out of its historical pattern of relative isolation from the global economy. However, this change required the acquisition of both foreign capital and technology, which were needed in conjunction with the exploitation of the region's agricultural potential and of its other resources. Initial investment in such activities, together with the attendant need for infrastructure expansion, necessitated borrowing from international capital sources or inviting foreign investors into the region under favorable terms. Commodity exports were never sufficient to cover the rising demand for imports, and external debts grew accordingly. By the turn of the century, foreigners controlled many financial and banking resources in the region.

Under Liberal control, Central America's economy was revitalized but not fundamentally changed. Agricultural commodities remained the key to prosperity, and economic success was tied to export markets where prices fluctuated considerably. By the late nineteenth century, coffee had become the leading export crop, except in Honduras and in Panama. At the same time, bananas began to emerge as a second major source of foreign earnings.

Coffee was introduced into Costa Rica during the 1830s, and it spread from there along the Pacific mountain chain, reaching El Salvador in the 1840s. Growers in the Matagalpa region of Nicaragua had established coffee haciendas by the 1850s. During the following decade, the Pacific slope of the Guatemalan highlands became a principal growing area. Expansion of the coffee industry was particularly dramatic after the completion of the Panama Railway by U.S. investors in 1855. The crop could now be more easily shipped to European markets. Honduras's failure to construct a railway into the mountainous interior prevented its participation in the "golden age" of the coffee export boom. Neither Honduras nor Panama became coffee exporters until after World War II.

Coffee haciendas were located in the cooler highland areas, which were also the more densely populated regions. Bananas were initially grown by small independent producers along both coastlines of the isthmus. Beginning in the 1870s, ships would take on fruit from the Caribbean side as supplemental cargo. By the 1890s, several North American companies had pioneered the cultivation of bananas on plantations in Costa Rica, Honduras, and Guatemala. El Salvador was the only Central American country that did not become a significant producer of bananas. Honduras had become the world's leading exporter by 1930.

Unlike coffee, banana production and export was an industry completely controlled by foreigners.[19] The industry required large amounts of labor, and foreign companies initially imported workers from the Greater and Lesser Antilles, Belize, and the Cayman Islands. Establishment of banana plantations also encouraged internal migration, with people moving from the highlands to the coast in search of jobs. The plantations remained economic and social enclaves; backed by foreign capital and managed by foreign personnel, their orientation was outward. The overall impact on national development was significant, but integration into the national economy was never fully achieved.

The banana enclaves did help create new socioeconomic groups and interests. Workers were brought together and organized "industrially," leaving behind their traditional values and social structures. Plantation workers were thus more receptive than other groups to new ideologies, and they soon developed a working-class identity. In some countries, such as Guatemala, Panama, and Honduras, enclave-spawned labor organizations were instrumental in spreading mass social awareness and in promoting broad national political participation.

Dictatorship and Political Order: 1930–45

World War I was an important turning point in Central American history, disrupting traditional trade patterns with the major European capitalist powers (Great Britain and Germany) and thus ensuring the future economic domination of the United States. U.S. investment and business activity expanded dramatically after the war until the economic crash of 1929 brought this era of expansion to an abrupt close. Producers laid off workers and offered lower wages to those who remained. Governments, heavily reliant on customs receipts and export taxes, were unable to take up the slack as incomes were reduced. The worldwide depression of the 1930s exposed the weaknesses of the Liberal model of economic growth and undermined the governments that had been supported by this model.

These economic stresses coincided with the widespread awakening of Central America's masses. Labor organizers began to win recruits among workers on banana plantations in Costa Rica, Panama, Honduras, and Guatemala. Communists and Socialists gained a sympathetic ear among such groups as well as among peasants and segments of the emerging middle class. Except in Costa Rica, where modest reforms were undertaken by President Ricardo Jiménez Oreamuno (1932–36), regional governments failed to act decisively in dealing with the social and economic consequences of the Depression. Rather, force was frequently used to quell dissent. Rural activism in El Salvador ended with the massacre of thousands in 1932, and early attempts at labor organization elsewhere in the region were quashed.

During the 1930s, a cadre of national caudillos emerged who imposed their will upon both masses and elites, often with the help of the armed forces. These included Maximiliano Hernández Martínez in El Salvador (1931–44), Tiburcio Carías Andino in Honduras (1932–49), Jorge Ubico in Guatemala (1931–44), and Anastasio Somoza García in Nicaragua (1932–56). *Continuismo*, the practice of maintaining oneself in power through constitutional alterations, became widespread in the region. Those elections that were held were manipulated, opponents were exiled, and censorship was widely practiced. This authoritarian style of personalistic leadership was accompanied by the careful maintenance of a minimal degree of political support from elites and from professional groups within the middle class. Such sectors looked to the caudillos for protection of their economic interests and reequilibration of the economy. During this period, the power of the national governments was shored up by the further strengthening and institutionalization of the armed forces.[20]

These dictatorial regimes survived until the end of World War II, when the pent up social and economic forces present since the Depression were released in a frenzy of change. In the immediate postwar period, national economic development once again became a central focus of public attention, as it had been during the era of Liberal reforms. Ironically, the dictatorial regimes that were the product and culmination of these Liberal reforms became the victims of those who demanded even more rapid and extended national development. Liberalism had apparently reached its natural limits, and the old structures now had to be adapted to postwar social and economic realities.

The Postwar Period: 1945–present

The release of political tensions in the years immediately following World War II was both the cause and the result of dramatic social and economic changes taking place within Central America. Increasing global demand for primary commodities and incipient industrialization altered intra-elite and class relations, which, in turn, forced realignments in domestic politics. As market prices for primary products rose, farmers and ranchers saw new opportunities to profit from lands already owned or readily available. Cotton, sugar, tobacco, and other crops generated new cash income. The rising demand for beef—in the growing urban areas and overseas—stimulated ranchers to increase their herds. New packing plants were built with government subsidies, as extensive use of refrigerated shipping facilitated the export of fresh meat.

This rapid commercialization of agriculture caused major changes in many rural areas. Traditional social relations were eroded as *hacendados* became agribusiness entrepreneurs who used credit, technology, and new machinery to produce a variety of export crops. Landholdings were expanded, often by dubious means. Previously idle lands were now cultivated or used for grazing. Subsistence farmers were evicted from areas that they had used customarily for free or with minimal rents.

In spite of the inroads made by new export crops such as cotton, traditional agricultural exports remained important. Coffee continued to represent a healthy proportion of total exports in Costa Rica, El Salvador, and Guatemala; bananas remained particularly important to Panama, Honduras, and Costa Rica. Yet the increasing diversification of crops grown in the region did not mean that Central America was significantly less dependent on the export of primary agricultural products. Between 1970 and 1980, thirteen primary products accounted for nearly two-thirds of all regional exports by value.[21]

The U.S. Point Four program paralleled and partially supported Central America's post–World War II "age of development." Technical and financial aid programs were sponsored by multilateral agencies such as the United Nations and the Organization of American States. Bilateral and multilateral aid was enlisted to revitalize and create administrative and physical infrastructure. Roads were built into areas formerly accessible only on horseback or by foot. Port facilities were renovated. Hydroelectric projects were planned. Technical assistance, financial aid, and credit facilities often necessitated the creation of new government agencies to administer the development programs. Human resource programs required still more new agencies or at least some bureaucratic restructuring. Educational, health, and hous-

Table 1.2. Contribution of five primary products to total value of merchandise exports, averages for 1970–74, 1975–79 (percentage)

Country	Total Five Products[a] 1970–74	1975–79
Costa Rica	68.3%	58.2%
El Salvador	60.2	71.2
Guatemala	57.9	64.3
Honduras	65.0	59.9
Nicaragua	59.6	63.8
Panama	53.7	33.3

[a] Beef, bananas, coffee, cotton, sugar

Source: IDB, *Economic and Social Progress, 1980–1981* (Washington, D.C., 1981), p. 447.

ing services and agricultural extension programs increased the number of people employed by the central government.

Transformation of the agricultural sector was paralleled by the growth of industrial productive capacity throughout the region. Higher national incomes and new development policies activated domestic and foreign investment in food processing, clothing manufacture, plastics, and other light industries. Chemicals, petroleum refining, and cement and gypsum production were secondary investments. Multinational corporations were attracted to the region with the formation of the Central American Common Market (CACM) in 1960.

Regional economic integration had been promoted by Latin American economists for many years. The concept was based on the creation of a larger and hence more viable consumer market, which could then support efficient regional industrial enterprises. When it was first launched the CACM included all the Central American states except Panama. Trade barriers were to be eliminated gradually among the member states and a common tariff imposed on all imports.[22] Trade among the five countries rose steadily until the disruption of the Common Market with the outbreak of hostilities between El Salvador and Hon-

Table 1.3. Central American intra-regional trade as a percentage of total trade, 1950–1975

Country	1950	1960	1965	1970	1975
Costa Rica	1.5	4.4	12.4	22.9	20.6
El Salvador	2.4	11.3	23.4	30.9	26.7
Guatemala	1.3	5.1	16.2	29.5	22.1
Honduras	10.1	10.6	18.9	19.5	12.3
Nicaragua	2.4	5.6	12.5	26.8	22.6
Panama	0.8	0.7	1.0	0.9	3.8

Source: International Monetary Fund

duras in 1969. Even so, the historical pattern of relative intra-regional isolation had been broken. El Salvador's trade with its neighbors surpassed 30 percent of its total world trade by 1970.

Differing levels of infrastructure development and a variety of other factors led to uneven development within the Common Market. Honduras, Nicaragua, and Costa Rica competed less successfully for industrial exports than did Guatemala and El Salvador. Trade deficits occurred, with Hondurans increasingly resenting their role as exporters of primary products and importers of consumer goods. The 1969 war provided Honduras with an opportunity to withdraw from the Central American Common Market and to demand some restructuring. Throughout the decade of the 1970s, CACM functioned through a series of bilateral trade agreements that Honduras signed with Guatemala, Costa Rica, and Nicaragua.

Central America's postwar economic growth was stimulated by rising global and domestic consumer demands, by government emphasis on national development, and by the initial success of the Common Market. Imports rose to meet the needs of industrial activity, infrastructure expansion, and new social services. Exports grew and became more diversified, with the cost of imports generally exceeding exports. The role of central governments inevitably expanded as public sector investments multiplied. Governments were now deeply involved in a wide range of economic and social activities. As new programs were created, public sector employment reached record levels.

Table 1.4. External public debt outstanding (millions of dollars)

Country	1960	1970	1980
Costa Rica	55	227	2,415
El Salvador	33	126	936
Guatemala	51	176	864
Honduras	23	144	1,609
Nicaragua	41	222	2,122
Panama	59	290	2,727

Source: Inter-American Development Bank, *Economic and Social Progress in Latin America: The External Sector* (Washington, D.C.: 1982), p. 387.

To a considerable extent, such postwar economic growth was dependent upon external financing. While foreign investments were helpful in creating new businesses, earnings were repatriated abroad. Differences between export and import prices were normally disadvantageous to Central America, and commodity export prices remained more volatile than those for imported manufactured goods. As a consequence, national expenditures tended to outpace incomes, with external debt financing making up the difference.

National development policies, economic diversification, and further integration into the global capitalist system led to considerable social and political change in the region. Traditional agrarian elites were challenged by new groups whose economic interests were related to aggressive urban industrial and agri-industrial investment policies, use of external capital sources, and a commitment to regional integration. The newer commercial-agribusiness sectors soon became impatient with inefficient and corrupt state bureaucracies. A struggle to control the government developed between old-line politicians and those whose political vision was based on more modern perspectives. Hotly debated issues included the question of tax credits for new industry and the necessity of land reform.

This pattern of intra-elite division was accompanied by expansion of the middle class. Regional economic growth increased the demand for white-collar, technical, and professional personnel in both the public and private sectors. Similarly, economic growth and diversification opened up new jobs for skilled and unskilled labor. The organized working class, formerly concentrated around large-scale agribusiness enterprises, became more complex as industrial and manufacturing plants were built. Unionized labor was able to extend its influence throughout Central America, in spite of a generally hostile reaction by regional governments to this process.

Postwar social and economic change had an equally dramatic effect on rural areas. Commercialization of agriculture and improved medical and social services combined to change relations between rural classes and the relationship of these classes to the land. The traditional landlord-tenant relationship was eroded in many areas as ranchers and farmers began to appropriate (legally or illegally) more territory for the production of export commodities. Peasant farmers now lacked a sponsor who in the past had been a source of informal credit, extra work, and political guidance. The eviction or exclusion of subsistence farmers from the land coincided with dramatic population increases. Land enclosure and population expansion forced people to migrate to other parts of the country. Here, they either settled on national lands, worked as seasonal migrant laborers on cotton or coffee ranches, or sought opportunities in the growing urban centers.[23]

Central America's unequal pattern of land distribution has changed little since colonial times, despite the existence since the 1960s of agrarian reform programs. Government-sponsored colonization efforts have proved expensive and difficult to administer. Corruption, inadequate funding, and resistance by both landowners and government officials have hindered effective redistribution. In many areas, the large estates have expanded even further as a consequence of the growth in export agriculture. This expansion has forced those peasants who still use precapitalistic methods of tilling the soil to move ever more increasingly to marginal or overworked lands.

As pressures on the land mounted, peasants and their families left for the cities and other less-settled regions in search of new lives. While these so-called push factors were important, the pull of growing urban centers in Central America also attracted rural inhabitants. With the traditional rural social structures weakening, fewer strings existed tying individuals to the countryside.

Table 1.5. Distribution of agricultural landholdings in Central America according to number and area, estimates for 1970

Country	0–7 Hectares	7–35 Hectares	Over 35 Hectares
Costa Rica			
Number of holdings	75%	14%	8.6%
Area of holdings	3%	14%	82.0%
El Salvador			
Number of holdings	92	5	2.2
Area of holdings	19	17	65.0
Guatemala			
Number of holdings	90	7	2.0
Area of holdings	19	15	66.0
Honduras			
Number of holdings	77	18	4.3
Area of holdings	12	27	61.0
Nicaragua			
Number of holdings	65	18	14.0
Area of holdings	3	11	95.0
Panama			
Number of holdings	57	28	15.2
Area of holdings	6	14	82.0
Regional Average			
Number of holdings	76%	15%	7.7%
Area of holdings	10%	16%	75.0%

Sources: Adapted from SIECA, VI *Compendio estadístico centroamericano, 1975,* p. 97; and SIECA, *VII Compendio estadístico centroamericano, 1981,* p. 115 (Guatemala, 1975 and 1981). Figures are rounded to include landless farmers (number of holdings) and do not total 100 percent since administrative lands are omitted.

Table 1.6. Population and urban population in Central America: 1960, 1980

	1960		1980	
Country	Millions	% Urban	Millions	% Urban
Costa Rica	1.2	34.5	2.6	45.7
El Salvador	2.4	38.5	4.7	44.0
Guatemala	4.0	33.6	7.7	38.0
Honduras	1.9	23.2	4.1	40.0
Nicaragua	1.4	40.9	2.8	54.0
Panama	1.1	41.5	2.0	54.0

Sources: Inter-American Development Bank, *Economic and Social Progress, 1980–1981* (Washington, D.C., 1981), p. 395; and SIECA, *VII Compendio estadístico centroamericano, 1981* (Guatemala, 1981), p. 30.

The vision of a radically improved life through enhanced educational opportunities and income-producing work increased the flow of migrants to the cities.

Originally settled as administrative centers, Central America's cities became economic and social centers as well. As late as 1950, the urban sector constituted less than a fifth of the region's total population. Three decades later, nearly 45 percent of the population was considered urban (see Table 1.6). The general level of urbanization and urban concentration varies among the six countries. In proportion to total population, Panama City appears to be the clearest example of a "primate" city. But when capital cities are considered in relation to other cities, Guatemala City and San José appear as the region's dominant urban centers.

Urbanization in Central America has been relatively steady when compared to other Latin American countries. Industrialization has not been as great a pull factor because the industrial sector has remained relatively small. The pace of industrial growth leveled off at the close of the 1960s, after disruption of the Central American Common Market by the soccer war. The impact of rising energy costs after 1973 further slowed both domestic and international investment in the region.

Economic, social, and demographic change has been particularly strong in Central America since the late 1940s. These have included structural changes in local economies, greater involvement in the global economy, and alterations in domestic social relations. For more than three decades, the several countries of the region have been in various stages of social fermentation, a process which has created new political forces. The emergent middle sectors, substantially literate and increasingly sophisticated, actively demanded wider participation in the political process. As labor organizations appeared, working-class demands reinforced the pressures for social reforms, more efficient government, and expanded political participation. And in some countries, rural peasant movements placed further pressure on existing governments with their calls for land and social justice.

Another less-visible component of change in Central America since World War II has been the strengthening of local military institutions. Except for Costa Rica, whose armed forces were dissolved in 1948, national armies emerged as significant contenders for political power. Institutional self-perceptions and defense roles were modified to include the concept of the national security state. The U.S. government tended to reinforce these trends by supplying arms, equipment, and training and by encouraging the formation of a regional defense organization—the Central American Defense Council (CONDECA). Through such activity, younger officers acquired new perspectives on the relationship between security and national development. They were taught that it was legitimate for the armed forces to be concerned about this relationship in an era of rapid social and economic transformation.

Regional governments and ruling elites responded in different ways to this new constellation of sociopolitical forces with its incessant demands for reform. The Costa Rican Revolution of 1948 and Guatemala's tumultuous decade (1944–54) followed by excessive repression offer examples of the extremes. In the region as a whole, the response can be characterized as mildly reformist. Social security legislation, new labor codes, policies to encourage industrial expansion, and legislation for agrarian reform were enacted in most countries.

Subtle yet important shifts in the bases of power took place as new economic elites established their independence from the traditional landed elites. Landed elites, whose control rested upon well-oiled political machines and patronage distributed through the state bureaucracy, were being displaced as traditional interpersonal relations were altered or dissolved. Thus, while extensive changes were affecting the entire social and economic spectrum of Central American countries, a major transformation was taking place within the governing classes. Elite factionalism and competition weakened administrations, delayed any effective actions to cope with critical issues of national development, and contributed to political polarization.

Rising levels of political and social consciousness were expressed through a wide range of reformist movements, labor organizations, community associations, cooperatives, and peasant leagues. New political parties were launched with varying degrees of success. Some were splinter groups of traditional parties; others, such as the Christian Democrats, sprang from new social bases and the revitalization of the Catholic church. Increased communication and urbanization and spreading literacy engendered a qualitative change in social and political relations. Such change led to the emergence of new class-based social and political formations and greater sectoral identity.

In some areas of Central America, the Catholic church became actively involved in community development and in religious revival movements. In turn, the church's attention to its rural parishioners became one of the motivating forces behind reform in the region. Many of the priests and layworkers who minister in rural areas are foreign born. This factor has, on numerous occasions, catapulted the church into the forefront of political conflict in a manner quite distinct from its traditional historical role.

Reform movements were resisted by entrenched elites in most Central American countries but particularly in Nicaragua, El Salvador, and Guatemala. Throughout the 1960s and 1970s, only token efforts were made to integrate reformist forces into the political process and frustration grew. Open alternative forms of political participation were seldom allowed to develop and, as a result, guerrilla movements surfaced in each of the decades following World War II.[24] Partly in response to threats posed by these radicalized forces and partly because of divisions within the ruling class, military rulers increasingly chose to govern directly. The nature of military government varied in accordance with the distinctive realities of each Central American republic, the institutional history of the military, and the international role that a particular country defined for itself. Whether as political arbiters, modernizers, reformers, or keepers of the status quo, the armed forces have become the repository of political power throughout most of Central America.

Since the beginning of the twentieth century, United States regional hegemony had defined the boundaries of Central America's domestic and foreign behavior. This condition prevailed until the mid-1960s, when the Cuban Revolution helped burst the hegemonic bubble. Regional forces supporting political change increasingly operated in a world of shifting global relations. Nationalism, national development, international solidarity among developing countries, energy scarcity, and the spread of new technologies have all altered the conditions that formerly allowed for U.S. regional dominance. Other areas of the world have become alternative sources for Central America's imports as well as part of a more diverse international export market. Thus, Central America's postwar domestic condition has come to be affected by a variety of global factors that provide the international context and dimensions for the current crisis.

Notes

1. Robert C. West and John P. Augelli, *Middle America: Its Lands and Peoples* (Englewood Cliffs, N.J.: Prentice-Hall, 1976), p. 24.
2. Ibid., p. 12; and Mary W. Helms, *Middle America: A Cultural History of Heartland and Frontiers* (Englewood Cliffs, N.J.: Prentice-Hall, 1975).
3. Franklin D. Parker, *The Central American Republics* (New York: Oxford University Press, 1964), p. 50.
4. Richard N. Adams, *Cultural Surveys of Panama–Nicaragua–Guatemala–El Salvador–Honduras* (Washington, D.C.: Pan American Sanitary Bureau, 1957).
5. Ralph Lee Woodward, Jr., *Central America: A Nation Divided* (New York: Oxford University Press, 1976), p. 35.
6. Miles L. Wortman, *Government and Society in Central America: 1680–1840* (New York: Columbia University Press, 1982).
7. Helms, *Heartland and Frontiers*, p. 169.
8. Mario Rodríguez, *Central America* (Englewood Cliffs, N.J.: Prentice-Hall, 1965), p. 74.

9. Wortman, *Government and Society*, pp. 23ff.
10. Miles L. Wortman, "Government Revenue and Economic Trends in Central America, 1787–1819," *Hispanic American Historical Review* 55, no. 2 (May 1975), pp. 251–86.
11. See Thomas L. Karnes, *The Failure of Union: Central America, 1824–1975*, rev. ed. (Tempe, Ariz.: Center for Latin American Studies, Arizona State University, 1976).
12. Helms, *Heartland and Frontiers*, p. 222.
13. Edelberto Torres Rivas, *Interpretación del desarrollo social centroamericano*, 7th ed. (San José: EDUCA, 1981), p. 88.
14. Dana G. Munro, *The Five Republics of Central America: Their Political and Economic Development and Their Relations to the United States*, ed. David Kinley (New York: Oxford University Press, 1918), p. 15.
15. Parker, *Central American Republics*, p. 222.
16. Woodward, *A Nation Divided*, p. 152; cf. Ciro F. S. Cardoso and Héctor Pérez Brignoli, *Centroamerica y la economía occidental (1520–1930)* (San José: Editorial de la Universidad de Costa Rica, 1977).
17. Torres Rivas, *Interpretación del desarrollo*, p. 41.
18. Woodward, *A Nation Divided*, pp. 99–100.
19. West and Augelli, *Middle America*, p. 388.
20. Woodward, *A Nation Divided*, p. 166.
21. SIECA, *Estadísticas macroeconómicas de Centroamerica, 1970–1980* (Guatemala, July 1981), p. 13.
22. See Isaac Cohen Orantes, *Regional Integration in Central America* (Lexington, Mass.: D. C. Heath, 1972); and Roger Hansen, *Central America: Regional Integration and Economic Development* (Washington, D.C.: National Planning Association, 1967).
23. See CSUCA/Programa Centroamericano de Ciencias Sociales, *Estructura demográfica y migraciones internas en Centroamerica* (San José: EDUCA, 1978).
24. Torres Rivas, *Interpretación del desarrollo*, p. 169.

2

Social Change and Political Revolution: The Case of Nicaragua

Stephen M. Gorman

Nicaragua can be considered something of a political enigma within Latin America generally, and Central America in particular. Long considered one of the most stable and durable of North America's clientele states in the region under the firm domination of Somoza family rule, Nicaragua has seemingly become the epicenter of violent revolutionary change throughout Central America. Not only has Nicaragua's Sandinista-led revolution inspired insurrectionary activity in neighboring countries by example (demonstrating that even a North American-backed military dictatorship can be defeated by armed action); it has also provided a safe base for revolutionary organizations in the region to prepare or direct other insurrections (or at least such is the assertion of Washington and other concerned governments). In reality, however, the social, political, and economic forces that helped precipitate the Nicaraguan revolution, together with the particular array of political actors and behavioral propensities within Nicaraguan society that facilitated the initiation of mass insurrectionary activity, are in many respects unique to Nicaragua.

This is not to say that pre-revolutionary Nicaragua did not share many characteristics with other Central American republics. The country's literacy and health problems, dependence on agro-export activities, limited communications, infrastructure, endemic structural unemployment and underemployment, skewed income distribution, and legacy of political turmoil were conditions common to one degree or another in most of the other Central American nations. But it remains to be explained why

HONDURAS
Puerto Lempira
Tegucigalpa
EL SALVADOR
INTER-AMERICAN HIGHWAY
NUEVA SEGOVIA
JINOTEGA
ZELAYA
Puerto Cabezas
Ocotal
MADRIZ
Somoto
ESTELI
Golfo de Fonseca
Estelí
Jinotega
Matagalpa
Río Blanco
Prinzapolka
Potosí
CHINANDEGA
Río Grande
MATAGALPA
Chinandega
LEÓN
Boaco
Corinto
León
BOACO
Lago de Managua
CHONTALES
Pacific Ocean
Rama
Juigalpa
Caribbean Sea
Managua
Masaya
Bluefields
Granada
Jinotepe
CARAZO
Isla de Ometepe
RIO SAN JUAN
RIVAS
Lago de Nicaragua
Rivas
San Juan del Sur
San Carlos
NICARAGUA
Road
Railroad
0
50 Miles
0
50 Kilometers
San Juan del Norte
COSTA RICA
INTER-AMERICAN HIGHWAY

a thoroughgoing revolution occurred first in Nicaragua (perhaps to be followed by other successful regional revolutions, and perhaps not). And even if the Nicaraguan Revolution is followed in the near future by others in Guatemala or El Salvador, the process of political change in these latter two countries already demonstrates that the insurrectionary process there will likely follow a course quite distinct from the one that brought the Sandinista Front to power in Nicaragua. Hence, it may be more profitable to concentrate on some of the unique aspects of Nicaraguan political development than on the country's commonalities with other Central American republics in attempting to explain the process of violent political change that transpired in that nation.

Man, Land, and Politics in Nicaragua

Nicaragua is both the largest of the Central American republics (with roughly 139,000 square kilometers) and the least densely populated (with less than 50 persons per square mile in 1980).[1] Nicaragua's settlement pattern also sets it apart from the rest of Central America. Like its neighbors, the vast majority of the Nicaraguan population lives on the Pacific side of the mountain chain that runs down the middle of the Central American isthmus, but the principal population centers are located at much lower elevations and therefore have a more tropical, less desirable, climate than is true for most of the region's other major urban centers. Geographically, the country is divided between a large, underdeveloped Atlantic or Caribbean region and a considerably more developed but smaller Pacific region. Separating these two areas is a string of mountains averaging 610 meters in elevation running about 400 kilometers from the southeastern frontier with Costa Rica. Another important range of mountains (including the rugged Segovia region) runs in a northeasterly direction along the remainder of the border with Honduras.

The Pacific region of Nicaragua is dominated by a low-lying basin containing two large lakes, and a narrow band of volcanos separating this basin from the Pacific. The bulk of the population lives within the confines of this semi-tropical basin or on the highlands of the surrounding mountains. Over the past three decades, the area of greatest population density has been the region in and around the capital of Managua, located generally between lakes Managua and Nicaragua. The population of this western region of Nicaragua is almost uniformly *mestizo* (mixed Spanish and Indian blood), and therefore relatively homogenous, although a very small minority may be considered *blancos* (or whites). In contrast, the Caribbean region of Nicaragua contains a variety of ethnic, racial, and linguistic minorities which together represent something between 5 and 10 percent of the national population. Most notable among these minorities are the Miskitu Indians and English-speaking descendants of African slaves.

The inhabitants of this Caribbean region of Nicaragua have never played an important role in either the economic or political life of the nation, and the entire area has remained largely marginal from the remainder of the nation throughout Nicaraguan history. Aside from the ethnic, racial, and linguistic, not to mention geographical, differences, the distance and even hostility between the peoples of eastern and western Nicaragua is also a consequence of divergent historical experiences. As Philippe Bourgois explains:

> The profound cultural antagonism between the Pacific and Atlantic provinces of Nicaragua arose out of their distinct historical experiences and social formations. It had its roots in the diametrically opposed trajectories of Spanish and British colonialism in the region.[2]

The Atlantic provinces' tradition of resistance to Spanish colonialism (which benefited from British assistance) has carried over into modern times in which the various minorities have resisted the authority of subsequent Nicaraguan governments.

To a greater extent than in most other countries, Nicaragua's political development has been influenced by its geography. In particular, the existence of a natural pass through the string of mountains that runs the length of Central America, and the close proximity of two large, low-level lakes, has long made Nicaragua an ideal location for a trans-isthmian canal. Recognition of this fact led to early British and North American political penetration of the country, much earlier and more direct in fact than was true for the rest of the region. This, as it turned out, had considerable ramifications for the subsequent evolution of political attitudes among certain groups. Anti-imperialism gained an early foothold in Nicaraguan thought as a result of concrete historical events. In many other respects, however, the political and especially economic development of Nicaragua, while similar in outline, lagged somewhat behind the rest of Central America during its first century of independence; another fact with important implications for the subsequent course of events in the country. Both points can best be demonstrated by a brief review of Nicaragua's first hundred years of independence.

Nicaragua gained its independence from Spain by declaration in 1821 along with the rest of Central America. After a brief inclusion of the region within the "Empire" of Mexico between 1822 and 1823, Nicaragua became one of the five constituent members of the United Provinces of Central America, with its capital in Guatemala. The axis of political competition within this confederation was between Liberals, with their anticlericalism and desire for a federalist system, and Conservatives who favored state support of church privileges and a strong central government. Nicaragua played a minimal role in the political life of the United Provinces of Central America. One questionable explanation that has been offered for this is that the population of Nicaragua at the time was of a generally lower calibre than in other provinces: "During colonial days this region attracted fewer energetic Spaniards than the settlements on the salubrious highlands of Guatemala and Costa Rica."[3] The unity of Central America began to deteriorate steadily after 1827 as factional political violence increased. By 1838, the United Provinces dissolved, and each of the member provinces became independent republics.

The rivalry between Liberals and Conservatives continued within the newly autonomous republics, but in Nicaragua the outcome differed from the regional pattern. By the second half of the century, Liberals were in the ascendance throughout most of the region but not in Nicaragua. At this point, the dominant political questions were beginning to center around economic issues with Liberals favoring expanded state assistance for the development of new agro-export industries. Thus, as Liberals displaced the more aristocratic and traditionalistic Conservatives, new forces of economic development were encouraged.

But in Nicaragua, "where the Liberals were tainted more than elsewhere" by virtue of their earlier alliance with North American expansionists "the Conservatives were able to hold on for much longer."[4] Between 1863 and 1893 Conservatives held undisputed sway in Nicaragua, and they were instrumental, as were the Liberals in other countries, in promoting the expansion of coffee, which was becoming an important cash crop for the rest of the region.

When a Liberal revolt led by José Santos Zelaya succeeded in ousting the Conservatives in 1893, Nicaragua again developed in a direction different from the regional pattern. Nicaraguan Liberalism under Zelaya's tenure (1893–1909) fostered a virulent anti-imperialism which ultimately led the United States to engineer the Liberals' overthrow and the restoration of Conservative rule. Subsequently, the United States maintained a military presence for nineteen of the twenty-one years between 1912 and 1933, both to insure collection of debts owed to New York bankers and to defend Conservatives against the armed conspiracies of the Liberals.[5] Significantly, however, the actual programmatic and philosophical differences between Nicaraguan Liberals and Conservatives all but disappeared during the 1920s, and in the factional strife that flared in 1925 partisan ambition was the dominant motivation. Thus, since the Liberal Party had discarded its extreme nationalism and anti-imperialism which it had acquired under Zelaya, the United States was able to install a Liberal president in 1928 without sacrificing even the least security for its interests in the country. The nationalistic, anti-imperialistic tradition was championed thereafter by movements outside the legal political system, beginning with the rebellion of Augusto César Sandino in 1927, and culminating with the revolution of the Sandinista Front on National Liberation in 1979.[6]

Extended Conservative rule, delayed economic development, and direct foreign intervention strongly influenced the country's political evolution. The Nicaraguan political system, in a manner of speaking, can be considered as falling somewhere between the Costa Rican and Guatemalan experiences. In Costa Rica, the Liberal and Conservative parties became the dominant structures of political competition early on, and by the beginning of the twentieth century a more or less agreed upon democratic framework for regulating that competition had already taken hold. In Guatemala, by contrast, political parties took a backseat to political *caudillos* who ruled the country by force of their personalities. Thus, only four individuals ruled Guatemala for 85 of its first 106 years of independence until, in the early post–World War II period, the military acting as an institution entered and monopolized the political arena.[7] In comparison to Costa Rica's political democracy predicated on party competition, and Guatemala's authoritarian tradition that rendered political parties irrelevant early in its history, Nicaragua presents a mixture of both patterns.

As we have noted, Nicaraguan political history was quite turbulent up to the 1930s as Conservatives and Liberals waged constant civil wars for control of the state. Political stability was only obtained after the establishment of the Somoza dictatorship in 1936 with direct United States assistance, including the training and equipping of a National Guard completely under Somoza's control. But Somoza elected to rule as a civilian under the guise of a democratically chosen leader, and to that end he converted the Liberal Party into a vehicle for his personal ambitions, and encouraged the continued existence of the Conservative Party as a token opposition. Over the next four decades one after another of the Somoza family continued to carry on the masquerade of "democracy" while placing ultimate reliance on a military apparatus which, significantly, never achieved the slightest degree of institutional autonomy and therefore was incapable of becoming an independent political actor. Thus, once firmly established, the somocista dictatorship effectively closed the road to democracy based on open party competition (as in Costa Rica) but also lessened the probability of institutionalized military rule (as in Guatemala). Ultimately, the prevailing political-economic order that rose up under the Somozas could be preserved neither through the "election" of a figurehead opposition leader, nor the imposition of a military junta. So completely did the Somozas penetrate the political system and the national military that they could not be destroyed without simultaneously destroying the prevailing political system and the national military. Hence, change, once it came, was as a revolution.

The revolution that toppled the Somoza dictatorship in July

1979 represents an intentional, popularly supported attempt to restructure the political and economic relations that took shape over an extended period of dependent capitalist development in Nicaragua. For our purposes, *dependent capitalist development* refers to economic activity in developing countries, which 1) treats labor as a commodity and relies on the state to keep the price of that commodity artificially low, 2) is oriented toward external markets with which close financial and political ties are maintained, and 3) is largely engaged in either the production of primary products desired by developed market economies or value-added industrialization in which the primary economic resource is extremely cheap labor.[8]

In the following sections of this chapter, it will be argued that the very nature of Nicaragua's economic development and the specific characteristics of the political system that came into existence to promote and protect that development eventually produced a level of lower-class mobilization and politicization that led to political decay. This is not to suggest that revolution was inevitable, only that it became more likely as the society became increasingly complex and the dictatorship became increasingly inflexible. The techniques of social control that facilitated the establishment of the Somoza dynasty in the 1930s became increasingly counterproductive as the society grew more complex and differentiated. The evolution of modern social and economic relationships required the institutionalization of new capacities on the part of political authorities. But the foundations of Nicaraguan economic development—the exploitation of cheap labor as the basis of efficient agro-export—contributed to political intransigence on the part of the dictatorship. As a result, the regime lost legitimacy and grew even more isolated. The inability or unwillingness of the traditional political parties to push effectively for any meaningful political change or economic reforms in turn provided an opening to more revolutionary solutions to the growing political crisis.

The Sandinista Front of National Liberation (Frente Sandinista de Liberación Nacional—FSLN) that became the political-military vanguard of the War of National Liberation successfully preempted other political groups in the revolutionary process. It did this by correctly identifying and utilizing certain political undercurrents produced by the country's dependent capitalist development. Specifically, the FSLN stressed the nationalistic, anti-imperialistic nature of the struggle against the United States–backed dictatorship. The theme of populism—which was completely ignored by the traditional political parties—also proved to be an important basis of appeal.[9] Finally, the FSLN's call for a united front against the dictatorship during the final stage of the insurrection allowed most of the upper classes (who had been unable to devise a viable solution to the political crisis on their own) to abandon the dictatorship in favor of a popular government of national unity dominated by the Sandinista Front.

In the following discussion, we will outline in some detail the social, political, and economic transformations that occurred in Nicaragua after the turn of the century that contributed to the self-destruction of the Somoza dictatorship and the establishment of a popular revolutionary government. The analysis will concentrate on four interrelated but distinct topics: 1) the emergence and development of dependent capitalism, 2) the escalation of social mobilization and the deepening politicization and organization of the popular classes, 3) the growth of political and armed opposition to Somoza which contributed to the gradual decomposition of the dictatorship, and 4) the consolidation of the revolutionary regime on the basis of new societal values and power distribution following the defeat of Somoza.[10]

The Evolution of Nicaraguan Dependency

The modern political economy of Nicaragua began to take root in the final quarter of the last century when the expansion of export agriculture tied the economy to foreign markets, restructured property and class relations, and led eventually to the establishment of a stronger and more centralized state apparatus. The introduction of coffee and the shift in power from Conservatives to Liberals that this promoted in Nicaragua between the 1870s and the 1890s was, as we have noted, part of a broader trend that was evident throughout Central America.[11] The original orientation of Nicaraguan Liberals under the presidency of José Santos Zelaya (1893–1909) was anti–North American.[12] But the promotion of coffee production strengthened the country's dependent integration into the global capitalist economy and subsequently increased North American influence in Nicaragua. Eventually, under Anastasio Somoza García, the Liberals became the representatives of North American interests in the country.

As historian Ralph Lee Woodward explains, the Liberals who came to power shortly before the turn of the century represented those members of the landed aristocracy and urban middle sectors whose interests Conservative governments had failed to serve.[13] He goes on to observe that they differed considerably from their Liberal predecessors in the immediate post-independence period both in their emphasis on material progress and their lack of faith in popular democracy. While they did not formally abandon democratic political philosophy, they now believed that economic growth and prosperity were necessary before true political democracy could be established.[14] Guided by this outlook, the Liberals proceeded rapidly to rationalize and modernize the economic and social mechanisms that had been created earlier by the Conservatives for the production and export of coffee.[15]

The period between the late 1870s and the 1940s witnessed the development of what has been termed primitive dependent capitalism.[16] The prosperity of the economy became increasingly dependent on the expansion of primary agricultural exports based on the exploitation of cheap and abundant labor. There was only limited expansion of the internal market, and the lower classes were unimportant as consumers of the economy's chief products. Thus, there was "little or no economic incentive for the privileged classes ... to make the sacrifices necessary to improve the conditions of the majority of the people."[17] The links between the country's political economy and the North American government and economy were further strengthened by the onset of an uninterrupted period of direct American political-military intervention between 1912 and 1933. Further reinforcing the ties between Nicaragua and the United States was the expansion of North American investment in the country after World War I. Very quickly, "United States economic interests became dominant in the country."[18] Throughout most of this period, coffee remained the dominant industry, except for a brief interlude between 1938 and 1949 when gold led exports.

The expansion of agro-export and, later, mining created the foundations of a modern, albeit largely rural, work force. For the most part, Liberals attempted to suppress labor organization, but by 1924 the first durable labor central (Obrerismo Organizado de Nicaragua—OON) came into existence (during a period of Conservative rule). The OON was founded and directed by Sonfonías Salvatierra, who became a close associate of Augusto César Sandino. After Sandino's assassination in 1934, however, Salvatierra lost control of the OON, which was then taken over by the Somoza dictatorship as an instrument of government that was directed at lower-class co-optation and manipulation. By the end of the 1930s the OON had dissolved and the labor movement was contained.[19]

The next major labor organization to appear was the CTN (Confederación de Trabajadores de Nicaragua), controlled by the Communists, which enjoyed limited acceptance during and immediately following the Second World War. The onset of the Cold War, however, provided the dictatorship with an excuse to dissolve the CTN in 1948, again leaving the working class with little or no effective representation. The acceleration of economic activity in the post-war period, nevertheless, brought about an expansion in the work force that made the suppression of labor organizations increasingly difficult. There was a proliferation of labor organizations, and the dictatorship returned to its earlier strategy of taking over the largest of these (the Federación Nacionalista de Sindicatos Democráticos—FNDS) as a means of controlling lower class mobilization.[20] During this period there was also a second round of peasant proletarianization, similar to the one that accompanied the expansion of coffee, as new areas of the countryside were converted to the production of cotton and other export products.

Cotton, like coffee, required a large cheap labor force that was mostly employed on a seasonal basis. It was also a crop subject to wild price fluctuations, contributing to the boom-bust cycle of the economy. Hence, the period between World War II and the Sandinista revolution, labeled by Thomas Walker and others as modern dependent capitalism, saw the rapid expansion of the rural proletariat and the deepening of Nicaragua's integration into the global economy as a primary products exporter.[21]

The nature of Nicaragua's dependent capitalist development after World War II differed from the earlier period in a number of ways, and therefore had more diverse sociopolitical impacts.

Most significantly, the diversification of export production contributed to a corresponding expansion of the rural proletariat. The expansion of cotton during the 1950s and thereafter, in particular,

> dislodged many peasants from land on which they had been used to plant at least enough to feed themselves, to marginal lands on hillsides and in remoter areas. In a country where 65 percent of the population lived off the land, this was having a catastrophic effect, and those who could not resign themselves to eking out a precarious existence from unprofitable smallholdings were forced to choose between employment as plantation hands, earning ... 85 cents a day during harvest time, or migration to the cities.[22]

Predictably, urban centers began to grow faster than before (as will be discussed shortly) and this, in turn, created new opportunities for political organization of the masses and broadened the range of socioeconomic problems demanding governmental attention.

The composition of the Gross Domestic Product (GDP) also underwent change, especially during the 1960s, as the share of agriculture declined relative to industry, services, and government.[23] While a large part of the industrial expansion was linked to the processing of primary exports, the advent of the Alliance for Progress and the infusion of foreign capital in the form of private investments, loans, and bilateral assistance also contributed to the expansion of the modern sector. Much of the growth of the economy was spurred by a rapid expansion of exports which tripled between 1961 and 1967, far outperforming the regional average. This allowed the economy to expand at a very respectable rate of over 7 percent per annum during the same period. The accumulation of capital that this facilitated permitted rising investment ratios throughout the decade, further increasing the importance of the modern economic sector.[24] The bulk of the population, however, did not share in this new wealth.

The modernization of Nicaragua's dependent capitalism brought about the mobilization of human, as well as material, resources. As a consequence, middle-class and working-class elements inevitably grew in size and importance, and began increasingly to demand the right to "participate in the society, effecting permanent alterations in ruling patterns ... Efforts to retain or restore the pre-war dictatorships required significant concessions to popular needs and demands."[25]

Anastasio Somoza García, the consummate political manipulator and balancer, was able to maintain his control during the first half of the 1950s partly because of his political skills and partly because the tempo of change was still within manageable limits. The changing political realities of the country, however, demanded *substantive* changes which Somoza was unwilling to make. Without making any real concessions toward effective democracy, or materially improving the well-being of the masses, Somoza was able to pass himself off as a progressive leader, and strengthened the bases of his external support by closely identifying himself with the United States in the Cold War. Discontent, nevertheless, was steadily growing and in 1956 Somoza García was assassinated by a young idealist.[26]

Somoza García was succeeded by his eldest son, Luis, who adopted a somewhat more enlightened approach to rule but remained committed to maintaining the family's hegemony within the country. As Woodward notes, "a discernible trend toward political liberalization followed the assassination of Anastasio Somoza, but there was no real progress toward restructuring the society."[27] Luis Somoza's "liberalism" consisted of permitting a broader expression of political views, and working to relieve the family of the responsibilities of directly governing the country (preferring instead to place trusted associates in the presidency). This approach was in fact a response to the politicization of new social elements who were becoming less willing to accept the legitimacy of direct Somoza family rule. Most significantly, the labor movement, which had had so many false starts, began to develop new momentum. Humberto Ortega Saavedra (an FSLN comandante and leading member of the post-revolutionary regime) notes that in the years following Somoza's assassination, the number of syndicates grew, and their willingness to confront openly the regime over workers' interests increased. Still, he notes, "the direction of these struggles was not very revolutionary."[28] Not until the political and economic crisis of the 1970s did the labor movement begin to assume a militant posture. All the same, a revolution of rising expectations was beginning to take place in which the growing sense of relative deprivation of large segments of the society was increasing pressures on the government to deliver material benefits to new socioeconomic groups. This, of course, was a direct consequence of the social mobilization brought on by economic development and urbanization.

Rising Social Mobilization after 1950

The Nicaraguan economy experienced considerable growth in the years following the Second World War as the country was more fully integrated into the international market and new productive activities came into existence. Although the growing economic prosperity that resulted from this did not benefit the bulk of the population significantly because of the economic relations that existed within the country, it did bring about important social changes that gradually impinged on the political system. The integration of new population groups into the mainstream of society, albeit in a subordinate role as rural or urban laborers, broadened the political awareness of the lower classes and opened new opportunities for political activation. At the same time, the growth of certain intermediate sectors such as the middle class and, especially, technocrats changed somewhat the relative political weight of those groups that had already achieved inclusion within the modern sector. In short, the 1950s and 1960s witnessed an increasing tempo of social mobilization in Nicaragua. That mobilization was both stimulated by, and reflected in, expanding urbanization, communication, education, and industrialization. The inevitable outcome was that political life became more complex as new actors attempted to place new or hitherto neglected issues on the national political agenda.

An essential ingredient in Nicaraguan social mobilization after the Second World War was the rapid growth of urban centers. This process was a partial by-product of both the expansion of cotton production that forced many rural families off subsistence plots, and the attraction of new, if limited, urban jobs. Between 1950 and 1971 the national population grew at an average annual rate of about 2.8 percent. But between 1950 and 1963 urban centers of 25,000 or more expanded at an annual average of 6.2 percent, and from 1963 to 1971 all urban centers expanded at an average annual rate of almost 5 percent compared to 1 percent per year in the countryside.[29] Not only did urban centers expand, but the population as a whole became more geographically concentrated. By 1971 over 48 percent of the population was urbanized and half of the entire population lived in a small triangular area between Granada, León, and the Pacific Ocean with Managua at its center (representing only 7 percent of the national territory).[30] The significance of urbanization is that it facilitates many of the other processes associated with modernization and social mobilization, including participation in a money economy, acquisition of education, and exposure to new communications channels. Correspondingly, the salience of national political issues increases for urban groups, as does their potential for acting on those issues.

Educational opportunities in Nicaragua, as in most other Latin American countries, have traditionally been greater in urban centers. Thus, increasing urbanization during the 1950s and 1960s fostered a growth in the number of children reached by education in both absolute and relative terms. By 1964 over 86 percent of all urban children had access to a primary education (compared with only 35 percent in the countryside). Secondary education, however, remained illusive since only 8 percent of those entering primary school finished the cycle and resources remained scarce. Even so, the majority of children obtained at least a rudimentary education, and by 1971, fully 57 percent of the population over 15 years of age possessed basic literacy by unofficial count.[31] Higher education also experienced a marked growth even though the absolute number of students remained quite restricted. The enrollment of the two leading universities (the Autonomous National University of Nicaragua and the Central American University) grew at an average annual rate of 17 and 21 percent respectively, between 1960 and 1971. Total enrollment, however, remained under 12,000.[32] Together with the students educated abroad, the graduates of Nicaragua's universities significantly increased the number of professionals within the country, fortifying the emerging middle class and thereby giving impetus to the reformist thought which is generally characteristic of the better-educated members of this social stratum in Latin America.

Urbanization and expanding literacy helped broaden modern channels of communication, especially the mass media. It has been recognized for some time that the growth of communications networks within a developing society contributes powerfully to social mobilization.[33] The expansion of communication appears almost as an inevitable consequence of economic development and urbanization, and controlling the flow and content of information often becomes a major preoccupation of authoritarian governments such as the one that existed in Nicaragua. One reason for this is that, as Gabriel Almond and Bingham Powell explain, "social mobilization is in large part a communications phenomenon," and communications through the mass media usually contain a lot of political information.[34] They go on to note that

> It is this exposure to new communications sources that creates the "revolution of rising expectations." The dilemma arises from the fact that political aspirations and expectations rise much faster than the system can develop the capabilities to meet them. Even more significantly, information can also lead to cynicism about politicians and institutions when these are ineffective and unresponsive. The resulting discontents make for a political instability often fueled by extravagant hopes built by political leaders.[35]

The expansion of mass media in Nicaragua was quite dramatic. By 1963 there were already 63 radio stations and more than 150,000 receivers in the country. And by 1968 there were fourteen daily newspapers, most of them in Managua. Of these, the seven largest had a combined circulation of over 101,000.[36] Attention to political issues was assured by the fact that the single largest daily was owned and operated by Pedro Joaquín Chamorro, one of the leaders of the traditional political opposition to the Somoza dynasty. The government also published its own daily with a high political content.

A final important development in the post-war years was the expansion of manufacturing which changed the composition of the Gross Domestic Product but did not open up adequate opportunities for the modern work force. While the expansion in manufacturing was considerable, it did not bring about a corresponding increase in industrial employment. Between 1960 and 1967, for example, industrial output increased by 102 percent, but the industrial labor force expanded by only 20 percent (from 51,601 to 62,600). The largest labor group in the country remained the rural proletariat associated with cotton and coffee production. And the fastest growing urban labor force was in the service sector, engaged in economic activities that were frequently incidental to the main productive activities of the society and less well remunerated. Thus, there emerged a sizeable lumpenproletariat that experienced a high incidence of underemployment.[37]

One of the principal characteristics of Nicaraguan manufacturing was a high degree of concentration of activity. As Jaime Wheelock noted,

> Of the 600 industrial firms with more than 5 workers, which represented a little more than 90 percent of the Gross Industrial Product, 136 firms generated 72 percent of the total value, and only 23 of them—in petrochemicals, plastics, metals, finished woods, beverages and alcohol—were responsible for 35 percent of manufacturing production in 1971.[38]

At the opposite end of the spectrum were as many as 13,000 small artisan work shops that produced only about 5 percent of the industrial product. The small group of Nicaraguan entrepreneurs who controlled the vast majority of the nation's industrial production were closely associated with either the Somoza family or foreign capital, or both. Throughout the 1950s and 1960s, they served as one of the key support groups to the Somoza dynasty, which adopted policies (such as low wages) that allowed for a high degree of capital accumulation. This government support, together with a relatively industrial labor force, allowed manufacturing to expand faster than any other sector of the economy.[39] But because manufacturing output did not satisfy growing lower-class consumption demands, and manufacturing employment did not expand in line with the growth of the urban labor force, industrialization produced a certain amount of popular frustration.

In spite of impressive rates of growth (averaging 9 percent per annum during most of the 1960s), manufacturing still accounted for only about 21 percent of the GDP and 12 percent of total employment in 1971.[40] The extreme concentration of wealth and the virtual stagnation in industrial employment meant that the vast majority of the urban population benefited only slightly from the country's economic development. This created a sense of relative deprivation which was only intensified with the steady expansion of literacy and mass communication. The increasing complexity of Nicaraguan society brought on by more than two decades of social mobilization required adjustments in the mode of political domination within the country. At a minimum, the government needed to accommodate a wider array of interests and improve its image of responsiveness to sustain the existing political framework. Two events, however, disrupted a gradual transformation of the political system and intensified political dissent: the death of the moderately reformist Luis Somoza in 1967 and the Managua earthquake of 1972.

Government and Opposition: 1967–78

Somocista power rested on three pillars: direct personal control of the National Guard, the National Liberal Party (Partido Liberal Nacionalista—PLN), and the Executive. Family control of these institutions was buttressed by close identification with the U.S. government and American business interests in Nicaragua, the encouragement of corruption within the National Guard to isolate troops from the rest of the population, political patronage coupled with selective coercion against opponents of the regime, and close controls of the legal opposition. The dictatorship, however, was not monolithic. At times the Somozas were obliged by circumstances to pay at least symbolic respect to democratic ideals, especially after the Second World War and again during the Alliance for Progress in the mid-1960s. This was normally accomplished by an ostentatious display of "constitutionalism" intended to disguise some new agreement for perpetuating the dictatorship under seemingly more legal auspices. At other times, the internal political climate forced the Somozas to offer various temporary power sharing formulas to the leaders of the legal opposition; arrangements which were quickly put aside after the immediate political difficulties of the dictatorship had been overcome. Through it all, however, the Somoza family remained firmly in command of the state apparatus.

Nevertheless, during the late 1960s and early 1970s the viability of the somocista power structure declined as a direct consequence of the changing nature of state-society relations. Although the earlier expansion of agro-export had helped consolidate a centralized government under strong leadership during the first half of the century, the role of the government within the overall political economy had remained fairly restricted. By modern standards, the state apparatus prior to the late 1950s was comparatively primitive. Economic growth, changing social norms, and an increasing professional class, however, encouraged an expansion of the public sector. As a result, the state began to penetrate the economy more fully and control a wider range of activities. This more complete articulation between the state and society brought a larger segment of society under the influence of the dictatorship operating through the expanded bureaucracy. Herein lies one of the principle causes of the growing social tension that gradually eroded the foundations of somocista power.

The societal-wide effects of the corruption and coercion of Anastasio Somoza García between 1936 and 1956 were constrained in one sense by the limited capabilities of the state apparatus. His ability to penetrate and control all facets of political-economic life in Nicaragua were correspondingly circumscribed. But the growth of the state apparatus after his assassination meant that similar political behavior would have magnified and more generalized consequences. As Samuel Huntington points out, modernization increases the opportunities for corruption. And to the extent that "corruption tends to accentuate already existing inequalities," the excesses of the somocista dictatorship after the 1950s intensified social conflicts associated with social stratification in Nicaragua.[41] In short, the somocista dictatorship became less tolerable because of the growing efficiency of the state apparatus as an instrument of graft and coercion.

The primary axis of political competition in Nicaragua prior to the 1970s was between Liberals and Conservatives. After assuming power in 1936, Somoza García had consolidated his control of the National Liberal Party while most of the opposition united in the Conservative Party. The Conservatives resorted to a variety of opposition strategies, including occasional participation in elections, more frequent boycotts of elections on the grounds they were rigged, and repeated attempts to topple the dictatorship by force. The armed actions of Conservatives, however, took the form of elitist putsches aimed at seizing power quickly with a minimum of lower class participation. Meaningful social reform was never a goal of the Conservatives. The largely upper-class Conservative Party provided the dictatorship with a symbolic but essentially ineffectual opposition that created the appearance of political democracy and prevented other, potentially more radical, groups from gaining a foothold in the political system. However, the growth of the middle and upper classes beginning in the late 1950s broadened the base of the Conservative Party and strengthened its ability to bring pressure to bear on the government. The new complexity of the Nicaraguan political economy, reflected in the expanding role of the state, economic growth, and mounting political opposition to dictatorship, brought about a brief era of reform under Luis Somoza.

Luis Somoza assumed the presidency on the death of his father, and was elected to a full term in 1957. While in office, he initiated a plan to extricate the family from direct responsibility for the government, preferring instead to direct events and protect family interests from behind the scenes through the PLN and the expanding bureaucracy.[42] At the end of his term in 1963, Luis Somoza arranged the election of a close family associate, René Schick, as president. His liberalization strategy also called for the eventual surrender of direct family command of the National Guard, headed by his younger brother, Anastasio Somoza Debayle.

Although Luis Somoza never intended to relinquish real power, his liberalization policies were opposed by his brother whose

> understanding of the mechanics of power was far more straightforward and unvarnished. Like his father before him, Tachito believed that the Somozas' only reliable constituency was the Guardia, and that to delegate any power at all was an exceedingly dangerous game.[43]

Taking full advantage of his command of the National Guard, Anastasio Somoza Debayle engineered his "election" as president in 1967. Shortly before his brother's inauguration, Luis Somoza died of a heart attack. Somoza Debayle's more open dictatorial style of rule after a period of moderation under his brother, as it turned out, accentuated political conflict within the country.

During his first term (1967–72), Somoza's approach was somewhat restrained in comparison to what it would become later. By 1970, the depth of the opposition to his government (together with the fact that he was constitutionally barred from election to a consecutive term as president) led him to propose a power-sharing formula to the Conservative Party. Under the terms of the agreement, the Congress dissolved itself in 1971 pending the election of a constituent assembly to frame a new constitution, and Somoza turned over executive power to a triumvirate (on which he had two loyal representatives) in May 1972. The dictator's intention in making an agreement with the Conservative Party was twofold: it served to diffuse the growing public opposition to his regime, and under the terms of a new constitution he would be eligible for reelection as president. Events, however, brought about a quick resumption of direct power by Somoza, and an intensification of coercion and corruption.

On the morning of December 23, 1972 Managua was devastated by a massive earthquake. In the aftermath of the disaster, Somoza demanded and received unlimited power from the constituent assembly to direct efforts at national reconstruction. Somoza employed this power to direct personally both international relief and the National Guard, and to extend his financial holdings into new areas at the expense of Nicaragua's emerging entrepreneurial class. The scope and aggressiveness of somocista corruption after 1972 virtually isolated the regime (even so, Somoza was able to use the National Guard to "win" election to another term as president under the terms of the 1974 Constitution). It was not merely the existence of corruption that intensified political opposition, but the nature of that corruption. As Samuel Huntington has noted,

> Corruption is not necessarily incompatible with political stability so long as the avenues of upward mobility through the political machine or the bureaucracy remain open. If, however, the younger generation of politicians sees itself indefinitely excluded

from sharing in the gains of the older leaders ... the system becomes liable to violent overthrow.[44]

After 1972 it was not just the younger generation that despaired at participating in the country's gains; established economic elites suffered from Somoza's greed as well.

Whereas the elder Somoza had enriched the family by acquiring a participating interest in new and existing economic activities in the country, Luis Somoza had relied on manipulation of government regulations to expand and promote family businesses. But Somoza Debayle began taking over entire business areas after 1972. This monopolization of opportunity deprived the dictatorship of support from even the privileged upper classes. According to John Booth,

> The Somozas' economic power came to affect profoundly the lives and well-being and interests of all Nicaraguans. This power at first promoted, but ultimately blocked, the complete unification of the capitalist class. Key elements among the nation's major investors in the end turned against the regime and, perhaps reluctantly, became rebels.[45]

And Somoza's growing resistance to even cosmetic reforms alienated other past and potential allies of the regime.

> Somoza increasingly closed channels for elite reformist efforts through established institutions after 1972. As a consequence, groups formerly coopted into collaboration or willingly sharing in power (the major national investor groups, certain Conservative Party factions, and certain liberal Nationalist Party elements) turned against the regime.[46]

It may well be that the increasing power of the state apparatus led Somoza to believe that it could serve as an autonomous base of domination, relieving him of the need to bargain for political support. But the opposite was the case. The increased articulation between state and society in Nicaragua meant that Somoza's abuse of the government adversely affected vast segments of the population to such an extent that the continuation of the dictatorship could no longer be tolerated by a broad cross section of the population.

Revolution and Consolidation

The literature on revolution suggests quite strongly that armed struggle in developing societies is frequently a response to the problems of modernization. Henry Bienen noted some time ago that "there has emerged consensus around the view that socioeconomic change lies behind any revolution."[47] We have said enough to agree that socioeconomic change in Nicaragua prior to the 1970s had accentuated a number of existing social, political, and economic problems, and also had created many new ones. But precisely how did this precipitate not only a revolutionary situation, but an actual revolution? To answer this question, we must first examine two things: the nature of revolutionary situations and the general characteristics of revolution itself.

Ted Robert Gurr writes that "a number of theorists ascribe revolution in the most general sense to the state's failure to adjust to changes in society."[48] At the most fundamental level, the viability of any state depends on a minimum balance between capabilities and responsibilities, and congruence between government policies and social norms. According to Gurr, the adaptability of a state, its ability to successfully adjust to social change, is conditioned by four key factors: 1) the skill, openness, and responsiveness of elites; 2) organizational efficiency in government adequate to satisfy the rising public expectations that accompany modernization; 3) compatibility in the attitudes of elites and masses concerning the political system; and 4) certain "structural-political" variables such as constitutions and political parties that promote congruence between the way authority is exercised in both government and underlying social institutions.[49]

In a somewhat similar fashion, Chalmers Johnson has attributed revolutions to the interactions of three variables: 1) multiple social dysfunctions; 2) the intransigence of elites; and 3) "accelerators" such as defeat in war, economic depression, or natural disasters. An example of a social dysfunction would be the continuation of feudalistic social relations within the context of expanding capitalist economic relations in a developing society. An intransigent elite is one that is either unwilling or unable to modify its behavior in line with the political forces that are released through modernization, or refuses to make necessary reforms in the political economy of the country. Accelerators, in turn, confront the political system with a major crisis which weak regimes will be unable to survive.[50]

But as James Malloy has pointed out, multiple social dysfunction, elite intransigence, and accelerators may create a revolutionary situation "but not necessarily a revolution per se."[51] For Malloy, and many others, an additional and perhaps critical factor is the legitimacy of the political system and the existing regime (which may be independent of these other considerations). It is quite possible, for example, for an inefficient regime to survive regardless of leadership capabilities as long as its legitimacy does not fall below some critical threshold, just as it is possible for a comparatively more efficient and well-managed regime to fall when it fails to elicit recognition of its legitimate right to exercise authority. The reality, however, is that modernization as a process comes to impose unique standards for government legitimacy which become progressively more difficult for oligarchies (much less autocracies like Somoza's Nicaragua) to meet.[52] Conflicts concerning legitimacy normally take the form of ideological competition in developing societies. When ruling elites definitively lose their ideological contest, yet still refuse to relinquish power or change their style of rule, revolution becomes more likely. Progressively after 1972, this was the situation in Nicaragua.

Turning to the second issue (the characteristics of revolution itself), revolutions can be distinguished from other forms of political conflict in the degree to which they aim at restructuring the political system as a whole. Gurr, working off Harry Eckstein's typology of political violence, considers revolution to be a type of "internal war." He defines internal war in the following terms:

> Highly organized political violence with widespread popular participation, designed to overthrow the regime or dissolve the state and accompanied by extensive violence, including large-scale terrorism and guerrilla wars, and revolutions.[53]

There are, however, significant differences between true revolutions and other forms of internal war such as peasant rebellions which are crucial for our understanding of their relationship to political change in modernizing societies.

S. N. Eisenstadt describes revolutionary movements as those that work at "(1) changing the rules of access to . . . the center; (2) broadening the bases of the collectivity . . ., and; (3) changing the pattern for the distribution of resources."[54] Malloy argues that revolutions aim at bringing about "(a) a redistribution of the capacity of groups to influence a society's authoritative mechanism; (b) the exclusion of groups with a previously high authoritative capacity from any future access to power; (c) the redefinition of a society's concepts and principles of authority; and (d) a redefinition of the goals which government authority usually pursues."[55] Both definitions highlight the fact that revolution is a profoundly transforming experience: it satisfies (or seemingly satisfies) long pent-up desires for fundamental changes in both social and political relations. Perhaps the most concise definition of revolution is offered by Samuel Huntington:

> Revolution . . . involves moral renewal. The manners and accepted patterns of behavior of the previously corrupt society are replaced by an initially highly Spartan and Puritan regime. In its negative phase, revolution completes the destruction of an already disintegrating code of morals and set of institutions. In its positive phase, revolution gives rise to new, more demanding sources of morality, authority, and discipline.[56]

Nicaragua fits all of these criteria and definitions. The overthrow of the Somoza dictatorship in 1979 represents only the fourth bona fide revolution in twentieth-century Latin America (the others being Mexico, Bolivia, and Cuba). In this final section, we will examine the internal decomposition of the Nicaraguan dictatorship and the rise of revolutionary politics.

The Sandinista Front of National Liberation (FSLN) that eventually toppled the Somoza dictatorship was formed in 1961 by a group of young Nicaraguan Marxists who received direct backing from Cuba. Although it was inspired by the anti-imperialist rebellion of Augusto César Sandino (1927–33), its principal goal was to carry out a socialist revolution by engaging the dictatorship in a protracted guerrilla war in the countryside (as outlined in the foco theory of the Cuban revolution). After a period of small-scale operations, the FSLN suffered a major military defeat in 1967 at the battle of Pancasán which set in motion a gradual reorientation in strategy.

Progressively after 1967, the FSLN augmented its activities in the countryside with increased urban organizational work. After a period of "accumulation of forces in silence," the Sandinista Front carried out a major action against the dictatorship in December 1974, when a number of close Somoza family members and associates were taken as hostages.[57] The hostages were exchanged for $1 million, the release of political prisoners, and the publication of FSLN political communiqués. This armed action provided the Sandinista Front with national recognition, but it also provoked a massive counteroffensive by the National Guard over the following three years. Although Somoza's counterinsurgency measures threw the FSLN completely on the defensive, his indiscriminate brutality produced new recruits for the Sandinista Front from all classes. This, together with the increasing corruption of the dictatorship that followed the 1972 earthquake, steadily eroded the legitimacy of the regime.

While the FSLN was gaining increasing national recognition as the leader in the struggle against the dictatorship, the severity of the counterinsurgency campaign caused the group to splinter over questions of strategy and ideology between 1975 and 1977. Three distinct factions or tendencies emerged. The Prolonged Popular War (GPP) tendency called for the concentration of activities in the countryside, and viewed the rural proletariat and peasantry as the leading revolutionary classes in Nicaragua. Another group, the Proletarian Tendency (TP) advocated greater attention to urban organizational activity, and argued that Nicaragua's recent capitalist development had turned the urban proletariat into the leading revolutionary class. Finally, a third group known as the *Terceristas* (or more correctly, the *Insurreccionales*) advocated the formation of the broadest possible front of opposition groups (including the progressive bourgeoisie) and the immediate initiation of nationwide insurrectionary activities.[58]

The Terceristas believed that the revolutionary potential of the general population was sufficiently high to begin a frontal assault on the dictatorship. The GPP and TP, in contrast, felt that many more years would be required to prepare the ground for a successful revolution. But when the armed actions of the

Terceristas elicited some popular support in October 1977, the other two tendencies were forced to reevaluate political conditions in the country, and the three groups began to move toward reunification. As James Petras noted later, the three tendencies discovered that their strategies were actually complementary.

> Both the guerrilla movement and the mass urban insurrectionary organizations were necessary for the maintenance of each other's struggle.... The insurrectionist activities of the Tercerista faction served to detonate action, while the GPP and TP groups contributed to the building of the mass organizations that sustained the struggle. The *audacity* of the former and the *organizational skills* of the latter were complementary—each requiring the other for the making of a successful revolution.[59]

After the October armed actions, the FSLN began to reassume the offensive. A series of political events were necessary, however, before the FSLN was able to consolidate its leadership of the nation against Somoza.

While the dictatorship had grown increasingly isolated after 1972, and politically inflexible after 1974, there was still no consensus among all the opposition groups on how to resolve Nicaragua's political impasse. At one end of the political spectrum were the Sandinistas who advocated revolution; at the other end stood the bourgeoisie which favored the removal of Somoza but did not seriously advocate sweeping reforms. Revolution was still avoidable so long as the bourgeois opposition continued to attract support from other social groups. Events during 1978 served to discredit the bourgeois opposition, and united the nation behind the FSLN.

In January 1978, Pedro Joaquín Chamorro, a nationally popular opponent of the dictatorship, was assassinated (apparently with the complicity of Somoza). This act galvanized the bourgeoisie into an open attempt to depose Somoza. In February, a large number of centrist political, social, and economic groups joined together to form the Broad Opposition Front (FAO) to end the dictatorship by means short of armed insurrection. The principal tactics of the FAO were economic pressure and, later, U.S. diplomatic pressure to force Somoza out of office and hold free elections. The FSLN regarded this as an attempt to create *somocismo sin Somoza* (the Somoza system without Somoza) since it would leave the National Guard intact and would not redress economic inequalities. When the FAO had failed to extract any concessions from Somoza by mid-year, the FSLN was able to begin consolidating popular support behind its revolutionary activities.

Taking advantage of years of organizational activities among the masses, the FSLN helped form the United People's Movement (MPU)—composed of student, peasant, and worker organizations allied with the Sandinistas—to coordinate the political attack on the dictatorship. Through the MPU, the FSLN issued a twenty-five point program calculated to appeal to a broad cross section of the population, and stressed the populist and nationalistic elements of its ideology. After an FSLN raid on the National Palace in August 1978, another nationwide insurrection broke out in September resulting in over 6,000 casualties and more than 30,000 refugees. In response to this increasingly revolutionary situation, the FAO made one last attempt to negotiate an end to the dictatorship. When this had completely failed, many of the more progressive members of the FAO began to openly support the Sandinista Front. To unify this growing support, the MPU organized the National Patriotic Front (FPN) in February 1979 which corresponded to the broad opposition front that had been advocated by the Terceristas. In the same month, the FSLN achieved its complete unification.[60]

The final assault on the dictatorship began in May 1979 and by early July the National Guard had been defeated in direct clashes throughout the country. A hard core of perhaps 5,000 Sandinistas were assisted by popular militias and spontaneous armed insurrection in lower-class neighborhoods, and on July 19, 1979, the FSLN took control of the government.[61] By the end, the revolution had resulted in over 40,000 dead and the destruction of over one-quarter of the economy.

After the fall of the Somoza dictatorship, the Sandinista Front moved quickly to restructure political relationships and carry out economic reforms. While most of the leadership of the FSLN were Marxists, the fall of Somoza did not bring about a communist or even socialist regime. Whatever the long-term objectives of the new revolutionary government, its orientation during the first three years in power was essentially that of a social democratic regime in policy matters. Even though there were expropriations of property, nationalization of certain economic activities, and a repudiation of the norms of bourgeois electoral democracy, a remarkable degree of pluralism was allowed and the private sector did not suffer from the collectivist orientations of the Sandinista rulers.

In the area of economic reforms, the Sandinistas limited expropriation mainly to the holdings of the Somoza family and its closest associates. The size of the somocista economic holdings (perhaps one-quarter to one-third of the Gross Domestic Product) allowed the government to carve out a state sector without directly harming the native bourgeoisie. Within a few months of the insurrection, the new regime had expropriated upwards of one-half million hectares of farm land, 180 business firms, and a large number of residential properties. Additionally, agricultural export and many areas of banking were nationalized, and measures were taken to cancel out the wealth that was taken out of the country by Somoza supporters during the final stage of the insurrection.[62] The agrarian policy that evolved after the insurrection emphasized the formation of state farms, voluntary collectives, and credit and technical assistance for medium- and large-scale producers.[63] In industry, progress was not as swift for two reasons. The extensive damage to the economic infrastructure that resulted from the revolution made industrial reactivation expensive, and credit for the private manufacturers became somewhat scarce as the FSLN channeled a large amount of national resources toward relieving the sufferings of the masses. The first obstacle was dealt with through a major program of national reconstruction, and the latter by appeal to foreign assistance (especially the United States) to provide financial assistance to the national entrepreneurial class. Alongside these economic reforms, a large number of social programs were initiated within the first year, including a massive literacy crusade and improvement in health services.

In the political arena, the state apparatus was immediately and completely overhauled. The new center of power became the nine-member Sandinista National Directorate (DNC) composed of the three ranking members of each of the old FSLN tendencies.[64] Ceremonial executive powers were vested in a five-member Government of National Reconstruction (JGRN) appointed by the DNC, and which originally included at least two representatives of the national bourgeoisie. In 1981 the JGRN was reduced to three members (including one representative from the DNC and another Sandinista leader) and became more openly subordinated to the DNC (as indeed it had always been). A quasi-legislative body, the State Council, was convened in May 1980 with forty-seven members appointed by traditional and popular organizations recognized by the DNC. While this body was given more powers than originally intended, careful control of its membership and direct DNC supervision of its deliberations insured that it fully cooperated with the Sandinista rulers. Finally, and perhaps most importantly, the old National Guard was completely disbanded, and in its place a new, ideologically indoctrinated Popular Sandinista Army was created with remarkable speed and efficiency. Reinforcing the new political arrangements was a unique collegiate leadership format within the DNC that reduced rivalry and discouraged *personalismo* among the FSLN leaders, yet allowed for considerable consistency in regime policy.

Underlying the new revolutionary order were a number of popular, grass-roots organizations closely aligned with the FSLN and supportive of the Sandinista vanguard role. Throughout the country, Sandinista Defense Committees were organized on a neighborhood basis to recruit reserves (militias) for the new army, and coordinate volunteer labor for social and economic programs. These committees were also important points of ideological indoctrination. In the agricultural sector, peasants and rural proletarians were organized into the Association of Rural Workers (ATC) which the FSLN had first created in 1977. The urban proletariat, in turn, was grouped into the Sandinista Workers Confederation which was formed on the basis of pro-Sandinista labor unions that had existed before the insurrection.[65] Aside from these bases of organized power among the lower classes, the Sandinistas received support from a wide variety of other social groups and institutions, including the Association of Nicaraguan Women, the July 19th Sandinista Youth, and certain segments of the clergy. Interestingly, however, the National Patriotic Front, and even the United Peoples' Movement, which had been formed during the insurrection to provide united front support for the FSLN, were allowed to fade away after the fall of Somoza. The likely reason is that the FSLN preferred direct linkages with its grass-roots support groups and opposed either of these groups becoming a formal political party in the new political system. The extensive organizational support that the FSLN enjoyed among the masses made it possible for the new government to tolerate a considerable degree of political organization on the part of the bourgeoisie (whose enthusiasm for the Sandinistas waned considerably not long after the fall of Somoza). By the end of the second year in power, however, the FSLN was beginning to take steps to contain the political activities of certain bourgeois opposition groups, partly out of concern that they might become the vehicle of external attempts to destabilize the new regime.

Conclusion

The Nicaraguan revolution was the result of the previous regime's incapacity to effectively respond to the pressures of political change. The anti-popular, pro-imperialist nature of the Somoza dictatorship was directly responsible for the popular, anti-imperialist nature of the Sandinista regime. The dependent capitalist development of the Nicaraguan economy and the authoritarian institutions of the Nicaraguan political system produced the social forces that after 1979 began pushing for a more socialized economy and popular forms of government. The Sandinistas have demonstrated a considerable amount of political skill, ideological flexibility, and sincere concern for the newly mobilized masses. The pressures of modernization and the demands of political and economic development, however, will continue to exercise profound influences on Nicaragua. Revolution, after all, is not in itself a solution to the socioeconomic problems associated with development. Revolutions simply open up new approaches to contending with those problems.

Notes

1. On this point, see Ralph Lee Woodward, Jr., *Central America: A Nation Divided* (New York: Oxford University Press, 1976), pp. 3–5.
2. Philippe Bourgois, "The Problematic of Nicaragua's Indigenous Minorities," in Thomas W. Walker, ed., *Nicaragua in Revolution* (New York: Praeger, 1982), p. 306.

3. Hubert Herring, *A History of Latin America,* Third Edition (New York: Alfred A. Knopf, 1968), p. 488.

4. Woodward, *Central America,* pp. 154–55.

5. See Thomas W. Walker, *Nicaragua: The Land of Sandino* (Boulder, Colo.: Westview Press, 1981), pp. 20–23; and Herring, *Latin America,* pp. 490–92.

6. See Harry Vanden, "The Ideology of the Insurrection," in Walker, *Nicaragua in Revolution;* and Humberto Ortega Saavedra, *50 años de lucha sandinista* (Managua: Ministerio del Interior, 1979).

7. See Woodward, *Central America,* pp. 149–76; and Herring, *Latin America,* pp. 472–78 and 496–501.

8. For a more complete treatment of dependency and dependent capitalist development, see chapter one of Ronald H. Chilcote and Joel Edelstein, *Latin America: The Struggle with Dependency and Beyond* (Cambridge, Mass.: Schenkman, 1974).

9. Stephen M. Gorman, "Power and Consolidation in the Nicaraguan Revolution," *Journal of Latin American Studies* 13 (May 1981), pp. 139–49; and Stephen M. Gorman, "The Role of the Revolutionary Armed Forces," in Walker, *Nicaragua in Revolution,* pp. 115–19.

10. The decision to focus on these four areas was influenced by the analysis of Jaime Wheelock in *Imperialismo y dictadura: crisis de una formación social* (Mexico City: Siglo XXI, 1975); and Humberto Ortega Saavedra in *50 años* both of which were considered in relation to the work of Samuel P. Huntington on social mobilization and political decay in transitional societies.

11. Woodward, *Central America,* pp. 149–53.

12. Vanden, "Ideology," p. 43; and Eduardo Crawley, *Dictators Never Die: A Portrait of Nicaragua and the Somoza Dynasty* (New York: St. Martin's Press, 1979), pp. 36–38.

13. Woodward, *Central America,* p. 167.

14. Ibid., p. 156.

15. Walker, *Nicaragua: The Land of Sandino,* p. 50–53.

16. Ibid., p. 49.

17. Ibid., pp. 47–48.

18. Woodward, *Central America,* p. 219.

19. Moises Poblete Troncoso and Ben G. Burnett, *The Rise of the Latin American Labor Movement* (New Haven, Conn.: College and University Press, 1962), pp. 119–20.

20. Ibid., p. 121.

21. Walker, *Nicaragua: The Land of Sandino,* p. 49.

22. Crawley, *Dictators,* pp. 121–22.

23. Inter-American Development Bank, *Socio-Economic Progress in*

Latin America (Washington, D.C.: Inter-American Development Bank, 1969), p. 235.
24. Ibid., pp. 2, 13, 16, and 20.
25. Woodward, *Central America*, p. 222.
26. Crawley, *Dictators*, pp. 115–17.
27. Woodward, *Central America*, p. 245.
28. Ortega Saavedra, *50 años*, p. 82.
29. John Morris Ryan, *Area Handbook for Nicaragua* (Washington, D.C.: American University, 1970), pp. 55–56; and Inter-American Development Bank, *Socio-Economic Progress in Latin America* (Washington, D.C.: Inter-American Development Bank, 1979), p. 259.
30. Inter-American Development Bank, *Socio-Economic Progress,* 1979, p. 259.
31. Ryan, *Area Handbook*, p. 116.
32. Inter-American Development Bank, *Socio-Economic Progress in Latin America* (Washington, D.C.: Inter-American Development Bank, 1972), p. 261.
33. See, for example, Karl W. Deutsch, *Nationalism and Social Communication* (New York: John Wiley and Sons, 1953); and more recently George Gerbner, ed., *Mass Media Policies in Changing Societies* (New York: John Wiley and Sons, 1977).
34. Gabriel Almond and Bingham Powell, *Comparative Politics: System, Process, and Policy,* Second Edition (Boston, Mass.: Little Brown, 1978), p. 153.
35. Ibid.
36. Ryan, *Area Handbook*, p. 196.
37. Walker, *Nicaragua: The Land of Sandino,* pp. 53–58.
38. Jaime Wheelock *Diciembre victorioso* (Managua: Secretaría Nacional de Propaganda y Educacíon Política, 1979), p. 29.
39. IDB, *Socio-Economic Progress, 1972,* p. 257.
40. Ibid., pp. 387 and 397.
41. Samuel P. Huntington, *Political Order in Changing Societies* (New Haven, Conn.: Yale University Press, 1965), pp. 67 and 100.
42. Walker, *Nicaragua: The Land of Sandino,* pp. 29–30.
43. Crawley, *Dictators,* pp. 130–31.
44. Huntington, *Political Order,* pp. 67–68.
45. John Booth, "Revolutionary Theory and Nicaragua's Sandinista Revolution" (Paper presented at the Southwestern Council of Latin American Studies, Arlington, Texas, March 1981), p. 3.
46. Ibid., pp. 19–20.
47. Henry Bienen, *Violence and Social Change* (Chicago: University of Chicago Press, 1968), p. 68.

48. Ted Robert Gurr, *Why Men Rebel* (Princeton, N.J.: Princeton University Press, 1971), pp. 148–49.
49. Ibid., pp. 149–53.
50. Chalmers Johnson, *Revolutionary Change* (Boston, Mass.: Little Brown, 1966).
51. James M. Malloy, *Bolivia: The Uncompleted Revolution* (Pittsburgh: University of Pittsburgh Press, 1970), pp. 6–7.
52. See Lucian Pye, *Aspects of Political Development* (Boston, Mass.: Little Brown, 1966), pp. 62–64 concerning the crisis of legitimacy that typically faces regimes during political development.
53. Gurr, *Why Men Rebel*, p. 11.
54. S. N. Eisenstadt, *Social Differentiation and Stratification* (Glenview, Ill.: Scott, Foresman, 1971), p. 222.
55. Malloy, *Bolivia*, p. 4.
56. Huntington, *Political Order*, p. 312.
57. Wheelock, *Diciembre*.
58. For details on the three tendencies, see *Latin American Perspectives* documents, "Sandinista Perspectives: Three Differing Views," Vol. 6 (Winter 1979), pp. 114–27; and Gabriel García Márquez, *Los sandinistas* (Bogota: Editorial Cveja Negra, 1979), pp. 169–243.
59. James Petras, "Whither the Nicaraguan Revolution," *Monthly Review* 31 (October 1979), pp. 11–12.
60. See Gabriel García Márquez, "Sandinistas Seize the National Palace," *New Left Review* (September 1978), pp. 79–88; and Neale J. Pearson, "Nicaragua in Crisis," *Current History* 76 (February 1979), pp. 79–80 and 84.
61. Gorman, "Power and Consolidation," and Roger Mendienta Alfaro, *El último marine* (Managua: Editorial Unión, 1980).
62. Daniel Ortega Saavedra, "Nothing Will Hold Back Our Struggle for Liberation," in Pedro Camejo and Fred Murphy, eds., *The Nicaraguan Revolution* (New York: Pathfinder Press, 1979), pp. 38–40.
63. David Kaimowitz and Joseph R. Thome, "Nicaragua's Agrarian Reform: The First Year (1979–1980)," in Walker, *Nicaragua in Revolution*, pp. 236–37.
64. Gorman, "Power and Consolidation," pp. 137–41.
65. Philip Wheaton and Yvonne Dilling, *Nicaragua: A People's Revolution* (Washington, D.C.: Ecumenical Program for Inter-American Communication and Action, 1979), pp. 84–85.

3

El Salvador: The Roots of Revolution[1]

Tommie Sue Montgomery

The Salvadoran regime has long contained the seeds of its own eventual destruction. Those seeds are both institutional and ideological, and have, over the last century, shaped a regime that is both unwilling and unable to adapt to new demands from the outside. It has, however, taken the emergence of other institutions and competing ideologies within the country but external to the regime to turn the predictable into the inevitable.

As we see in the other chapters of this volume, the regime in each Central American country is a distinctive product of that country's particular history. The confluence of events in Nicaragua produced a family dynasty. In Guatemala class antagonisms have been exacerbated by ethnic divisions and multinational corporations. In contrast, El Salvador has had none of the above. It is an overwhelmingly *mestizo* society that has endured a long series of civilian, then military, petty dictators, and in which multinationals entered usually at the sufferance of and in joint-venture capital projects with the local economic elite, known as the oligarchy.

The roots of the oligarchy lie deep in the colonial period. Until December 1931 a small group, who came to be known as the "Fourteen Families," controlled both the political and economic life of the country. A coup d'etat, however, established the military in power, effecting a division of labor that continued into the early 1980s. These two actors, the oligarchy and the military, comprised the Salvadoran regime: the oligarchy ran the economy and the military ran the state. Periodic challenges to this arrangement were always successfully, if bloodily, beaten back—

GUATEMALA
INTER-AMERICAN HIGHWAY
HONDURAS
Indefinite boundary
Lago de Guija
Metapán
SANTA ANA
CHALATENANGO
Chalatenango
Santa Ana
Ahuachapán
Chalchuapa
Lago de Coatepeque
Suchitoto
Sensuntepeque
CABAÑAS
CUSCATLÁN
AHUACHAPÁN
SAN MIGUEL
MORAZÁN
Sonsonate
San Salvador
Cojutepeque
SAN VICENTE
San Francisco Gotera
Nueva San Salvador
Santa Rosa de Lima
Acajutla
SONSONATE
LA LIBERTAD
Lago de Ilopango
San Vicente
El Triunfo
Zacatecoluca
USULUTÁN
LA UNIÓN
La Libertad
San Miguel
LA PAZ
Usulután
La Herradura
Puerto El Triunfo
Laguna de Olomega
La Unión
EL SALVADOR
Road
Railroad
0
50 Miles
0
50 Kilometers
GOLFO DE FONSECA
PACIFIC OCEAN
NIC.

until the 1970s, that is. During that decade two other actors emerged that in different yet complementary ways began to challenge the regime. Those actors were the Roman Catholic Church and the contemporary revolutionary organizations.

By 1980 it was clear that the regime's days—or years—were numbered. After 1970 the social forces unleashed by the church's pastoral work and harnessed by the mass "Popular Organizations" of the left meant that those organizations (and the "political-military organizations" with which they were affiliated) would have to be included in any political settlement. By 1981 the guerrillas had enough military power to veto any political arrangement of which they did not approve. By late 1982 it was clear that the only force sustaining the Salvadoran military was continued United States military assistance.

The institutional and ideological characteristics of the Salvadoran regime may be summarized as follows:

1. A pattern of increasing concentration of land and wealth from the sixteenth century onward coupled with a concentration of political power, first in the oligarchy and later in the army.

2. After 1931, the development of the institution of the army, which was reinforced by the *Tanda* system of military school class cohesion and by a systematic process of corruption.

3. A political ideology that may be described as Thomas Hobbes with a vengeance: classical liberalism that assigned to government the sole responsibility of maintaining order so that the economic elite could pursue laissez-faire economic policies.

4. An unwillingness to implement any reforms, in either the economic or political sphere that in any way affected the economic interests of the oligarchy or the political interests of the military.

Only on occasion have external actors sought to influence the Salvadoran regime. The most prominent of these actors has been the United States, although in the nineteenth century Great Britain had a greater presence in the country and during the 1930s Nazi Germany had direct influence on the Salvadoran army. Only in the 1980s, as the civil war in El Salvador threatened to become a regional war, did other external actors attempt to exert some influence; they included other nations of the region and the Socialist International.

In this chapter we will examine each of these actors—the

oligarchy, the military, the church, revolutionary organizations, and external groups—and their respective ideologies. We will see that on the part of the Salvadoran regime there was a continuing unwillingness (for avaricious or institutional reasons) and an incapacity (for ideological reasons) to adapt to new demands; that at every juncture since 1931, when modest but real socioeconomic reforms could have bought off the peasantry and/or industrial workers, the opportunity was rejected in favor of preserving the status quo. The result, in a metaphorical sense, is Gulliver struggling to free himself from the bonds imposed by the Lilliputians. Once he began to free himself from his captors, to tear out the cords that bound him, he began to destroy the system. And once he stood up, the system was destroyed forever.[2]

The Oligarchy

The first attempt, in 1524, to settle El Salvador, called Cuzcatlán by its native Pipil and Lenca Indians, failed when the outraged Indians chased the Spanish conquistadores back into Guatemala in less than a month. It took the Spaniards four years to establish a permanent settlement and another eleven to establish sufficient control over the Indians to consider them "subjects of the royal service." The colonists in Cuzcatlán, like their predecessors in Mexico and Peru, sought instant wealth that could be returned to Spain. Unfortunately for the settlers, however, there was little gold, silver, or other natural resources. They soon discovered that Cuzcatlán's wealth lay in its land, which at the time was producing considerable riches for a great many Indians through the cultivation of cacao.

With no natural resources to exploit, the search for the "key to wealth" began[3]—and ended with the recognition that, through the *encomienda* system, the colonists could force the Indian landowners to deal only with them. By the early 1540s the export of cacao was dominated by only three *encomenderos*; thus began the Salvadoran oligarchy.

Cacao quickly gained popularity in Europe, where it became the drink of kings and queens. The first massive fortunes for the encomenderos, their children, and approximately 200 creole and mestizo merchants who benefitted from the trade were made from this source. Plantations remained in Indian hands, but as the demand for cacao grew there was a corresponding need for more labor on the plantations, which were located primarily in the southwestern part of the country. Meanwhile, the indigenous population, which was highly susceptible to imported diseases, was dying in large numbers. Indians began to migrate from the highlands but were unacclimated to the hot coastal zone. By the middle of the sixteenth century, so many Indians had died that the Spaniards imported a large number of black slaves from Africa.

The exploitation of cacao and its subsequent decline by the end of the sixteenth century represented the first of three economic cycles that had played themselves out in El Salvador by the middle of the nineteenth century. These cycles shared several characteristics, including 1) the discovery of a new crop, 2) the rapid development of that crop, 3) a period of great prosperity from export of the crop, 4) a dramatic decline or stagnation, 5) an economic depression during which an intense search for a replacement occurred, and 6) the discovery of a new crop and the beginning of another cycle.

Cacao was followed by indigo, a natural blue dye that became the second key to wealth in El Salvador. Unlike cacao, which was labor-intensive, indigo required little human care. In fact, cattle could be turned loose in indigo fields, as natural "weeders" eating everything but the indigo plants. By 1600 indigo had replaced cacao as El Salvador's principal export, although it was another century before the "boom" arrived. When it did, it lasted for 150 years. Eventually the demand for indigo declined as a synthetic dye was developed in Europe, and as civil war in the United States closed shipping lanes through the Caribbean. Even before that, however, the Salvadoran landowners had discovered that the volcanic soil of west central El Salvador was well-suited to coffee, which would become the third key to wealth by the late nineteenth century.

The development of a monocrop economy, in which the cycles of development and decline were similar and only the crop changed, produced a set of enduring consequences for the country's later history. These consequences may be summarized as follows:

1. The decline of cacao and the extended economic depression

that followed in the seventeenth century created a need for the colonials to quickly find a means of survival. This led to development of the hacienda system, which was not unlike plantations in the antebellum South in that they were largely self-sufficient.

2. The development of haciendas led, in turn, to the creation of new relationships between landowners and Indians or peasants, that could for the most part be characterized as feudal. These new relationships were established primarily through debt peonage, a means of permanently binding the Indians to a hacienda, usually by tricking them into a debt they could not repay. Such indebted persons came to be known as *colonos*, or serfs, living on the hacienda and depending on the landowner (*patrono*) for their very existence. A variation of this relationship was *aparcería*, or sharecropping, in which the Indians gave either part of the harvest from their small plot or worked several days a week for the patrono.

3. The expansion of haciendas with each succeeding depression also had the effect of concentrating land in fewer and fewer hands. Most of this expansion by the Spanish landowners was accomplished through usurpation of communal or ejidal lands, without compensation to the former owners.

4. Not surprisingly, the same landowners also had firm control over the political life of the colony by the late eighteenth century. This pattern of economic and political control would continue into the twentieth century.

5. The pattern of land concentration led to vast underemployment and unemployment among the peasantry, particularly during the second and third cycles. This was because both indigo and coffee required minimal labor nine months of the year but enormous numbers of seasonal workers during the harvest season.

6. The emphasis on a monocrop economy produced, from the sixteenth century onward, a need to import foodstuffs, including basic grains. While the landowners and the small middle class could afford to pay for the imported goods, the peasantry could not.

7. The usurpation of land led, during the colonial period, to periodic revolts by Indians and peasants. These revolts, which not only continued, but grew in magnitude during the nineteenth

century, required the creation of local, then state, "security forces" which were, from the beginning, in the pay of the landowners and always at their beck and call.

When agitation for independence from Spain began in the late eighteenth and early nineteenth centuries, a plurality of the land in El Salvador continued to be held by the Indians or mestizos in traditional communal lands or *ejidos*. Between one-quarter and one-third of the total land area was divided among large haciendas with an average size of 800 hectares. Of the remaining land, much was in the hands of small property owners or occupied by squatters who had been pushed off their small plots as the haciendas expanded.

By 1821, the year of independence, one-third of the total land area was concentrated into 400 haciendas, most of which were devoted to the cultivation of indigo. The historic mentality of the landowners was a single-minded desire to maximize earnings.[4] This attitude was rooted in an understandable fear of being financially wiped out by an economic depression. The view that what was good for the landowners was good for the country took hold; until they perceived the need for certain forms of internal development (roads, railroads, and water lines) which coffee would require, development was a nonexistent issue.

Thus there were growing economic inequities, which were accompanied by increasing class and ethnic antagonisms. Tribute (a forced payment in labor or crops by the Indians to the Spaniards) was abolished by the Spanish parliament in 1811. But it continued to be collected in El Salvador until 1814, when a priest told his parishioners of the abolition three years earlier. The enraged Indians descended on the local mayor and demanded a refund. They were driven off but their anger festered. Meanwhile, usurpation of communal lands became more frequent as the protection of the crown was withdrawn following independence. These conditions provoked a major revolt in 1832. Led by the Indian *cacique* (chief) Anastacio Aquino, three thousand peasants battled government troops for a year—until Aquino was captured, shot and decapitated. His head was prominently displayed as a warning to other would-be rebels.

The development of coffee, the third "key to wealth," contributed greatly to El Salvador's economic strength and stability, at least on a national level. But in order to facilitate the transition from indigo to coffee, an 1881 law mandated that all communal property be subdivided among the owners or become the property of the state. The next year all communal lands were abolished by decree. The common lands, said the decree, were "contrary to the political and social principles on which the Republic was established," i.e., the unfettered right of private property. In accordance with this decree, the indigenous people were evicted from their ancestral lands, often violently. Though five popular uprisings broke out in the coffee-growing areas between 1872 and 1898, within a few years the best land was concentrated in the hands of the "Fourteen Families." In the latter part of the century most presidents were both generals and major coffee growers: Francisco Dueñas, Tomás Regalado, Pedro José Escalón, Fernando Figueroa, and Francisco Meléndez. Into the 1980s these family names identified many members of the economically dominant oligarchy.

The ideology shared by the oligarchy, and therefore shaping the Salvadoran regime, came from the classical liberalism expounded by Thomas Hobbes, John Locke, and Adam Smith. There were differences of emphasis, in that some members of the oligarchy stressed the economic themes of the liberal creed, while others stressed political themes, especially free speech. All agreed, however, on the basic ideas that would shape the Salvadoran regime and nation: encouragement of coffee production, construction of railroads to the ports, elimination of communal lands, passage of laws against vagrancy, and repression of rural unrest. The 1886 Constitution guaranteed that these policies would be pursued without obstacle. It established a secular state, decentralized state authority by allowing for the popular election of municipal authorities, and confirmed the inviolability of private property and the abolition of communal lands.

Though the booming coffee market fueled the construction of roads and railroads, the social costs included a literacy rate of less than 30 percent in 1900, and high levels of malnutrition. Because the regime wanted to maintain a sufficient work force for the coffee harvest, there was no effort to create alternative sources of employment. Rural family life came under strain as thousands of people, mostly men, were forced to take up a nomadic existence in search of work. By the late 1920s Alberto Masferrer, El Salvador's most eloquent social critic, was warning that "as long as justice is not the same for everyone, none of us is safe."⁵ Masferrer declared:

> The conquest of territory by the coffee industry is alarming. It has already occupied the high lands and is now descending to the valleys, displacing maize, rice, and beans. It is extended like the *conquistador*, spreading hunger and misery, reducing the former proprietors to the worst conditions—woe to those who sell! Although it is possible to prove mathematically that these changes make the country richer, in fact they mean death. It is true that the costs of importing maize are small in relation to the benefits of the export of coffee, but do they give the imported grain to the poor? Or do they make them pay for it? Is the income of the *campesino*, who has lost his land, adequate to provide maize, rice, beans, clothes, medicine, doctors, etc.? So, what good does it do to make money from the sale of coffee when it leaves so many people in misery?⁶

By January 1932 the Salvadoran peasantry reached similar conclusions in the wake of deteriorating social and economic conditions, an increasingly militant labor union movement, and experience with authentic electoral democracy for the only time in El Salvador's history. Labor unions developed early in the century, although the first ones tended to be oriented more toward mutual assistance and savings among the membership than toward political goals.⁷ In the early 1920s, however, radical union organizers from Guatemala and Mexico began to change the largely mutualist character of the union movement to something more militant. The Great Depression increased social tensions, and labor's increasing militancy in the form of demonstrations and strikes inflamed the situation.

This period was made more interesting because the country was enjoying the first presidential administration in its history committed to allowing political organizations of all kinds to participate in political life. In this context, the Communist Party of El Salvador (PCS), the country's first revolutionary organization, was founded. President Don Pío Romero Bosque insisted that there not be an "official" candidate (from the oligarchy) for the presidential election of 1930. Thus Arturo Araujo, a wealthy landowner who had once addressed a national workers' congress, who paid his employees double the going wages, and who had become known as a friend of the working class and peasantry, was elected president.

Unfortunately, Araujo's election aroused hope among the poor and fears within the regime, especially within the army whom he had courted by naming General Maximiliano Hernández Martínez as his vice-presidential running mate. Loyal to his class, Araujo was unprepared to honor the more extravagant campaign promises his labor supporters had made in his name. Nevertheless, the oligarchy refused to lend its support to his administration by accepting governmental appointments, thereby denying its expertise to the government at one of the most critical junctures in Salvadoran history.

The social, political, and economic situation deteriorated from the day of Araujo's inauguration. Denied the support of the oligarchy and beset by increasing social unrest, Araujo was unable to deal with the crisis. The result was a coup d'etat on December 2, 1931, by young officers who installed the constitutional successor, General Martínez, as president.[8] Salvadoran historian Jorge Arias Gómez captures the significance of these events:

> December 2, 1931, marks an era in the political life of the nation which has continued for almost 40 years. On that date, the oligarchy ceased to govern directly. If before the coup d'etat the political idea that only civilians must serve as president had triumphed and been consolidated, afterwards the opposite idea was pursued. If before, forces of the oligarchy were thrown into the struggle for power, organizing more or less successful parties and electoral movements, exciting the masses, afterward the entire oligarchy withdrew from the political game in order to leave it to military tyranny. . . . In a few words, political power passed, on December 2, 1931, into the hands of the army. That was transformed, in practice, into the great elector and into a type of political party permanently in arms.[9]

The Salvadoran left greeted the coup with cautious optimism, but its hopes were dashed when the legislative and municipal elections in early January were characterized by the familiar fraudulent procedures of the past. In the western part of the country, where the newly formed Communist Party was strong, the elections were suspended. The PCS claimed victory in other towns but the government refused to certify the elections. Augustín Farabundo Martí, the PCS secretary-general and a labor organizer for a decade, along with other radical leaders concluded that the Martínez regime would not let them take office. They planned simultaneous uprisings in several towns and army barracks on January 22, 1932, but the government learned of the scheme several days before it was to be executed. The result was a disorganized uprising that met with a swift and brutal response. In the aftermath 30,000 people were killed, of whom 10 percent may have participated in the uprising. Martí and two students were tried by a military tribunal and shot.

The military consolidated its hold on the government and there was no more pretense of popular political participation. Peasant unions were outlawed, and all other political organizations were prohibited. The PCS went underground. The oligarchy achieved the social peace it wanted and considered necessary to rebuild a shattered economy.

The Military

The relationship between oligarchy and military after 1931 was summed up by a Salvadoran oligarch in 1980. "We have traditionally bought the military's guns," he said in an interview, "and have paid them to pull the trigger."[10] The cyclical economic patterns that had evolved in the centuries after the conquest had their counterpart in politics. Just as the first pattern served to consolidate economic power in the oligarchy, the second pattern perpetuated political power in the hands of the army. State security forces whose origins lay in private armies, organized by the oligarchy to keep the peasants in line and keep them working, were headed by army officers.

The army itself began to form in the late 1850s when a Colombian general was asked to build a professional force. Later French and Spanish officers spent extended periods in the country training infantry, cavalry, and artillery units. During this time El Salvador lived under constant fear of invasion, so the attention of the army focused on national security and the task of maintaining order was left to the security forces. Not until the late twentieth century would the army be used to control the people.

Elements of the private forces became the Rural Police and

Mounted Police by decree in 1884 and 1889, respectively, in the western third of the country. An 1895 decree extended their authority over the entire country. Ultimately, the Rural Police became the National Police. Then, in 1912, the National Guard was formed and trained by Spanish officers. Designed to function as an adjunct to the army, its duties overlapped those of the National Police: patrolling towns, villages, ports, and roads, and providing police services to haciendas. The National Guard was mandated by law to respond to the call for help of any landowner. A third contemporary security force, the Treasury Police, was created in 1936.

Each political cycle, beginning in 1931, followed a consistent pattern. First, a group of progressive, young military officers who pledged to break with the past and institute needed reforms overthrew an increasingly repressive regime. Next, the most conservative elements of the army, influenced by members of the oligarchy, reasserted themselves and let the reforms lapse. This produced civil unrest which, in turn, led to increased repression by the regime. This often repeated relapse became known in El Salvador as *derechización,* or a drift to the right. Following this drift, a group within the army became disaffected once again, ultimately producing yet another coup.

Six such cycles occurred after 1931, producing five progressive coups or coup attempts between 1944 and 1979. In 1944 and 1960 the progressives held power for only three or four months before giving way to conservatives. In 1948 the more conservative elements reasserted themselves much more slowly. The coup attempt in 1972 simply failed. Seven years later derechización began even before the coup d'etat of October 15, 1979.

Throughout the decades following the assumption of power by the army, two goals remained paramount. One was protection of the interests of the oligarchy, which meant maintaining the economic status quo and social order. The second was the preservation of the institution of the armed forces. Although civilians participated in each coup and staffed government ministries, the dominant elements within the army remained unwilling to give up control of the state. They were reinforced in that position by two other institutions: the tanda system and corruption.

A tanda is a graduating class at the Salvadoran military academy (*escuela militar*) and, beginning in the 1930s, *tandas* developed a strong sense of cohesiveness. During the officers' thirty-year careers,[11] they make alliances with officers in tandas just ahead or behind them in preparing to take political power and to share the benefits that are available through a thoroughly institutionalized system of corruption.[12]

For many years after 1931 that system relied on the largesse the oligarchy could bestow on officers it sought to influence. A hotel manager in San Salvador once described in an interview how the system might work for him: An officer would be invited to dinner at the hotel, to return and bring his family, to use hotel facilities, gratis, for a birthday party, to accept use of the manager's beach house for the weekend. Later the officer would be offered the opportunity to buy 10 percent of a business with guarantees that if he needed a loan one would be available at attractive interest rates, courtesy of a bank owned by members of the oligarchy. This, the manager said, was only one example of how a "very elastic system" of corruption worked.[13]

On another occasion an officer who had been a senior official in ANTEL, the national telephone company, related how he had been approached at a funeral and offered $80,000 by a cabinet member to help a certain supply company win a bid from ANTEL. The officer declined the offer, only to have a company officer offer him $40,000 more, with the advice that the country was about to collapse and the money would provide a cushion for him in exile. The officer said that once again he refused, then added that "corruption has been a tool of the oligarchy [and has] yielded economic profits to the oligarchy—the ultra right—and political profits to the far left."[14]

Beginning in 1980, as the oligarchy sent tens of millions of dollars out of the country, as newly nationalized banks and external commerce provided new opportunities for graft, and as United States economic and military assistance increased, the army became less and less reliant on the oligarchy for additional income and thus less beholden to its longtime benefactors. An Agency for International Development memorandum in 1981 charged that millions of dollars intended for the agrarian reform had simply vanished.[15] Former U.S. Ambassador Robert White, among others, charged that Salvadoran army officers were selling arms to the guerrillas.[16] Carolyn Forché and Leonel Gómez wrote in late 1982: "The Salvadorean Army is held together ... by a vast network of corruption which now controls the country's nationalized banks, 15 percent of its best farmland, all export-import activities and a good portion of U.S. aid."[17] The net effect of these developments was to give the army an increasing sense of independence from the oligarchy and to strengthen the army's own agenda, which gave priority to preservation of the institution.

For three and a half decades after the fall of Hernández Martínez in 1944, this long-term goal could be most clearly seen in the recurring political cycles referred to earlier. Prior to 1979, the coup that best illustrates this recurrent cycle of broken promises is that of 1948. Inspired—or pressured—by developments in Guatemala, where a 1944 revolt had succeeded and a progressive government headed by the army was making significant social and economic reforms, young Salvadoran officers acted to restore political rights and initiate needed economic and social reforms. Within two years, however, the Central Election Council, which had been created by the junta immediately after the coup as an independent agency to collect and count votes, lost its autonomy and came under the control of the official (army) party. Citing a fear of communism, the regime so restricted the activities of opposition parties in the 1952 and 1954 elections that they withdrew their candidates in protest. As a result, the army was, once again, virtually alone in the political arena.

The regime, which fourteen months after the coup came to be headed by Oscar Osorio, initiated a series of public works and other programs intended to encourage industry and trade, increase production, and diversify agriculture. This represented a marked departure from previous governments, especially that of Hernández Martínez, which had done almost exactly the opposite in accordance with the wishes of the oligarchy. But in the early 1950s housing construction, health care, and sanitation projects were initiated. Labor unions were legalized in 1951, although agricultural unions continued to be banned. The oligarchy, predictably, began complaining about the reforms, but when the government reminded it of the "communist threat" next door, the complaints died away.[18]

The economic model embraced by Osorio and the oligarchy was "developmentalist," that is, encouraging growth and modernization of the industrial sector and diversification of agriculture. The government also embarked on a program of developing the country's infrastructure: roads, dams, and bridges were constructed. By 1955 José María Lemus, who was handpicked by Osorio to succeed him after fellow officers rejected his first choice of a civilian candidate, was praising the 1948 "revolution":

> The dispossessed classes have progressed in cultural and spiritual respects that concern the value of work and the enjoyment of human treatment regulated by law. And there has not been present, in the course of this great experience, the explosions of angry capitalists or the dangerous condition of mass discontent. The Revolution has constructed modern school buildings, raised educational standards in the most remote regions, sought a solution to the problem of urban housing by providing facilities for the proletariat and middle class, and has organized rural communities through which the problems of housing, work, and production in some zones have been resolved.[19]

This self-congratulatory passage ignored what Alastair White recognized fifteen years later, that the Osorio and Lemus administrations,

> in attempting or appearing to effect a general expansion and improvement through industrial development... tended to achieve only an expansion of job opportunities for a new salaried middle class, and in attempting or appearing to introduce modern government provision for social development... tended to create a relatively privileged sector within the working class, those with access to such innovations as social security, collective wage bargaining through the legal unions, and the government housing and rural land settlement schemes. These benefited a very small percentage of the poor, but could be represented demagogically as a social revolution being carried out by the government.[20]

The developmentalist policies followed by the 1948 "revolution" did nothing to upset the oligarchy's control over the economy. Indeed, in the long run, the policies enabled the oligarchy to increase its wealth and to include the tiny industrial sector and technocrats in the process. High coffee prices on the world market and increased production of "the golden grain" gave the oligarchy profits that it had to invest somewhere. Much of the money was poured into "import substitution," and industries developed through joint-venture capital of the oligarchy and multinational corporations. This industrial expansion created an internal contradiction because the import-substitution model implicitly assumed an expanding domestic consumer market to absorb the goods that were being produced. But the regime's lynchpin was an understanding that El Salvador's first key to wealth, the land, was untouchable. Thus the possibility of developing through agrarian reform a class of small farmers which would acquire purchasing power was negated. In addition, the country continued to be a net food importer. As prices rose, the problems of the poor, which Masferrer condemned thirty years earlier, were exacerbated rather than ameliorated.

In the long run neither industrialization nor agricultural diversification created new sources of employment. In fact, the number of jobs available, relative to the size of the population, declined. Two examples illustrate the problem. In the industrial arena, prior to the arrival in the 1950s of the ADOC shoe factory, which was jointly owned by six oligarchic families,[21] there were several thousand shoemakers and assistants in El Salvador. ADOC created several hundred industrial jobs, but it put most of the shoemakers out of business. In the agricultural sector, the expansion of cotton production from 9,800 hectares in 1942 to 19,030 hectares in 1951, and from 43,000 in 1960 to 122,300 hectares in 1965, took place at the expense of forests, cattle ranching, and subsistence farming. From the perspective of the growers, the return on investment made it worthwhile. By 1964 cotton accounted for 24 percent of all exports.[22] Meanwhile, thousands of tenant farmers and squatters were pushed off the land that had previously provided them with subsistence crops.[23] The effect was noted by William Durham in his study of the ecological origins of the 1969 war between El Salvador and Honduras: "From a balance of payments point of view the country as a whole is better off with land in export crops. But the problem is ... that most Salvadoreans do not derive much benefit from export production."[24]

The last years of the 1950s were characterized by growing labor and political unrest, as the "trickle-down theory" of development proved as vacuous as the regime's promises of improved living standards for the majority of Salvadorans. In October 1960 yet another coup d'etat was carried out by a new generation of military and civilian progressives in response to the deteriorating conditions. Committed to the development of a completely open electoral process and the elimination of illiteracy, the new civilian-military junta lasted exactly three months. Its announced intent to hold free elections and permit the participation of all political groups provoked a countercoup that returned the conservatives to power. The October coup and January countercoup were notable for another reason: it appears to be the first time the United States openly allied itself with the oligarchy and conservative army officers—or at least actively supported, and participated in, the countercoup.[25]

The January coup occurred just days after the inauguration of President John F. Kennedy, who quickly appointed Murat Williams to be the new U.S. ambassador. Williams took seriously the aims of Kennedy's Alliance for Progress, which was developed in the wake of the Cuban revolution as a "third way" between the Scylla of leftist revolution and the Charybdis of right-wing military dictatorship in Latin America. Under pressure from Williams the new Salvadoran government headed by Colonel Julio Adalberto Rivera undertook a series of political reforms that enabled a legal opposition to emerge and develop for the first time in three decades. Proportional representation was instituted in the unicameral National Assembly, and the Christian Democratic Party (PDC), which was founded in 1960 along with other opposition parties, began to gain political support throughout the country. With each biennial election for the assembly the opposition, especially the PDC, gained seats. By the end of the decade the opposition was only two seats shy of an absolute majority in the assembly. The question then, as Stephen Webre put it in his study of the Salvadoran Christian Democratic Party, was "not whether the opposition would continue to make gains, but what the PCN (the official National Conciliation Party) would do when the electoral solution became absolutely incompatible with its survival as the dominant party."[26]

The answer to that question came in the 1972 presidential election. A coalition of Christian Democrats, Social Democrats (Revolutionary National Movement—MNR), and the PCS (legal front of the National Democratic Union—UDN), joined together in a coalition to run José Napoleón Duarte (PDC) and Guillermo Manuel Ungo (MNR) for president and vice-president. When it became clear, on the night of the election, that Duarte and Ungo were winning, the government banned further announcement of election returns and impounded the ballots. An attempted coup, led by young officers and publicly supported by Duarte, failed. Duarte was arrested, tortured, and shipped off to exile in Venezuela. Thus the electoral solution in El Salvador suffered from a logical flaw. As Webre observed, the 1960s' democratic opening "encouraged an active opposition but, by definition, forbade that opposition to come to power."[27]

During this period economic reform efforts also ran into difficulties. Industry expanded during the 1960s and 1970s as import substitution gave way to production for export, but the number of jobs increased less rapidly. With agrarian reform prohibited by political realities, the regime began to regard the economic integration of Central America as a means of partially alleviating unemployment. Together with its neighbors, El Salvador created the Central American Common Market (CACM) in 1961 with the hope that the unrestricted flow of capital, people, and goods within the isthmus would create additional markets for industrial goods, new opportunities for investment, and a means of relieving the growing population pressure in El Salvador. As a result, intra-regional trade increased 32 percent each year between 1962 and 1968, and the increase averaged 26 percent between 1960 and 1972.[28]

Another economic innovation was a 1965 minimum wage law for agricultural workers which officially discouraged the longtime feudal arrangement between *colonos* and *aparceros,* on the one hand, and the landowners, on the other. According to David Browning, "the *colono* or *aparcero* was expected to become a laborer whose sole connection with the property that he worked on [was] the wage paid to him by the owner."[29] The impact was dramatic. The 1971 census recorded a decline in the number of colonos during the 1970s from 55,800 to 17,000. At the same time the number of landless *campesinos* increased from 30,500 (12 percent of all rural Salvadorans) in 1961 to 112,100 (29 percent) ten years later. By 1975 the number had increased to 167,000 landless people (41 percent).[30]

Another reason for the increase in landless peasants and the economic downturn was the 100-hour "soccer war" between El Salvador and Honduras in 1969 (so-called because it followed a series of bitterly contested games between the two countries during the qualifying rounds for the 1969 World Cup). There were, however, three other, far more profound reasons for the conflict. First, the two countries had long been at odds over their common border. Second, unlike El Salvador, Honduras's balance of trade within the isthmus was on the decline, while trade outside was favorable. This meant that Honduras was subsidizing the industrial development of its neighbor. Third, and most important, there were at least 300,000 Salvadoran settlers in Honduras. Many of them were second generation, and most were successful small farmers.

In April 1969, Honduras enacted a new agrarian reform law giving Salvadoran farmers thirty days to leave their land. In June, the country reversed its immigration policy and closed its border. El Salvador responded by closing its border to those trying to return and filing a complaint with the Inter-American Commission on Human Rights. Then, on July 14, El Salvador invaded Honduras. Four days later the war ended, thanks largely to U.S. pressure in the form of threatened economic sanctions against El Salvador.

Within El Salvador the war temporarily took people's minds off the country's growing economic problems, but nationalist sentiment soon wore thin. The Honduran market, which in 1968 absorbed $23 million in Salvadoran goods, vanished. El Salvador's overland route to Nicaragua and Costa Rica was temporarily closed. The Central American Common Market (CACM) lay in shambles. El Salvador found itself with tens of thousands of new landless and jobless citizens inside its boundaries. Economic woes led once again to popular protests. These were joined by labor unions, and the unrest spread as teachers and workers went on strike. The response of President Fidel Sánchez Hernández was to blame the discontent on the communists.

Spiraling economic problems, increasing unemployment, growing repression, and renewed electoral fraud in 1972 contributed to a regime crisis that would never be overcome. They also contributed to the growth of new institutions and ideologies that would, in different but complementary ways, challenge the regime and undermine the status quo. The institutions were the

Roman Catholic Church and the revolutionary organizations. The ideologies, respectively, were liberation theology and uniquely Salvadoran blends of Marxism, Leninism, *fidelismo*, and nationalism.

The Church

Until 1970 the Roman Catholic Church was a silent presence in El Salvador, supportive of the status quo by its inaction, occasionally sallying forth to warn the faithful against communism. In the summer of 1960, for example, the government trucked in 20,000 peasants to San Salvador for an anti-communist rally. Archbishop Luís Chávez y González concluded the rally with a Mass. Seven years later the bishop of San Vicente, Pedro Aparicio, threatened to excommunicate parishioners who had the temerity to ally themselves with the Renovating Action Party (PAR), whose presidential candidate, Fabio Castillo, had been one of the civilian members of the short-lived 1960 junta.[31] Then, two weeks before the election, the Episcopal Conference issued a declaration reminding Salvadorans of the church's blanket condemnation of communism.[32]

The Second Vatican Council (Vatican II), which ended in 1965, and the Second Conference of Latin American Bishops (CELAM II) at Medellín, Colombia in 1968 presaged a dramatic change in the church's role. The new doctrines defined the church as in and of this world, a community of equals by baptism, with concerns well beyond the purely spiritual. Criticism of communism was combined with an equally strong critique of capitalism's abuses. At Medellín the bishops called on the church to "defend the rights of the oppressed," promote grass-roots organizations, denounce outside intervention, and make a "preferential option for the poor."

The primary means for achieving these ends was the development of Christian Base Communities (Comunidades Eclesiales de Base—CEBs), small, homogeneous, closely knit groups within parishes that met regularly for Bible study. In the Salvadoran context, the CEBs were truly subversive. In the first place, they provided a means where people with shared interests could meet together on a regular basis. Second, they provided an opportunity for leadership to emerge. Leaders, called catechists (lay teachers) and delegates of the Word (lay preachers), were chosen by the people themselves, not by the priest or nun working with them. Third, the CEBs offered an experience in participatory democracy. Beyond the Bible study, which was structured by the priest or nun, the people decided what they wanted to do in their CEBs. This ranged from sending one of their number off for paramedical training to the development of agricultural cooperatives. Fourth, the message CEB members heard in their Bible study and in the Mass was radically different from the church's message during the previous four centuries. No longer were people told to accept their lot—their poverty—and await their reward in the hereafter. Now they heard that God is a God of justice who acts in history on behalf of the poor and oppressed, that God sent Moses (for example) to lead His people out of slavery and oppression in Egypt, and later sent His son, Jesus, to proclaim "good news" to the poor, to "set free the oppressed."[33]

The new medium and the new message produced hundreds of CEBs and thousands of catechists and delegates between late 1968 and 1979. Fifteen thousand catechists were trained in seven centers set up around the country specifically for that purpose. In highly polarized El Salvador, such pastoral work had inevitable political consequences: the poor began to cast off their centuries-old fatalism and to gain a strong sense of self-confidence. A Salvadoran campesino from the parish of Suchitoto recalled years later that when Father José Alas arrived in December 1968 and began developing CEBs, "it was the first time anyone ever asked me what I thought."[34] Hundreds of these people later went into Salvadoran revolutionary organizations as community organizers, political education instructors, and, ultimately, guerrillas.

By the time Monseñor Oscar Arnulfo Romero became archbishop of San Salvador in February 1977, succeeding the aged Chávez y González, much of the church in El Salvador was identified with a "preferential option for the poor." Indeed, Romero's installation marks a transition from one period of Salvadoran church history to another, just as Medellín had marked an earlier period of transition from a conservative, pre-Conciliar orientation to an era of new and expanded pastoral action through the CEBs. The base communities continued to thrive under Romero, but the political situation was becoming such that attention was increasingly focused on the diminutive archbishop. Romero spoke for the poor and the oppressed and refused to be intimidated by the government. Fully recognizing the consequences of his stance, he explained (shortly after two priests were assassinated by right-wing death squads and state security forces in the spring of 1977) that as soon as anyone defends the poor in El Salvador, he is labeled a subversive.

Romero soon became known as "the voice of those who have no voice." His message reached into every corner of the country through the archdiocesan radio station, YSAX. In an effort to diminish his influence, the YSAX transmitter and antenna were bombed ten times, seven times between January and September 1980.[35] Nevertheless, the 8:00 Mass on Sunday became the most-listened-to program in the nation. By 1980, with the largest newspapers and radio stations in the hands of the oligarchy, many Salvadorans had come to regard the church as the only place "the truth could be spoken" in El Salvador.

For its efforts the Salvadoran church was forced to pay an extremely high price. The kidnapping of Father José Alas in 1970, just hours after he had presented the church's position in favor of agrarian reform at a National Agrarian Reform Congress, and the murder of Father Nicolás Rodríguez, after he was abducted by National Guardsmen in 1972, were the first recorded acts of persecution. Father Rutilio Grande's death in March 1977, however, initiated a wave of persecution the likes of which the Latin American church has rarely experienced. Within a month, a second priest, Alfonso Navarro, was assassinated. In July 1977, flyers appeared in San Salvador's wealthy neighborhoods demanding "Be a patriot. Kill a priest!" Between 1977 and June 1982 eleven priests, one archbishop, one seminarian, four nuns, and one lay missioner were murdered by state security forces or death squads. In the same period at least sixty priests were expelled or exiled, including José Alas in 1977. These deaths were the most outrageous but not the only attacks against the church. Between January 1980 and February 1981, for example, there were 300 attacks of various types against the church, including assassinations of catechists, bombings, shooting at various church buildings, and robbery.[36]

Of these attacks the assassination of Archbishop Romero on March 24, 1980 was the most notorious.[37] Romero was replaced by the bishop of Santiago de María, Arturo Rivera y Damas, who pledged to continue the work of his predecessor. Under strong pressure from the Vatican to heal the rift that had developed in the church hierarchy during the Romero years (because the other three bishops were all politically reactionary)[38] Rivera initially chose to adopt a cautious line. Indeed, both members and observers of the Salvadoran church believed that the Vatican was keeping Rivera on a "short leash" by naming him apostolic administrator and leaving him in that position for three years. Rivera was finally named archbishop just days before Pope John Paul II arrived in El Salvador on March 6, 1983. Nonetheless, by fall 1981 Rivera was speaking out against the violence of both the left and the right and arguing in favor of negotiations between the parties to the conflict. And as *Estudios Centroamericanos* (ECA), the journal of the Jesuit-run Central American University, noted in mid-1982, "In reality Monseñor Rivera has been careful not to appear publicly with the powerful, unlike CEDES [the Episcopal Conference] and the nuncio whose members frequently appear with the country's political and military authorities in the [Constituent] Assembly, in the garrisons, even going to bless helicopters."[39]

In May 1982 an individual close to the archdiocese and to the progressive wing of the church talked about Rivera. She noted that Rivera is different from Romero, that one of Rivera's major concerns is the tremendous reduction in the number of priests, nuns, and catechists. She believed that Rivera's intention was to strengthen the church in this respect and not to take positions that would lead to the assassination of other priests or of himself. "There is no doubt," she continued, "that if Rivera had followed in Romero's footsteps, he would already be dead—and he knows this." But, she continued, "Rivera has the mental clarity to see with objectivity the present situation in the country. He is not fooled or deceived by the situation."[40]

While the hierarchy continued to be divided, so too did the church at the base. In late 1979 a new organization, the National Conference of the Popular Church (CONIP), appeared. This was an organization of priests, nuns, and CEBS that included the most radical Catholics in the country. By September 1981 CONIP claimed to represent at least 70 percent of the CEBs, although that figure could not be verified because so many had disbanded or had been destroyed by the repression. In a political context, however, CONIP's significance lay in its open recognition of the revolutionary organizations as the authentic representative of the Salvadoran people.

The Revolutionary Organizations

CONIP's support for the Farabundo Martí Front for National Liberation (FMLN) and the Democratic Revolutionary Front (FDR) was symptomatic of conditions in the country, if not representative of the entire church. With the church telling people after 1968 that they had a right to organize, the revolutionary organizations found more people disposed to listen to their message and join them.

Rebellion in El Salvador has a long history. Indeed, it includes the rebellions of 1524, 1832, and 1932 together with those already mentioned. In 1970 fifty-year-old Salvador Cayetano Carpio, himself a former seminarian, baker, and union leader, resigned as secretary general of the Salvadoran Communist Party (PCS), and went underground with a small group to begin building the Popular Forces of Liberation (FPL). He criticized the PCS in a 1980 interview for their shortsightedness: "If there had not arisen a stubborn majority that at all costs blocked the advance towards the political-military strategy that the people needed for moving towards new stages of struggle, no need would have arisen to create a revolutionary organization such as the FPL."[41] The PCS, as noted earlier, had created a legal front three years earlier and had begun to participate in electoral politics.

Differences of opinion likewise led in 1975 to a split in the second of the political-military organizations, the Revolutionary Army of the People (ERP). It had been founded in 1972 by an amalgam of Young Communists, members of the left wing of the Christian Democratic Party, and radical members of the middle class. It incorporated two distinct groupings, one arguing for a large guerrilla army and an exclusively military strategy, the other advocating mass political work as well. The second faction called itself the "National Resistance." In the early 1970s it quietly worked with peasants in Suchitoto, north of San Salvador. Father José Alas had begun organizing these peasants in CEBs in

Table 3.1. The structure of the Salvadoran Left

Political-Military Organization	Mass Organization	Armed Forces
Popular Forces of Liberation (Fuerzas Populares de Liberación) (FPL—1970*)	Popular Revolutionary Bloc (Bloque Popular Revolucionario) (BPR—1975)	Popular Forces of Liberation (Fuerzas Populares de Liberación) (FPL—1970)
National Resistance (Resistencia Nacional) (RN—1975)	United Popular Action Front (Frente de Acción Popular Unificada) (FAPU—1974)	Armed Forces of National Resistance (Fuerzas Armadas de Resistencia Nacional) (FARN—1975)
Party of the Salvadoran Revolution (Partido de la Revolución Salvadoreña) (PRS—1977)	28th of February Popular Leagues (Ligas Populares 28 de Febrero) (LP-28—1978)	Revolutionary Army of the People (Ejército Revolucionario del Pueblo) (ERP—1972)
Communist Party of El Salvador (Partido Comunista de El Salvador) (PCS—1930)	Nationalist Democratic Union (Unión Democrática Nacionalista) (UDN—1967)	Armed Forces of Liberation (Fuerzas Armadas de Liberación) (FAL—1979)
Revolutionary Party of Central American Workers (Partido Revolucionario de los Trabajadores Centroamericanos) (PRTC—1976)	Popular Liberation Movement (Movimiento de Liberación Popular) (MLP—1979)	Revolutionary Party of Central American Workers (Partido Revolucionario de los Trabajadores Centroamericanos) (PRTC—1976)

*Years cited are dates of founding

December 1968. After several confrontations with large landowners and the government, they concluded that a more formal political organization was needed. Accompanied by Alas and joined by some labor unions and student and teacher organizations, they met in San Salvador's Basilica of the Sacred Heart in April 1974. There they formed the first of the "Popular Organizations," the United Popular Action Front (FAPU).

Among the ERP leaders active in FAPU was Roque Dalton, El Salvador's leading contemporary poet. Dalton's adherence to the "Resistance" faction led a handful of hardline ERPers to charge him with treason, try him in absentia, find him guilty, and condemn him to death. His assassination in May 1975 split the ERP. Dalton's faction immediately organized a separate party, the National Resistance (RN), and named its armed branch the Armed Forces of National Resistance (FARN). FAPU automatically became its mass organization.

In addition to the FPL, ERP, and RN, two other political-military organizations appeared. The Revolutionary Party of Central American Workers (PRTC) was founded as a pan–Central American party in 1976. Finally, in the late 1970s, the PCS decided the time for armed struggle had indeed arrived and created its own guerrilla force, the Armed Forces of Liberation (FAL).

In 1975, only a year after FAPU's formation, differences emerged that led to yet another split. The departing faction called itself the Popular Revolutionary Bloc (BPR). It identified with the political line of the FPL and became that group's mass organization. FAPU and the BPR (or the RN and FPL) remained far apart until late 1979. They debated, among other things, the best approach to building popular organizations. Though agreeing on the merits of a worker-campesino alliance, they differed over the role of the middle class and military. The FPL wrote off those sectors, while the RN directed part of its efforts to allying with them. FAPU's conception of working with unions was to build support from the base—the membership—through its political education classes, a tactic it shared with the PCS. The FPL's approach was to try to seize control of a union from the top. By 1980 the BPR had become the largest of the mass organizations with a total membership of over 60,000 and nine affiliated organizations. FAPU's membership was estimated at half that size and more of its leadership was older, middle-class, and in the unions.

FAPU acquired a reputation on the left for incisive analysis of the Salvadoran situation and helped in developing the unified political program that emerged in early 1980. Ultimately, its platform of revolution *and* democracy and its policy of alliances with progressives in the church, the Central American University, the Christian Democrats and other middle sectors such as professionals and technicians, became the official policy of the FMLN–FDR.

The third of the mass organizations was the February 28 Popular Leagues (LP–28), so-called in commemoration of a massacre following the 1977 presidential elections, which the army once again had stolen. It was founded by ERP sympathizers within the national university in February 1978. By 1980 it was also the third-largest popular organization, with about 10,000 members. LP–28's founding was the result of a belated recognition by the ERP that if it did not create its own mass organization it was going to be left in the dust by the FPL and RN. By killing Dalton, even though those responsible were expelled from the organization and forced into exile, the ERP had made itself the outcast among the groups. It was only in the spring of 1980 that the breach began to heal.

The fourth of the popular organizations, the Popular Liberation Movement (MLP), is the youngest and contains the fewest members. The fifth, the National Democratic Union (UDN), was the legal front of the PCS.

Throughout the 1970s the most prominent characteristic of the Salvadoran left was its sectarianism. Thus the demonstrations, occupations of embassies, government ministries, and churches, and kidnappings of oligarchs and foreign businessmen for ransom were all carried out by the various popular organizations or political-military organizations acting on their own. The fifty-two kidnappings, which netted at least $65 million, represented the most direct and effective assault on the regime during this period. For the revolutionaries, the rationale behind the kidnappings was simple: the oligarchy had exploited and impoverished the people while making millions and living in luxury. Kidnapping for ransom, in the words of one RN leader, was a means of "recouping some of this wealth for the people, to shape and develop the political struggle for their liberation." He denied that all the money had been used to buy arms. "Much of it has been used to build the popular organizations. The armed struggle is necessarily a part of the struggle," he said, "not because we would have chosen that path but because there is no other way to wrest political and economic power from the dominant forces and change the structures to a more just and humane system."[42]

The sectarianism diminished, however, as proximity to power increased. In late December 1979 the FPL, RN, and FAL created a coordinated command. On January 11, 1980 the popular organizations papered over their remaining differences, called a press conference, and proclaimed unity. Eleven days later, on the forty-eighth anniversary of the 1932 peasant uprising, they staged the biggest mass demonstration in Salvadoran history. At least 200,000 people gathered in the capital from all over the country in a show of power characterized by discipline and order.

What began as a peaceful march ended in chaos as state security forces fired on the demonstrators along the line of march. When the shooting was over forty-nine were dead and hundreds injured. The government claimed it had confined all forces to barracks for the day. Eyewitnesses said shots came from the roofs of fourteen public and private buildings in the center of the city. Later, an army officer said there had been a conspiracy among the minister of defense, the vice-minister, and members of the oligarchy to disrupt the march and to provoke the left into a confrontation. In that they failed.[43]

Three months later, and three weeks after the death of Archbishop Romero, the mass organizations came together in the Democratic Revolutionary Front (FDR). In May the coordinated command, created the previous December, was joined by the ERP to form the Unified Revolutionary Directorate (DRU). On October 10, creation of the Farabundo Martí Front for National Liberation (FMLN) was announced by the four political-military organizations. They were joined by the PRTC a month later after the party had separated into its national units. It appeared that the Salvadoran revolutionaries were on their way to repeating the triumph of the Sandinistas in Nicaragua the previous summer, but disputes continued to flare up, threatening the measure of unity that had been achieved.

The October Coup,
or The Regime's Last Chance[44]

"Whenever the [Salvadoran] army feels threatened as an institution," a U.S. military officer with long experience in El Salvador observed in early 1980, "it joins together and moves to the right."[45] This process, called "derechización" in El Salvador, had occurred several times since 1944. In 1979, it began even before the October 15 coup d'etat, thus dooming any possibility that the regime could adapt enough to continue to survive. It was absolutely essential that those who made the coup and those who joined the new government accomplish two goals: rid the army of the most conservative and corrupt officers, thus breaking the decades-old alliance with the oligarchy, and implement socioeconomic reforms, which would have broken the oligarchy's economic stranglehold on the country.

The coup was engineered by the October 15 Movement, a group of progressive young military officers who shared these goals and who plotted for five months to overthrow the repressive government of President/General Carlos Humberto Romero. In November 1978, as popular unrest grew, the government passed the law for the Defense and Guarantee of Public Order, legalizing press censorship and outlawing public meetings, strikes, and the dissemination of any information which "tended to destroy the social order." Though the law was repealed in early 1979 in an effort to appease the Carter administration, officially sanctioned violence continued unabated. In late 1978 and early 1979 national and international human rights groups condemned the Romero government for systematic torture, murder, and persecution of political dissidents.

There was at least one other inspiration for these young officers. They were keenly aware that, far from ensuring tighter control over the populace, government repression had increased the vulnerability of those in power. More people were being radicalized, and the left itself was turning increasingly to violent means of protest such as bombings and kidnappings. The victory in July 1979 of the Sandinistas and the rout of the Nicaraguan National Guard had a profound impact. Many former guardsmen fled through El Salvador, and the Salvadoran officers saw men who had lost everything—homes, money, and country. Now clearly before them was a warning of what they, too, would suffer if they failed to address the demands of the growing revolutionary organizations.

In August 1979 a Military Coordinating Committee, composed of five officers working in tandem with a group of civilians, began feeling out officers around the country. Archbishop Oscar Romero warned the committee *not* to include Colonel Jaime Abdul Gutiérrez, commander of the army's repair shop, who was known to be corrupt. But Gutiérrez learned of the plot in August, whereupon Romero advised the committee to include him in order to watch him. This meant that Gutiérrez was in on the plot from the beginning. Later on the archbishop sent the committee a message, stating that he opposed the inclusion of either Gutiérrez or of Colonel José Guillermo García in the new government for the same reason—corruption. On October 6 Colonel Arnaldo Adolfo Majano, a reform-minded and incorruptible officer from the military academy, was brought into the coordinating committee. Two days later the plotters held a secret meeting and elected Majano and Lieutenant Colonel René Guerra y Guerra as the two military members of the junta. Colonel Guerra was the prime mover behind the plot and, like Majano, was regarded as principled, honest, and intelligent.

The next day Gutiérrez and García called another meeting and began the process of derechización. They challenged Guerra's election, arguing that he was junior in rank. Colonel Gutiérrez's name was placed in nomination, and because the dissident group had assembled all its allies but not those of Guerra, Gutiérrez replaced him on the junta.

The coup itself was virtually bloodless—a bad omen for Salvadorans. "*Cuando no hay balazos,*" the saying goes, "*el golpe es malo.*" (When there are no bullets, the coup is worthless.) There was widespread agreement among the members of the October 15 Movement that the first civilian member of the junta should be the rector of the Jesuit-run Nicaragua University (UCA), Román Mayorga Quiroz. Mayorga agreed to serve on the junta if the second civilian were chosen from the Popular Forum, an ad hoc group of political parties, unions, and mass organizations that had been meeting for many months to discuss the country's growing problems. The forum selected Guillermo Manuel Ungo, a Social Democrat and UCA administrator. The third civilian,

Mario Andino, a moderately conservative businessman, was selected by Majano and Gutiérrez after consulting the private sector.

By the night of October 17 El Salvador had a new government. The five members of the junta broke with the past by pledging to support the principles of the Proclamation of the Armed Forces. Drafted over the summer by civilians, the proclamation acknowledged that the previous regime had "violated human rights," "fomented and tolerated corruption," "created an economic and social disaster," and "profoundly discredited" the armed forces in the eyes of the country. It called for dissolution of ORDEN, a right-wing paramilitary peasant organization founded a decade earlier; respect for human rights, beginning with a general amnesty for all political prisoners; implementation of a process of agrarian reform; reform of the financial sector and external commerce; and political freedom—in particular, freedom for the popular organizations.

Gutiérrez gave verbal support, but was unsure how far he wanted the proposed economic reforms to go. He saw himself as a minority of one on a radical junta. He wanted political reinforcement, and for this reason he took it on himself, without consulting anyone, to name Colonel García minister of defense just hours after President Romero had fled the country. Two days later the junta and the October 15 Movement accepted García's appointment as a *fait accompli*. In so doing, they revealed two weaknesses that would ultimately prove fatal for the new government. One was a lack of unanimity and decisiveness. The other was the great political naiveté of the young officers.

García promptly appointed Colonel Nicolás Carranza his viceminister of defense. Along with Gutiérrez, these two men had worked earlier in ANTEL, which had long been a breeding ground of corruption. Indeed, the three were known as the "ANTEL mafia." In the days following the coup the three demonstrated how little they shared the priorities of the Armed Forces Proclamation or of the October 15 Movement. Two days after the coup, García and Carranza argued in an officers' meeting that the first priority should be the restructuring of the army and that reforms should wait until afterward. Meanwhile, according to an officer present, Colonel Majano talked of nothing but "changes, changes, changes."[46]

Informed observers have said that 90 percent of those in the government between October 15, 1979 and January 3, 1980 were the "cream of the country." Ten senior officials, for example, were UCA professors or administrators. Other able and honest Salvadorans returned from exile to accept top government positions. Despite these encouraging developments, Salvadoran political reality subverted the goals and ideals of the October 15 Movement and its civilian allies and led directly to the resignation of the government on January 3, 1980. Essentially, the problem was that Gutiérrez and García refused to take the army out of politics, and Majano was too vacillating to challenge his colleagues. The young officers had naively believed that by getting rid of seventy senior officers and installing new leadership in the Salvadoran High Command they could automatically bring the various state security forces under control. Unfortunately, the new members of the high command were no more disposed than their predecessors to control the security forces.

The new government also suffered from the young officers' fear of institutional destruction akin to that which had befallen the Nicaraguan National Guard. This the oligarchy exploited, working hand in glove with García. They argued that the triumph of the left in a revolution would mean the dissolution of the army and security forces, and that the economic changes proposed were leftist-oriented and would signal the triumph of communism in one more country. These arguments, of course, had been used before—every time, in fact, that reforms offending the oligarchy's self-interest were proposed.

As repression mounted, civilians in the government became increasingly disenchanted. The final crisis came on December 26 when García, accompanied by the high command, appeared at a meeting of the cabinet. According to officials present at the meeting, a "screaming match" ensued during which the new director of the National Guard, Carlos Eugenio Vides Casanova, told the ministers they were going too far with their proposed reforms. The ministers told García, Vides, and their military cohorts that the reforms were none of their business. In a country where civilians had taken orders from the army and oligarchy for half a century, that was an intolerable heresy.

The ministers appealed to the young officers to intervene, but they declined. So, on January 3, 1980, Mayorga, Ungo, the entire cabinet except the minister of defense and his vice-minister, and all heads of state-owned companies resigned. Mario Andino left the junta the next day. Mayorga went into exile. Three months later, Ungo led his small National Revolutionary Movement (MNR) into the Democratic Revolutionary Front. He became its president following the assassination in November 1980 of Enrique Alvarez Córdova and five other FDR leaders by state security forces.[47]

The mass resignation of the government shook the young officers out of their political apathy. On January 15 in a meeting of the officer corps about 75 percent of those present voted to demand the resignation of García and Carranza. That same day copies of a letter addressed to the junta circulated in all major army posts. The letter, signed by 186 officers, demanded the immediate dismissal of the minister and vice-minister of defense. When the letter was given to Majano and Gutiérrez they apprised García and Carranza of its contents, and then did nothing. The civilian members of the junta never saw the letter, and no one ever responded to its demand. The power of García and Carranza remained unshaken.

The semblance of a civilian-military coalition was maintained when the Christian Democratic Party agreed to join the government under certain conditions. The most important of these were that the army publicly commit itself to a program of economic reforms, that the repression cease, that the army agree to open a dialogue with the popular organizations, and that no representatives of business organizations be appointed to the junta or the cabinet. The army accepted these conditions, whereupon José Antonio Morales Erlich, a former mayor of San Salvador, and Héctor Dada Hirezi, who had served as foreign minister from October 15 to January 3, joined the junta.

A rightist coup remained a constant threat throughout 1980 and a periodic threat thereafter. Indeed, right-wing coups were derailed at least eight times between February 1980 and February 1983.[48] At the end of February 1980 the United States Embassy foiled an attempt in which García was a participant. From the embassy and from the State Department in Washington the word went out that any change in the government which excluded the Christian Democrats was absolutely unacceptable. Members of the high command and the oligarchy were called to the embassy and given this message. Salvadoran oligarchs living in Miami were informed that if the coup took place, their residence visas would be revoked.

Another coup attempt at the end of April also stalled not only because of pressure from the United States, but also because the Majano supporters in command positions made it known that they would oppose such a coup. Majano himself ordered the arrest of Roberto D'Aubuisson as the principal conspirator. D'Aubuisson was caught with a suitcase full of incriminating documents, held for three days, then released for "lack of evidence." Majano, meanwhile, was relieved of his post as commander-in-chief of the armed forces, and Gutiérrez was named to replace him. Majano threatened to resign from the junta, but was persuaded to remain by U.S. Ambassador Robert White.

On September 1 the army's order of the month transferred all Majano supporters from command authority and sent several overseas. In December Majano himself was removed from the junta and ordered to Spain as ambassador. He refused and went into hiding, from where he gave a series of clandestine press conferences charging the government with supporting the death squads.[49] García issued a warrant for Majano's arrest. He was not found until February 20, 1981, at which time the army threatened to court-martial him. After a month in custody, with the regime under extreme pressure from Panama's General Omar Torrijos, who had been Majano's classmate at the military academy, he was sent into exile.

Meanwhile, the United States was insisting that El Salvador had a "moderate, reformist government" and that the proof of this lay in the presence of the Christian Democratic Party. That argument was increasingly strained, however, as first Héctor Dada, then other Christian Democrats resigned from the government in protest over the growing repression. On March 10, 1980, Dada and others resigned from the party as well, charging that the government had degenerated into "something neither democratic nor Christian."[50] Threats against his life immediately drove Dada into exile. Of the Christian Democratic officials who resigned from the party then and in the following months, all but two joined the newly created Popular Movement of Social Christians (MPSC). This organization also helped form the Democratic Revolutionary Front.

Divisions within the PDC deepened at the party congress, called on March 9 to select Dada's successor on the junta. José Napoleón Duarte, who had returned from exile days after the coup, and who continued as party leader, handpicked a majority of the delegates with help from his supporters. Duarte and his son lobbied hard for his election. On the other side, all Christian Democratic ministers opposed Duarte, and Majano called Duarte personally to tell him the progressive officers did not want him on the junta. During the convention, Morales Erlich spoke twice in opposition to Duarte. But it was all prearranged: Duarte won, and with that the left wing of the party walked out.

With the removal of Majano in December, a shuffling of positions occurred in which Duarte became president of the junta, Gutiérrez vice-president, and Morales Erlich head of the agrarian reform. Washington chose to interpret this as a sign that the influence of Duarte was increasing, with the implication that civilian control over the miitary was emerging. Nothing could have been farther removed from reality. As the progressive isolation of Majano demonstrated, the real power in El Salvador lay in the hands of the minister of defense and his followers. Duarte himself, far from exercising a moderating influence on García, helped only to preserve the government's legitimacy before the Christian Democrat–led governments of Venezuela and Costa Rica, and within the United States. Without Duarte, the Salvadoran regime would have had almost no friends but the United States, Guatemala, and Honduras.

The resignation of Dada and the election of Duarte to the junta took place in a week that also saw the promulgation of the long-awaited agrarian reform and bank nationalization. These reforms, heralded by the United States as the most sweeping since the Mexican Revolution, were the result of heavy pressure from the U.S. government and the young military and were only approved at an extremely high price. There was, in a word, a trade-off. The United States and the young military got the reforms. García and the conservatives got carte blanche to carry out a systematic program of repression against the very people the agrarian reform was supposed to benefit: the rural poor.

The agrarian reform had three stages. Phase I nationalized 376 farms of more than 500 hectares. These farms were largely pasture land, cotton or diversified crop farms. Phase II, which affected about 2,000 farms of between 100 and 500 hectares, was announced and postponed indefinitely. It included most of the coffee farms, and its postponement thus signaled once again that El Salvador's first source of wealth and those who profited from it would not be touched.

Phase III (Decree 207) was promulgated on April 27, 1980. Called "Land to the Tiller," it mandated that all rented land now belonged to those who cultivated it. The phase was widely touted as "self-implementing," but that proved to be an overstatement. Indeed, a lengthy report by an AID official, who spent five weeks visiting numerous nationalized farms in the spring of 1980, disputed official U.S. claims that the reform was working and was draining support from the left. Monitoring groups, such as Amnesty International, documented the fact that any positive effects of the reforms were more than offset by an accompanying wave of repression. Moreover, a July 18, 1980 memorandum from the University of Wisconsin Land Tenure Center discussed forty-seven different problems with Decree 207, concluding:

> In general, this is a very hastily and poorly drafted law. . . . It sets the stage for a top-down land reform process tightly controlled by the government, with no significant participation by *campesinos* at any level. Also, it creates a cumbersome two-tier bureaucratic structure for acquiring and distributing land, which is very inefficient and likely to lead to large inequities.[51]

By the spring of 1982 *Estudios Centroamericanos* reported that (1) as of the previous October (1981) 326 of the 376 Phase I farms had actually been acquired; (2) as of December 1981 67, or 20.5 percent of the 326, had been abandoned; (3) by late 1981 only 96 of the cooperatives were receiving technical assistance from personnel of the Ministry of Agriculture, the Development Bank, and the Agrarian Transformation Institute; and (4) as a result of these and other deficiencies, there was a 10 percent decline in production in the farms affected by Phase I. The UCA study concluded that, "without exception, the reforms have been and continue to be poorly administered, profoundly affected by the war and consistently rejected by the oligarchy, which tries to reverse the process of reform to benefit its own exclusive interests."[52]

"Reform with repression," coupled with growing pressure from the guerrillas, led to hard economic times by late 1980. The economy declined by 4 percent that year. Earlier, in 1979, the Inter-American Development Bank had characterized the economy as "adversely affected by prolonged strikes in industry, interruptions in the harvesting of certain crops and extraordinary flights of private capital."[53] The situation deteriorated further in 1981. Net exports declined 28.8 percent between 1978 and 1981. Investment declined in the same period 61.3 percent. The gross internal product was off 14.8 percent.[54] U.S. officials charged in early 1983 that economic sabotage by the insurgents had cost the country $600 million.[55] Not surprisingly, then, government dependence on the United States increased. A State Department source suggested that without continuing U.S. and multilateral assistance, the Salvadoran government would be bankrupt within days.[56]

After Duarte replaced Dada on the junta, conversations between the private sector and the government, which the former had suspended during the second junta, resumed. The oligarchy and business organizations created the Productive Alliance in mid-1980 in an effort to gain support for their position, especially in the United States. The alliance immediately sent a delegation to Washington to call the attention of the United States government to the importance of private sector cooperation in achieving a climate of tranquillity in El Salvador and reducing unemployment.[57] The leadership and membership list of the alliance was studded with names of the most conservative oligarchs.

Influence from Outside: The United States

Prior to 1980, official United States concern with El Salvador was confined to moments of perceived crisis. The Hoover administration, citing a 1923 treaty that proscribed recognition of governments created extralegally, broke diplomatic relations following the 1931 coup d'etat. President Franklin D. Roosevelt restored relations in 1933. During that decade, however, Martínez became progressively enamored of the fascist regimes in Italy and

Germany—to the point that, by 1938, a German officer became director of the *Escuela Militar* and Salvadoran officers were receiving training in those countries. By 1940, however, a deteriorating economy and increasing dissent among officers not sympathetic to the Axis forced Martínez to do a sudden about-face. The United States had already offered to become El Salvador's primary arms supplier, and in June 1940 Martínez requested 35,000 rifles. He was assured by the military attaché that "our exceptionally loyal friends" would not be disappointed.[58]

By 1948 a U.S. army colonel was director of the *Escuela Militar*, yet the United States was completely in the dark when the coup occurred that year.[59] The United States appears to have been similarly ignorant of the October 1960 coup, which occurred less than two weeks before the U.S. presidential election. As we have seen, however, the U.S. embassy actively supported those in the military and oligarchy who opposed the reforms the junta was trying to implement, and embassy personnel were involved in the countercoup in January 1961. We have also seen that the period of Murat Williams's tenure as ambassador is the only time that the United States has followed a policy of consistently pressing for fundamental reforms. The irony, of course, is that those reforms created contradictions with which the regime ultimately could not cope.

In 1972 the United States was again in a position to influence events in the direction of reform, as it had been in 1960. But the U.S. ambassador, Henry Catto, maintained absolute silence as the military denied Duarte and Ungo their rightful electoral victory. The arrival of Jimmy Carter in Washington, and the emphasis by his administration on human rights as a criterion in the conduct of foreign policy, quickly placed the United States at odds with the Salvadoran regime. The government of President Arturo Molina was being widely criticized for human rights violations, and Carter ordered Secretary of State Cyrus Vance to communicate the White House's concern over a public threat to kill every Jesuit in El Salvador if they were not out of the country by June 30, 1977.

At that point the presidency was passing to General Carlos Humberto Romero. Miraculously, following Vance's intervention, Romero gave public assurances to the Jesuits and the crisis passed. But Romero was enraged at the U.S. interference and later in the year suspended U.S. military assistance—before the Congress had an opportunity to act. Military aid remained suspended until after the October coup, whereupon the Carter administration offered the junta new military aid and increased economic assistance. The administration also fell silent in the face of continuing—and increasing—repression by the security forces who refused to be bound by the commitments of the October 15 Movement or of the junta.

Instead, U.S. policy began operating on two levels. Publicly, the United States announced support for the junta and for the reforms it proposed. Privately, the U.S. embassy, primarily through the ambassador, Frank Devine, and the military attaché, Lieutenant Colonel Gerald Walker, threw their support to the oligarchy, which was vehemently opposed to the proposed reforms, and to the most conservative sector of the military, which was more interested in restructuring and modernizing their institution than in supporting the Proclamation of the armed forces. The United States began encouraging a law-and-order line within the Salvadoran military. It did this primarily through frequent conversations between Colonel Walker and the high command, who interpreted these conversations as a carte blanche for repressions.

When the governmental crisis erupted in late December, the embassy made no effort to support the junta, although one embassy official expressed "consternation" at the resignation of the government. Rather, there was a feeling within the embassy that the government was, perhaps, a little too radical and that it would be easier to work with a government in which the Christian Democrats were the primary civilian actors, rather than the coalition of Social Democrats, Christian Democrats, independents, and communists who made up the government of the first junta.

Ambassador Devine's departure at the end of the year brought James Cheek to El Salvador as chargé d'affaires. Cheek tried to persuade the Christian Democrats that their job was to fight a "clean, counterinsurgency war" and that they should pass laws that would make it easier for the military to capture and hold "subversives" indefinitely. Cheek's logic was that if "subversives" could be held under a permanent suspension of habeas corpus (which is, of course, unconstitutional in the United States), the armed forces would have an incentive to capture rather than kill their quarry. The Christian Democrats responded, however, that sufficiently repressive laws already existed in El Salvador.[60]

The multilevel U.S.–El Salvador relationship became more complex when Robert White arrived as U.S. ambassador in early March 1980. Committed at first to talking to all sides, he ruffled feathers on both extremes of the political spectrum within three weeks of his arrival. He upset the left by announcing (erroneously) the death of BPR secretary general Juan Chacón and then accusing the left of causing the violence at Archbishop Romero's funeral. He enraged the oligarchy by telling them that they shared responsibility for the situation in El Salvador through their greed and their lack of social conscience. White insisted that El Salvador had a "revolutionary government," that José Napoleón Duarte (who had been elected to the junta just days after White's arrival in the country) was a champion of democracy, and that the junta was caught between two warring extremes of left and right. He minimized the differences between the October, January, and March juntas, and yet he was the first U.S. official to openly acknowledge that elements of the security forces were implicated in much of the violence. He maintained that the greatest danger in El Salvador came not from the left but from the right. White encouraged Majano to remain on the junta through 1980, strongly supported Duarte, and yet apparently he did nothing to get rid of the first obstacle to any meaningful reform: Minister of Defense García.

After Romero's funeral and after the left's mixed success during the summer to mount three general strikes, White and the Carter administration became convinced that the popular organizations were a fading political threat. In fact, the funeral marked the end of an era in the history of El Salvador's revolutionary organizations—the era of *la lucha de masas*, the mass struggle. The months between April 1980 and January 1981 may now be clearly seen as a period of transition from mass struggle to armed struggle. The growing repression forced the organizations to decide against mass demonstrations, which clearly had become an invitation to a massacre. The efforts to mount general strikes during the summer were intended to mobilize the workforce and to demonstrate in a different way the power of the left.

But the last strike, in August, led to the arrest of several of the country's top labor union leaders and the effective decapitation of the most militant labor union federation in the country, FENASTRAS. At the same time, that strike demonstrated the budding potential of the left to coordinate political and military actions in the cities and in the countryside. Yet the United States chose to ignore this potential in favor of the view that the left was finished.

Through the fall there were rumblings that the left was preparing for a major action in January—and the long-awaited "general offensive" began on January 10. For three days the insurgents had the Salvadoran army on the run, but then the tide turned. The FMLN had no unified war plan. There was little coordination among the commanders, a problem exacerbated by a shortage of radio-communications equipment. There were many tactical errors. So the rebels beat a retreat to their "controlled zones" in the northern and eastern parts of the country. Meanwhile, the Carter administration in its closing days decided to send $5 million worth of weapons to the Salvadoran army. Days later the United States had a new president, Ronald Reagan, who quickly sent an additional $10 million in military assistance and nineteen military trainers and maintenance personnel.[61]

Robert White initially supported Carter's last-minute decision to send military assistance, and then days later he opposed the move. Ten days after Reagan's inauguration, White was recalled to Washington. He had appeared on a Reagan transition team "hit list" of ambassadors to be replaced because they were too liberal.

The Reagan policy was, in its fundamentals, a continuation of the Carter policy. Both shared a common objective: to prevent the left from coming to power. The only significant difference was Reagan's conviction that Carter had paid too little attention to the international dimensions of the Salvadoran conflict. Reagan and company imbued the struggle with a vast East-West significance that Carter had avoided. The first indication of this change came with the publication, just a month into the new administration, of a State Department "White Paper." In it the anonymous authors charged that "the insurgency in El Salvador has been progressively transformed into another case of indirect armed aggression against a small Third World country by Communist powers acting through Cuba."[62] The "supporting documents" for the "White Paper" did not, however, support the exaggerated claims of arms shipments to the FMLN or of Soviet or Cuban control of the revolutionary forces.[63] Further, neither U.S. allies in Europe and Latin America nor the U.S. Congress were swayed by the administration's campaign. Indeed, the Congress soon voted to bar all military assistance and advisers unless the president certified that the Salvadoran government had met six conditions designed to prevent human rights violations and to promote democratic reforms.[64]

In spite of the opposition from allies, Congress, and public opinion,[65] the Reagan administration plunged ahead single-mindedly with its policy. In early March 1981 military assistance was increased by $25 million, and by late March fifty-six military "trainers" were in El Salvador. The game plan was to "win a military victory in sixty to ninety days." By midsummer, however, the FMLN had reviewed its mistakes of the previous January, had rectified many of them, and had launched a new offensive. The new U.S. Ambassador, Deane R. Hinton, began cabling the Department of State that the Salvadoran army was not winning the war, that there was a military stalemate, and that the army was losing. He requested more military assistance and trainers.[66]

To justify a growing commitment in the face of equally growing domestic opposition, the administration began describing the Salvadoran government as "transitional," and it developed a political game plan whose focus was national elections for a constituent assembly in March 1982.

The FMLN, meanwhile, staged a military resurgence that sufficiently impressed France and Mexico, who, in August 1981, issued a joint declaration recognizing the FDR and FMLN as a "representative political force" that must be involved in any political settlement. Several other European and Third World nations endorsed the Franco-Mexican declaration. In October the FMLN opened up yet another offensive, in which the most devastating action (in military, economic, and psychological terms) was the blowing up of the *Puente de Oro* (Bridge of Gold), a $10 million suspension bridge that was the major link between the eastern and western halves of the country. Indeed, with the August offensive a pattern emerged that continued into 1983. The pattern was simply that each successive military offensive initiated by the insurgents lasted longer, inflicted increasing numbers of casualties on government forces, placed growing amounts of territory under FMLN control, and revealed ever greater military coordination and unity within the FMLN. The August offensive was notable for another reason as well. For the first time the FMLN officially took prisoners of war, announced they would be treated under the Geneva Conventions, and called on the International Red Cross (IRC) to come and take them. It took one year, however, for the Salvadoran government to agree to allow the IRC to do so. The reason was that the handing over of POWs by the FMLN and their receipt by the IRC constituted a tacit recognition of the insurgents as a belligerent force under international rules of war.

The FMLN policy of taking prisoners, treating them well, and releasing them began to pay tremendous dividends in both political and military terms. In June 1982, for every 100 casualties among government troops, there were 8 POWs. By January 1983, that ratio had increased to 44 for every 100. Clearly the message had spread through the army that it was better to surrender than to risk being killed. The results were political credit on the international and domestic levels. By the fall and winter of 1982–1983, entire garrisons were surrendering to the FMLN without a fight. By June 1983 the Salvadoran army was having a serious problem with reenlistments. According to a *Washington Post* story, "About half the nearly 7,000 Salvadorean officers and troops the United States has trained to combat leftist guerrillas . . . have left the army since President Reagan began the training program in 1981. . . ."[67]

President Reagan's early insistence that the Salvadoran conflict was aided and abetted by the Soviet Union, acting through Cuba, expanded to include Nicaragua by 1982. This justified an unpublicized policy that was clearly formulated by June 1982 and involved nothing less than the regionalization of the conflict. In short, the policy was, in this order, to achieve a military victory over the FMLN, to overthrow Nicaragua's revolutionary government, and finally, to destabilize Cuba with the ultimate objective of overthrowing that government as well. With the growth of Nicaraguan counterrevolutionary forces based in Honduras and funded by the CIA to the tune of at least $19 million, and with the growing strength of the FMLN, the priorities changed. By early 1983 the number one objective was the overthrow of the Nicaraguan government. The shift in priorities seems to have been a pragmatic one: Nicaragua by early 1983 appeared more vulnerable than it had several months earlier.[68]

With regard to El Salvador, however, this policy was played out through a "two-track" approach. Domestic and international opposition to a military solution required the Reagan administration to pay lip service to the desire for a political solution. This took the form of accepting negotiations with the FDR/FMLN—over their participation in elections, while pushing for ever greater amounts of military assistance. The FDR/FMLN, meanwhile, was making periodic offers for open and unconditional negotiations with the Salvadoran government.[69] Their position was that elections should be part of an overall political solution for the country and that the current government could not guarantee the safety of their candidates, since it clearly could not protect people (like Christian Democrats) who were participating in the government.[70] The extent of the Reagan commitment to a political solution could be measured by the decision in May 1983 to remove Thomas Enders, the Assistant Secretary of State for Inter-American Affairs, and Ambassador Hinton, both of whom had had the temerity to argue for a political solution. Neither man could, by any reasonable measure, be called a "moderate." Enders, for example, had directed the secret bombing of Cambodia from the U.S. Embassy in Phnom Penh, in direct violation of U.S. law, during the early 1970s.[71]

By early 1983 it was clear that the *logic* of U.S. policy in El Salvador would ultimately leave no alternative but to send troops. In a speech to a joint session of Congress on April 27, President Reagan did not say the U.S. "will not" send troops. He said they were "not thinking of" sending troops and that troops had not "been asked for." With the FMLN continuing to make considerable military advances, no one was talking in 1983, as they had in late 1981 and 1982, of a "military stalemate." There was even occasional public acknowledgment that the army was losing. Indeed, Lieutenant General Wallace H. Nutting, head of the U.S. Southern Command in Panama, said in an interview in May 1983 what everyone in the administration had been thinking for a long time. Acknowledging that Central America was at war,

Nutting asserted that the United States "is engaged in that war." Noting that the Reagan administration "has said that we will not allow a Marxist government to take office in San Salvador, our government as a whole and our people as a whole have not followed up that commitment with a willingness to take those steps necessary to bring that about."[72] Nutting complained that "the guerrillas are winning the psychological war" and that the debate over policy in the United States must end with a national consensus behind the president to do whatever is necessary in order to convince the guerrillas that "they can't win."[73] Public opinion polls, however, suggested that the consensus Nutting (and the administration) wanted, would not be forthcoming. The shadow of Vietnam was too long.

The Future of the Regime

By the summer of 1983 it was clear that the Salvadoran insurgents had sufficient military power to veto any political arrangement that did not include them and their political allies in the FDR. It was also clear that, short of direct and massive U.S. military intervention in the form of tens of thousands of troops or blanket bombing, the situation was not likely to change. Meanwhile, however, the United States sought to legitimize the existing regime through elections.

In March 1982 the Reagan administration endorsed El Salvador's elections for a constituent assembly in the expectation of legitimizing then–junta president José Napoleón Duarte and the Christian Democratic Party. But the elections legitimized instead Roberto D'Aubuisson, an army major cashiered after the October coup, and his fascist ARENA (Nationalist Republican Alliance) party. Only extraordinary pressure from the United States on the Salvadoran army high command prevented D'Aubuisson from being elected as El Salvador's provisional president. That outcome, of course, would have made the administration's job in persuading the Congress to continue appropriating military and economic support funds far more difficult, if not impossible. D'Aubuisson, after all, had been directly implicated in the assassination of El Salvador's archbishop, Oscar Romero, and was reputed to have close ties to the death squads.

More to the point, the elections did not change the character of the regime. The same army that had been running the country since 1931 was still in control. There was still a civil war going on. Nevertheless, the United States plunged ahead with plans to hold elections in March 1984 for a permanent national assembly and a national president. As the military situation deteriorated in early 1983, however, the administration pressured the Salvadoran government to move up the date, to December 1983. With reluctance, the Salvadorans went along. There were at least two reasons for their desire to put off the elections. One was that the country was virtually bankrupt, and to remain solvent it was dependent almost entirely on U.S. largesse and what the United States could pressure international lending agencies to provide.[74] The second reason was a practical one: there was no master registration list of electors. With over 40,000 people dead since 1979, between a half-million and a million either in exile or internally displaced, and somewhere between one-fourth and one-third of the national territory under FMLN control, compiling such a list was a difficult task.

But political exigencies in the United States required that elections go forward. Without a "legitimate" government, the Reagan administration would have an extremely difficult time in persuading the Congress to continue supporting its policy.

Thus, the only conclusion one could draw in mid-1983 about the Salvadoran regime was that it was being maintained by the United States government. It was clear that, if military assistance were to be withdrawn, the army would collapse in less than a month. Without economic assistance, the government would be bankrupt immediately. Yet the Reagan administration, for ideological reasons, remained unwilling to consider the one alternative that held some promise of resolving the crisis: negotiations with the opposition. Thus the Salvadoran regime promised to remain a regime in crisis, a regime whose days were numbered.

Notes

1. This chapter draws on evidence and arguments I've developed elsewhere: see Tommie Sue Montgomery, *Revolution in El Salvador: Origins and Evolution* (Boulder, Colo.: Westview Press, 1982), and

Montgomery, "El Salvador: The Descent into Violence," *International Policy Report* (Washington, D.C.: Center for International Policy, 1982). I am grateful to the Maryknoll Sisters, and especially to Sisters Joan Petrik and Ellen McDonald for providing both a tranquil place in which to finish this chapter and a lot of moral support.

2. I am grateful to Dr. Charles Clements for this metaphor.

3. Murdo J. MacLeod, *Spanish Central America: A Socioeconomic History, 1520–1720* (Berkeley: University of California Press, 1973), p. 49.

4. For a fuller discussion, see Montgomery, *Revolution in El Salvador*, pp. 31–43.

5. Alberto Masferrer, "Como anda la justicia en esta San Salvador" [How justice operates in this San Salvador], *Patria*, November 30, 1928.

6. Masferrer, "La crisis del maíz" [The Maize Crisis], *Patria*, April 4, 1929.

7. Alejandro Bermudez, *Salvador al vuelo* [El Salvador: An Overview] (San Salvador: n.p., 1917), pp. 171–72; Carlos Urrutia Glamenco, *La ciudad de San Salvador* [The City of San Salvador] (San Salvador: n.p., 1924), p. 208.

8. Normally in Spanish, an individual uses his or her first last name which is the father's name. But Hernández Martínez's mother was not married to his father. So the general carried only his mother's name, Hernández, from childhood. Later, he added Martínez, his father's name, in order to be more socially acceptable.

9. Jorge Arias Gómez, "Augustín Farabundo Martí (Esbozo biográfico)" [Augustín Farabundo Martí (Biographical sketch)], *La Universidad* 96, no. 4 (July-August 1971), p. 230.

10. Privileged interview.

11. It is thirty and out, no exceptions, as General José Guillermo García found out when he tried to continue as Minister of Defense in 1983. For any officer to violate the thirty-year rule upsets the next *tanda*, who have been waiting for their turn at the spoils.

12. See Carolyn Forché and Leonel Gómez, "The Military's Web of Corruption," *The Nation* 235, no. 13 (October 23, 1982), pp. 391–93.

13. Privileged interview, San Salvador, 1980.

14. Privileged interview, San Salvador, 1979.

15. Agency for International Development, *Agrarian Reform Project Number 519–0263 Audit Report*, 1981, p. 8.

16. White, quoted in Forché and Gómez, "Military's Web," p. 391. I have had FMLN officials tell me that corrupt army officers in both El Salvador and Honduras were selling them arms.

17. Ibid.

18. Robert Varney Elam, "Appeal to Arms: The Army and Politics

in El Salvador, 1931-1964" (Ph.D. dissertation, Stanford University, 1968), p. 147.

19. José María Lemus, *Entrevistas y opiniónes* [Interviews and Opinions] (San Salvador: Imprenta Nacional, 1955), p. 29.

20. Alastair White, *El Salvador* (Boulder Colo.: Westview Press, 1973), p. 105.

21. The families are Palomo, Simán, Dueñas, Hill, Alvarez Meza, and Meza Ayau. Eduardo Colindres, *Fundamentos económicos de la burguesia salvadoreña* [Economic Fundamentals of the Salvadoran Bourgeoisie] (San Salvador: UCA Editores, 1977), p. 131, 400-428.

22. 1964 represented the apogee of Salvadoran cotton production, however. By 1969 overuse of fertilizer and insecticides, coupled with rising costs, forced out speculators and reduced the area planted to half the 1965 levels. David Browning, *El Salvador: Landscape and Society* (Oxford: Clarendon Press, 1971), pp. 232, 234-35, 240. By the mid-1970s cotton production rebounded to levels exceeding those of 1960, only to plummet once again in the early 1980s by a third.

23. White, *El Salvador*, p. 131.

24. William Durham, *Scarcity and Survival in Central America: Ecological Origins of the Soccer War* (Stanford, Calif.: Stanford University Press, 1979), p. 36.

25. For a fuller discussion of the U.S. role, see Montgomery, *Revolution in El Salvador*, pp. 73-74; and U.S. Congress, House of Representatives, "Human Rights in Nicaragua, Guatemala, and El Salvador: Implications for U.S. Policy," hearings before the Subcommittee on International Organizations of the Committee on International Relations, 94th Congress, 2d session, June 8 and 9, 1976, pp. 47-48.

26. Stephen Webre, *José Napoleón Duarte and the Christian Democratic Party in Salvadoran Politics, 1960-1972* (Baton Rouge: Louisiana State University Press, 1979), p. 105.

27. Ibid, p. 181.

28. "Central American Patterns of Regional Economic Integration," *Bank of London and South American Review* (June 1979), pp. 340-42; *NACLA Report on the Americas* 14, no. 2 (March-April 1980), p. 11.

29. Browning, *Landscape and Society*, p. 87.

30. Melvin Burke, "El sistema de plantación y la proletarización del trabajo agrícola en El Salvador" [The plantation system and the proletarianization of agricultural labor in El Salvador], *ECA* 31, no. 335-36 (September-October 1976), p. 476.

31. *Diario de Hoy* (San Salvador), January 15, 1967. Dr. Castillo, a pharmacologist, had served in the interim as rector of the University of El Salvador where he had significantly upgraded the quality of edu-

cation, expanded enrollment, and begun providing scholarships for needy students.

32. Nevertheless, in the election PAR garnered 14.6 percent of the national vote, against 21.6 percent for the PDC; in San Salvador, however, the PAR led the PDC 29 to 25 percent, with the PCN gaining only a plurality, 41 percent. Nationally, of course, the PCN carried the day with 54.4 percent of the vote.

33. Exodus 3:7–17.

34. Interview with Dr. Charles Clements, May 1983. Clements, a Quaker medical doctor, served in 1981–1982 in the Guazapa Front, one of the areas of El Salvador under guerrilla control. Guazapa includes part of the Suchitoto parish.

35. Equipo de trabajo del departamento de letras de la UCA, "Los medios de comunicación, un arma más en la contienda" [The media, one more weapon in the conflict], *ECA* 37, no. 403–4 (May-June 1982), pp. 486–90.

36. Interview with Socorro Jurídico, 1981.

37. Former U.S. Ambassador Robert White testified before a Senate committee in 1981 that "there is compelling, if not 100 percent conclusive evidence," that the mastermind of Romero's assassination was Roberto D'Aubuisson, an army major who had been in charge of intelligence for the National Guard and was cashiered following the October 1979 coup. On April 15, 1983, Craig Pyes wrote an article in the *Albuquerque Journal* which cited two secret cables from the U.S. Embassy in San Salvador to the State Department that contained extensive evidence that D'Aubuisson had indeed been the ringleader and that he had drawn straws with other officers for the "honor" of killing the archbishop. I subsequently had the opportunity to ask White if one of those cables was the basis of his testimony and he confirmed that it was. Conversation with White, Amherst, Mass., April 30, 1983.

38. San Miguel's bishop, Eduardo Alvarez, is a colonel and chaplain in the Salvadoran army. San Vicente's bishop, Pedro Aparicio, submitted to the government in the summer of 1982 a list of about thirty names of priests he suspected of collaboration with the insurgents. Marco René Revelo, of Santa Ana, is best known for going to Ilopango Air Force Base, east of San Salvador, in 1981 to bless some newly arrived warplanes.

39. Ivan D. Paredes, "Evolución de la iglesia salvadoreña: 24 de marzo 80/28 de marzo 82" [Evolution of the Salvadoran Church: 24 March 80/ 28 March 82], *ECA* 37, no. 403–4 (May-June 1982), p. 443.

40. Privileged interview, San Salvador, May 1982.

41. Mario Menéndez, "Salvador Cayetano Carpio: Top Leader of the

Farabundo Martí FPL" (written for *Prensa Latina*), February 1980 (mimeo).

42. Privileged interview, San Salvador, 1980.

43. All information on the demonstration is from my own experience and interviews with several dozen people that day and in the following days.

44. Privileged interview.

45. All information on the coup, unless otherwise noted, comes from individuals who had firsthand knowledge of the event, including René Guerra y Guerra.

46. Privileged interview.

47. Juan José Martell, the MSPC member of the FDR executive committee, survived because he was late. He related in an interview that, on November 27, security forces surrounded a Catholic school in which the FDR Executive Committee was to hold a press conference. Men in civilian clothes entered the school and forced the six committee members who had already arrived to go with them. Hours later the bodies of the six, including Alvarez, BPR Secretary General Juan Chacón, and UDN Secretary General Manuel Franco, were found along roads near San Salvador. At a press conference commemorating the first anniversary of the assassinations, Martell related that he had avoided being a seventh victim by sheer luck; as he approached the school he could see the troops. So he immediately went to a safe house where he remained for some time.

48. Those attempts occurred in February, April, and May 1980; September 1981; July and October 1982; and January and February 1983. The last two times took the form of a barracks mutiny on the part of the commanding officer, or threat thereof.

49. It is well known in El Salvador that the death squads are, for the most part, members of the security forces in civilian clothes. Refugees have told me of cases where death squads came into their villages looking for people, and some of the men were recognized out of uniform. In addition, a former member of the Treasury Police, which has a reputation for being the most brutal, said in an interview that the death squads are a special section of each of the security forces and that he had been offered the opportunity to join them, with a salary supplement of 1200 colones ($480) per month. He declined and subsequently deserted to leave the country.

50. "Carta de renuncia al Partido Democrática Cristiana" [Letter of resignation to the Christian Democratic Party], March 10, 1980 (mimeo).

51. Memorandum from the University of Wisconsin Land Tenure

Center to Tom Mehen, Development Support/Rural and Administrative Development, July 18, 1980.

52. Instituto de Investigaciónes Económicos, "Evaluación económica de las reformas" [Economic evaluation of the reforms], *ECA* 37, no. 403-4 (May-June 1982), pp. 507-39.

53. Inter-American Development Bank, *Economic and Social Progress in Latin America, 1979 Report* (Washington, D.C.: Inter-American Development Bank, 1980), p. 250.

54. Héctor Lindo, "La economía en epoca de guerra" [The economy in a period of war], *ECA* 37, no. 403-4 (May-June 1982), pp. 493-506.

55. "El sabotaje a la economía" [Economic Sabotage], *Proceso*, no. 110 (May 6-22, 1983), p. 7.

56. Privileged interview.

57. Press release, Productive Alliance of El Salvador, June 26, 1980.

58. Elam, "Appeal to Arms," pp. 50-51.

59. See Montgomery, *Revolution in El Salvador*, pp. 63-64; Elam, "Appeal to Arms," pp. 129-32.

60. See Montgomery, *Revolution in El Salvador*, pp. 164-65, for a fuller discussion.

61. Cynthia Arnson, "Background Information on El Salvador and U.S. Military Assistance to Central America," Update no. 4, Institute for Policy Studies, Washington, D.C., April 1981 (mimeo).

62. "Communist Interference in El Salvador," Special Report, no. 80, United States Department of State, February 23, 1981.

63. For example, see Jonathan Kwitny, "Apparent Errors Cloud U.S. 'White Paper' on Reds in El Salvador," *Wall Street Journal*, June 8, 1981.

64. John M. Goshko, "Panel Rejects Reagan Cuts," *Washington Post*, April 30, 1981.

65. Six weeks after the "White Paper" was published, 29 percent of the respondents to a Gallup poll said they thought that the United States should "stay completely out of the situation." ("Is El Salvador 'Another Vietnam'?" *Tampa Tribune*, March 26, 1981.) A year later that figure had grown to 54 percent. ("A *Newsweek* Poll: 'Stay Out'," *Newsweek*, March 8, 1982.) In the spring of 1983 that particular question was not being asked, but a Harris poll conducted after President Reagan's speech to a joint session of Congress on April 27 revealed that the president had not persuaded the public of the correctness of his policy. By a 64-31 percent margin, the public rated the president negatively on his handling of the situation in El Salvador, while 69 percent opposed the Reagan policy of "sending $700 million in economic and military aid to El Salvador since 1981." (Louis Harris, "Public is Negative on Reagan's Central American Policy," *The Harris Survey* [New York: Tribune Company Syndicate, Inc., 1983]).

66. Privileged interview.

67. George C. Wilson, "Salvador Strives to Retain Troops," *Washington Post*, June 14, 1983.

68. Information in this paragraph is based on a series of privileged interviews in Central America in March 1983 and in Washington, D.C., in June 1983.

69. The first, formal offer was made in a speech by Commandante Daniel Ortega to the General Assembly of the United Nations on October 10, 1981. The FDR/FMLN repeated their offer periodically thereafter, each time becoming somewhat more flexible, though always insisting that the "dialogue" or "negotiations" had to have an open agenda.

70. For example, at least sixty Christian Democratic mayors, local officials, and members were killed by death squads between March 1980 and March 1982.

71. See William Shawcross, *Sideshow: Kissinger, Nixon and the Destruction of Cambodia* (New York: Washington Square Press, 1979), p. 264.

72. Karen DeYoung, "General Urges Aid to Central America," *Washington Post*, May 22, 1983.

73. Ibid.

74. For a detailed discussion of U.S. pressure on the International Monetary Fund, the World Bank, and the Inter-American Development Bank, see Jim Morrell and William Jesse Biddle, "Central America: The Financial War," *International Policy Report*, March 1983, pp. 1–6.

4

Origins of the Crisis of the Established Order in Guatemala

Julio Castellanos Cambranes

Translated by David O. Wise

Colonial Legacies

Known in the United States of America as a tourist attraction, as a region of earthquakes and political disturbances, and as a "banana republic," Guatemala has become one of the two principal centers of violence in the Western Hemisphere. The other, El Salvador, was paradoxically the richest Guatemalan province during the period of Spanish colonial domination. In both El Salvador and Guatemala, this violence can be traced back to the beginnings of foreign domination in the first half of the sixteenth century. It is the most genuine reflection of the degree of deterioration which has occurred in the structure of power and control implanted by the conquerors more than 450 years ago.

The conquest of Latin America was promoted by the feudal landlords and the merchants of the Iberian Peninsula with the primary objective of gaining control of the mineral wealth of the New World. In those places where neither gold nor silver existed in large quantities, exploitation involved use of the land and forced labor of the native population. In 1512, Fernando V, "the Catholic," wrote in a royal ordinance that the principal wealth of the Indies was "the benefits derived from the Indians."[1]

For the Guatemalan population, arrival of the Spanish conquerors in 1524 meant a war of extermination and slavery for the survivors. Tens of thousands of natives were killed and thousands more died of the diseases brought from Europe. The Spanish crown declared all the agricultural lands of the native peasants to be *realengas* and distributed them among the conquerors and

MEXICO
PETÉN
Tikal
Lago de Petén Itzá
Flores
BELIZE
INTER-AMERICAN HIGHWAY
San Luis
GULF OF HONDURAS
HUEHUETENANGO
Francisco Vela
ALTA VERAPAZ
IZABAL
Livingston
Puerto Barrios
QUICHE
Lago de Izabal
Cobán
Huehuetenango
Sacapulas
Los Amates
SAN MARCOS
TOTONICAPÁN
BAJA VERAPAZ
ZACAPA
Santa Cruz del Quiché
Salamá
EL PROGRESO
HONDURAS
San Marcos
Totonicapán
Zacapa
CHIMALTENANGO
Quezaltenango
Sololá
GUATEMALA
El Progreso
Chiquimula
SOLOLÁ
Chimaltenango
JALAPA
Coatepeque
Lago de Atitlán
CHIQUIMULA
Antigua Guatemala
Guatemala
Jalapa
SUCHITEPEQUEZ
SACATEPEQUEZ
Retalhuleu
Mazatenango
RETALHULEU
Escuintla
Cuilapa
Champerico
Jutiapa
Chiquimulilla
JUTIAPA
GUATEMALA
ESCUINTLA
SANTA ROSA
Road
Railroad
San José
EL SALVADOR
PACIFIC OCEAN
0
50 Miles
0
50 Kilometers

the first European colonists, as well as among the native *caciques* willing to cooperate with the colonizers. The colonial authorities, in pursuing with all the means at their disposal (civil, military, and religious) the subjugation of the native population, laid the institutional bases for the violence and terror that today rule Guatemala. Guatemalan historian Julio César Pinto states that:

> The Conquest was fundamentally an act of violence, and this fact was reflected, most of all, in the arbitrary form in which land was distributed to the native communities. This meant that from the outset, not the slightest correspondence existed between the number of natives in a given town and the lands that were assigned to it. Thus the land received by each Indian family was necessarily inadequate, a situation that would only become more acute as the native population began to recover in numbers and as the socioeconomic laws of colonial society came into operation, laws whose dynamics favored, precisely, the systematic concentration of land in the hands of a parasitic minority.[2]

In 1538, the bishop of Guatemala, Francisco Marroquín, was instructed to concentrate the natives into settlements so that they could be more effectively controlled.[3] Marroquín was only able to carry out the instructions he had received after cajoling and deceiving the natives who had sought refuge from the Spaniards in mountains, caves, and ravines. This policy of concentrating Indians accustomed to living in a dispersed and independent fashion into Spanish-style settlements continued throughout the period of colonial domination, and was later adopted by the authorities of the Republic of Guatemala.

Several things motivated the Spanish crown to recognize part of the native communities' ancient rights to the lands they cultivated. The crown wished to avoid extermination of the population and its flight to inaccessible regions which would depopulate zones of agrarian production controlled by the Spaniards. The Spaniards soon requested *encomiendas* of natives, who were obliged to pay tributes in foodstuffs (corn, wheat, beans, salt, honey, fish) and in commercial products such as cacao. They were also forced to provide personal services in sowing and cultivating agricultural products, and in constructing houses, public buildings, churches, and roads. By the middle of the sixteenth century, 84 *encomenderos* had managed to bring thousands of natives under their control.[4] By the end of this century, approximately 200 encomendero families had divided up the greater part of the estimated half-million natives living in the kingdom of Guatemala.[5]

The outrages committed by the encomenderos against the native population were sanctioned by the Spanish authorities who believed these acts to be the determining factor of power in the colonial socioeconomic and political structure. The king of Spain ceded the native tribute which was due him in the form of encomiendas to the most important captains, soldiers, and functionaries in recognition of services rendered to the crown, and as a reward for readiness of the encomenderos to be permanent instruments of terror and repression among the native population.[6] Fully aware that they were the official representatives of Spanish colonialism, the encomenderos began to exert pressure on the native communities in order to get possession of part of their lands. Recognizing that things had gone too far, the king of Spain ordered the president of the Audiencia de los Confines (Guatemala) not to permit the encomenderos to force the authorities of the native communities to sell them their lands. "It is said they persuade the caciques and prominent Indians to sell the lands to them, as a result of which the aforesaid Indians suffer harm," the king pointed out in his ordinance dated April 29, 1549.

The encomienda as an economic institution did not imply the encomendero's ownership of the land where the native population lived. By royal grant, the land legally belonged to the natives who cultivated it, and in theory these natives, although vassals of the king of Spain, were free men. The encomenderos, however, did not respect these stipulations, seizing both land and natives as they wished.

> Since the land was the most important means of production, it was logical that the dominant groups would try to bring it under their control. . . . With this dynamic as a base, a struggle for the possession of land . . . began between the poor peasant masses and the dominant minorities. This struggle was necessarily decided in favor of the parasitic minorities who were favored by their privileged social position reflected in, among other things,

the complicity of local authorities when it came time to rule on lawsuits involving land.[8]

The circumstances under which Spanish colonialism was implanted in Guatemala—massacres of natives, agrarian plundering, temporary slavery and permanent semi-slavery—gave rise to sharp contradictions in the rural areas of Guatemala. These contradictions drove many natives to mass suicide, to flight from their communities, or to rioting. Although crushed militarily, riots instilled a fear of the natives in the Europeans and their descendants, a fear which persists until our day in the greater part of Guatemala's white and *mestizo* population.

The readiness of the crown to tolerate the usurpation of native lands by means of the so-called *composiciónes de tierras* that began to spread in Guatemala after 1591 led to heightened tensions in the countryside and to an open struggle over the possession and ownership of land. In order to avoid even greater social tension and to prevent the total usurpation of communal lands, the crown forbade the encomenderos to reside in the native towns. However, the encomenderos were easily able to get around the royal ordinances. The king of Spain was far away and the colonial bureaucracy, in many cases, had its own special interests. The majority of the officials charged with enforcing colonial law in the rural areas (the *corregidores* and *alcaldes mayores*) were encomenderos or large landowners. We read in a document from 1713 that these authorities "not only do not provide the Indians with land to establish their towns, but rather, if they have any, take it away from them violently, selling their children as slaves and carrying off their wives to their own houses, to serve them by sewing, weaving, and embroidering without paying them for their labor, with the result that the towns which were founded with great effort by the missionaries are dying out . . ."[9]

During the *repartimientos* of the sixteenth and seventeenth centuries, the growing number of mestizos were not taken into account. A Guatemalan historian has asserted that the exclusion of the mestizos from agrarian control came to be a principle of the colonial authorities' economic policy.[10] It is possible that this was the case during the first century of Spanish domination, since all the land near the native settlements suitable for cultivation was snatched up by the Europeans. However, the mestizos were officially granted the right of *denuncia*[11] and the acquisition of land by the royal ordinance of October 15, 1754. By 1804, more than 4,000 mestizo smallholders existed in Guatemala.[12]

The acquisition of land was quite complicated for individuals of limited economic means. It meant involvement in vexatious bureaucratic proceedings and legal disputes. Also, there were the outlays of money that land claimants had to make before acquiring confirmation of their property deeds. For these reasons, the great majority of the mestizos found themselves obliged to rent and cultivate the unused lands of the European proprietors and their descendants. There were 10,000 such renters in Guatemala at the beginning of the nineteenth century.[13] In the *Gaceta de Guatemala* of November 11, 1799, a Creole calls these small producers "the ones who provide us with food, who chased from pillar to post, expelled from one place, rejected at the next, always searching for someone who will rent them a piece of land under the harsh condition of personal service."[14]

Independence

Guatemala's poverty and underdevelopment can be traced back to the inheritance that Spanish colonialism left at the time of national independence (September 15, 1821). Another legacy of Spanish colonialism was the highly stratified social and economic order whose base was formed by an economy totally subordinated to the interests of a few families of landowners and merchants with direct links to the old feudal colonial system of domination. Guatemala also inherited a monocultural economy characterized by intensive use of labor and prejudice against the laboring class. Racism was the principal characteristic of this mentality, and the basis for the Spanish colonist's ideology of domination.[15]

Independence was a tactical maneuver by the Creole families which left the colonial economic and social structure essentially unchanged. In the first article of the Declaration of Independence, the Creole oligarchy stated its reasons for separation from Spain: "in order to forestall the consequences, which would have been fearsome, if the people themselves should declare it [independence]."¹⁶ The old Spanish colonists gave up political power, although most of them stayed in the country, preserving their economic interests. The survival of the latifundium, the basis of the colonists' political and economic power, meant the survival of the system of peonage and serfdom in the countryside.

The Liberals won the struggle for political power that broke out soon after independence between the Liberal and the Conservative sectors of the dominant class. However, their minimal political influence among the bulk of the population, as well as their own interests, prevented them from shaping the development of the agrarian economy in a way that would have meant a change in the forms of land ownership. Intermittently in power from 1823 to 1839, they tried to promote Guatemala's development by means of free trade, foreign investments, and European immigration. Despite the fact that they expropriated church property, they left the great non-church agricultural holdings untouched. This is not surprising if we consider the fact that many of these Liberals were also landowners, and that despite their developmentalist mentality, they were unable to overcome the same prejudices the Conservatives held against the peasant masses.

The extent of the Liberal's identification with the Conservatives became clear in 1829 when the Legislative Assembly passed laws favoring the development of commercial agriculture. Both parties considered it expedient to restore officially the old practice of forced labor common under the Spanish regime but subsequently abolished by the colonial authorities in 1820.¹⁷ On the grounds that agriculture was being neglected, a law was passed requiring all persons who owned no property, as well as the members of the indigenous communities, to work on the haciendas of the dominant families. This law gave the *hacendados* the right to request all the men they might require for agricultural tasks from the mayors of the towns. If a laborer became indebted to a landowner, he was not permitted to leave the hacienda before paying his debt.

The Liberals' belief that European immigration was equivalent to economic development led them to grant an English settlement company (the Eastern Coast of Central America Commercial and Agricultural Company) more than 6 million hectares of land in 1834 and 422,100 additional hectares in 1838. This grant involved areas of Verapaz, Petén, Izabal, Zacapa, and Chiquimula and did not take into account the fact that these lands were occupied by tens of thousands of Indian and mestizo peasants.[18] As a result, Guatemala's first guerrilla movement emerged, bringing its leader, Rafael Carrera, to power.

Establishing himself as dictator, Carrera soon fell under the influence of the Conservatives. The Conservatives governed the country much as they wished, reestablishing the institutions of political and military domination of the Spanish colonial period. In the rural areas, the corregidores regained the paramount position they had held prior to independence. Military detachments, whose principal functions were to repress any armed uprising and to collaborate with the local authorities in supplying workers to the hacendados, were established in major towns. The Conservatives ordered that all mayors keep a book in which they would list the names of men "suitable for field work" who resided in their jurisdictions.[19] As a result of these measures, thousands of peasants were required to work for the rich landowners, who in many cases did not even pay them the wages they had promised.[20]

In the middle of the nineteenth century, use of violence against the peasantry was common. When the peasants resisted forced labor, thugs would enter their homes in the middle of the night to arrest them. Peasants would then be beaten in the presence of their families or taken as prisoners to the hacienda jails where they were put in the stocks and flogged. These feudal forms of oppression were similar to the social injustices that peasants had to endure during the period of Spanish domination.

A limited number of families of foreign origin monopolized the best land for the production of cochineal (the main export product), for cattleraising, and for the cultivation of sugar cane. Peasant renters who worked on the property of the rich had to turn over to them from 50 to 75 percent of all grain they produced and most lived in permanent debt. Of every thousand children born, a third died before reaching legal adulthood. In some regions, deaths reached over 500 for every thousand births. There were only 33 physicians for a national population of more than 700,000 in 1863, and most of these lived in Guatemala City.[21]

Economic resources that could have been invested in the development of Guatemala's agricultural and stockraising industries were destroyed during the early nineteenth century civil wars or confiscated to cover the costs of military operations. While many Conservative merchants and landowners did not survive the period of economic recession into which the nation plunged, the arrival of a new wave of foreigners and their capital helped to strengthen the old economy of the colonial period. Commercial agriculture remained oriented toward the cultivation of a single product. Cochineal was grown in Guatemala until the 1860s, when the discovery in Europe of chemical dyes caused the decline of this crop.

Coffee Culture and Land

The second half of the nineteenth century was very important for Guatemala's agricultural development, due to the growth of coffee cultivation. Unlike cochineal, which was cultivated only in the central region and in a few eastern departments, coffee was grown in most parts of the country. Its cultivation strengthened Guatemala's ties to foreign markets and expanded commercial agriculture geographically. Coffee production required the creation of a transportation network. New and better roads were built, new ports were fitted out on the Atlantic and Pacific coasts, railroad lines were laid linking important coffee-producing zones to ports of embarkation, and steam navigation of inland rivers began. Thousands of people were employed in new jobs connected with maintaining and expanding this infrastructure. All this, in turn, permitted a slow expansion of the internal market as the buying power of the population increased. Commercial houses located in the capital city opened branch offices in the hinterland, and new trading firms sprang up in some provincial cities to distribute foreign manufactured goods.

Foreign investors attracted by the profits to be made in cochineal and in coffee established large agricultural enterprises in Guatemala, businesses capable of producing the profits that the developmentalist sector of the colonial landowners needed to transform itself into an agrarian bourgeoisie. Coffee cultivation and the development of the agrarian bourgeoisie went hand in hand from the beginning. The history of the first decades of commercial coffee cultivation have often been presented as the story of a generation of enterprising men who, struggling against serious obstacles, succeeded in laying the base for the principal source of national wealth and well-being. Such historical presentations have not taken into account the nation's major productive force, the peasantry. Peasants cleared the jungle, planted the coffee shrubs, constructed the owners' residences and the sheds for processing the coffee, hauled on their backs the thousands of *quintales* of coffee that were exported, and built the roads, the railroads, and the network of telegraph stations.

The lands most suitable for coffee cultivation belonged to native communities, who used them to grow subsistence crops. When it was discovered that the areas were highly desirable for coffee growing, they were invaded by speculators and foreigners interested in fast and easy profits. The developmentalist sector of the dominant class believed it was necessary to seize the coffee-suitable lands of the Indian peasants and to turn them over to national and foreign entrepreneurs. "There has always been opposition from the natives to giving the lands that they don't cultivate to others who do," a corregidor and rich landowner wrote to the Minister of Government in 1858.[22]

The first outsiders who settled on lands belonging to the native communities had to face the open hostility of the peasants. Such hostility took the form of physical attacks and the destruction of the newly-planted coffee shrubs. Reports of corregidores and other rural authorities mention constant "disturbances in the settlements," "Indians who have started to destroy the newly-planted coffee groves," "insults and threats against some of the coffee growers," "demands that lands be vacated," "secret agreements between members of the different communities to attack the mestizos who are planting coffee without the permission of the municipal authorities." By 1863 the illegal planting of coffee on community lands was so widespread that the peasants of the southwestern region of Guatemala were perceived as being "implacable enemies of coffee cultivation."[23] In 1864 the Conservative government learned that the *comuneros* were planning to destroy the coffee plantations "in all places where they existed."[24]

Indian peasants believed that the violence and tensions that had sprung up in the rural areas were caused by the distribution of communal lands to individuals who made use of them for speculation. "We natives," declared the peasants, "seek in agriculture only the means of survival and not those of building up fantastically great fortunes."[25] In a memorandum sent on February 27, 1864, to President Carrera, Indian comuneros informed him:

> The maneuvers which the coffee growers have employed to gain control over almost all our land are well known. We deplore the fact that the honorable coffee entrepreneurs want to treat us in the same way the European colonists treated the natives in the country that now forms the great Republic of North America. And it is possible that they will try to make use of this historic precedent against us, we who do not have the resources of large amounts of capital for profitable enterprises, nor the advantage of arts and industry, and try to take away our only means of survival by expelling us from our homes and lands, turning us and our coming generations into nomads without a permanent home, without the ties and duties to which a home and property give rise.[26]

In Alta Verapaz, a predominantly Indian region and presently one of the major centers of the guerrilla struggle, the comuneros held great stretches of land with frequently imprecise boundaries marked off by mountains, rivers, and barely accessible ravines. Here, occupation of the communal lands was possible only by means of violence, coercion, and trickery. "We are being tyrannized and the best lands we till and own to pasture our animals are being taken away from us," the peasants of Alta Verapaz declared in 1866 to President Vicente Cerna. "They have already taken over a great deal of land and we know that they want to take an area where more than sixty peasants have their corn fields, and many outsiders are arriving to settle . . ."[27] Between 1860 and 1867, the value of coffee exports increased dramatically from $15,350 to $415,350.[28] Agrarian entrepreneurs were able to bring greater pressure to bear on the authorities, demanding more community lands and a larger number of laborers for their plantations. Their progressive enrichment led them to see the state as an instrument to be manipulated to satisfy their needs and to safeguard their interests.

The Liberals and Barrios

During the Conservative period, liberal ideas had spread in Guatemala, especially after the Liberal seizure of power in Mexico. The example provided by Benito Juárez's reform laws gave new impetus to Liberal movements in the different Central American states. As Liberal ideology spread in Guatemala as the result of differences between the great landowners of colonial origin and those within the coffee sector, opposition to the Conservatives increased. However, the agrarian bourgeoisie was still weak and incapable of acting independently of other social forces. Above all else, it needed a caudillo and support of the masses. It obtained this mass support by offering to return to the peasantry the lands which it had usurped.

The peasants were extremely hostile to the Conservative government, not only because of the land thefts of which they had been the object, but also because of the continual demands of the authorities to work on the coffee plantations.[29] These circumstances led in February 1867 to an armed revolt headed by Serapio Cruz, a former officer in the army of Rafael Carrera. Rebel activity took on the character of a guerrilla war which spread from the eastern to the western region of the country.[30] The reelection of Vicente Cerna in January 1869 heightened political, economic, and social tensions and led to an intensification of the armed struggle. Serapio Cruz was killed in 1870 and Justo Rufino Barrios took his place. Up to that time one of Cruz's lieutenants, he was a coffee plantation owner from western Guatemala. Led by Barrios, the Liberals took power on June 30, 1871; their political domination lasted until 1944.

All of the measures adopted by the Liberals to foster Guatemala's development were in fact designed to consolidate and strengthen the economic, political, and social position of the minority that had controlled the destiny of the country since 1524. Most of the Conservatives who had previously held power continued to enjoy their old privileges. The Liberals expropriated only the holdings of the church, which they divided among themselves. Guatemala's peasants continued under the yoke of the dominant minority.

Such domination was made possible because the Liberals took advantage of the arrival of foreign entrepreneurs who introduced scientific and technical knowledge, including modern military techniques. Many of the Germans who settled in Guatemala as agrarian entrepreneurs were former cavalry officers accustomed to receiving and giving orders as well as to discipline and hard work. Most of the measures taken by the Liberal dictators who governed the country from 1871 until 1944 appear to have originated with the German entrepreneurs who had these measures passed into law by corrupt Guatemalan politicians.

It is no exaggeration to say that Guatemala's rural society was militarized after 1871, and that this militarization greatly contributed to the subjugation, oppression, and exploitation of the Indian peasant and mestizo laborer. One of the first measures implemented by Barrios created urban militias made up of large landowners, merchants, doctors, lawyers, and other people of high social rank. It also created active militias made up of the urban and rural poor, and reserve militias made up of all plantation laborers and renters. In this manner, the agrarian entrepreneurs retained the right to punish their workers by putting them in the stocks or in jail, or by public whippings if they shirked work or were "insubordinate."

Plantation laborers were enrolled in "squadrons" under the control of landowners who were required to submit a weekly report on the condition of the militia under their command to the nearest *jefe político*. Article 9 of the decree of August 9, 1871 (which put the population on a military footing) stipulated that

> absences from the squadron can take place only through the death of the soldier (the rural laborer), a discharge granted by his patron, or through flight. In the case of flight, the escaped militiaman shall be considered a deserter and pursued both inside and outside the department. Therefore, under pain of the appropriate penalty, the patrons will not omit a single absence from their weekly reports, nor shall they grant discharges unless the petitioner demonstrates the consent of his natural superior (*jefes natos*).[31]

The regulation of forced labor on the great estates was achieved by the so-called Reglamento de Jornaleros (Day-Laborers Statute) of April 3, 1877, and with Decree 222 of May 14, 1878, the so-called "Anti-Vagrancy Law." Using the agrarian legislation of the country, foreign entrepreneurs were able to legalize the forcible recruitment of the workers that they needed on their estates, especially at harvest time. According to these laws, every able-bodied man was required to carry a "laborer's passbook" which vouched for his honesty, productivity, and solvency. Anyone found without this passbook was considered a vagrant and was liable to pay a fine in cash, or to work it off through labor on public work projects. If an estate owner paid the fine, the laborer was turned over to him and remained on his plantation until he had paid off the sum with his labor. Since the fine varied from $5 to $25, it was practically impossible for a man ever to regain his freedom. These laws were drawn up by the Swiss plantation owner Gustav Bernouilli.

In 1934, the anti-vagrancy law was modified to stipulate that peasants work at least 150 days per year on the plantations, with the number of days they worked to be written down in the passbook they were required to carry. If a peasant was found without his passbook or if it was determined that he had not worked the required number of days, he faced jail, public whipping, or road labor. Road labor in most cases was equivalent to a death sentence, because it took place in tropical areas under harsh conditions. This law was issued at the urging of the German-Jewish planter Erwin Paul Dieseldorff, who adapted it from the agrarian laws in force in the German colony of Southwest Africa (now Namibia).

Justo Rufino Barrios and the entrepreneurs who supported him decided to gain control of community land "legally," maintaining that the communities' title deeds issued by the Spanish colonial authorities were "old and invalid papers."[32] The land grants issued personally by the dictator before 1877 led to the massive invasion of community lands in zones suited to coffee growing. By Decree 170 of January 8, 1877, all community lands passed to the control of the Liberal state and were auctioned to the highest bidder. Since the rich entrepreneurs were the only ones who could afford to purchase land, the communities' property came into their hands, thus ruining the majority of the peasants. Barrios became the largest landowner in the country, and the dictators who followed him in power were also the most important agrarian entrepreneurs of their time. However, the best coffee plantations gradually came under the control of German owners and consortia. Today this situation remains unchanged, in spite of the expropriation of the German properties in 1943.

The expropriation of communal lands was not accepted passively by the Indian peasantry, nor was it forgotten. Many individuals who acquired community lands at auction, or by a personal grant from the dictator, had to request police protection in order to take possession.[33] Some communities appealed to the president of the republic and other government authorities, requesting the annulment of Decree 170.[34] "Our poverty is well known," comuneros who had been deprived of their lands wrote to the Minister of Government in 1879; "we cannot abandon our tasks and see our hopes shattered."[35] Resistance to expropriation also appeared in the form of mysterious fires that destroyed coffee groves, processing sheds, and even laborers' dwellings.[36] On other occasions, groups of comuneros threatened plantation owners with machetes and clubs.[37]

The demands of the peasants met with two replies from the Liberals. First, police posts were reinforced in order to capture anyone who openly resisted the expropriations. By 1873, the plantation owners had founded the National Army as a repressive instrument whenever circumstances might demand. Second, Barrios distributed some community lands to other communities with the intent of dividing the peasantry and breaking the opposition to the Liberal dictatorship. In this manner, he gained the support of the favored sector of the peasantry while at the same time embroiling the communities in endless lawsuits and interregional rivalries.

From 1871 until the present, foreign estate owners have been the real source of power in Guatemala's established order. There have been numerous local dictators famous for their brutality through the years, and yet the real power behind the throne was (and is) exercised by families almost completely unknown to most Guatemalans. The old dominant class tied itself through business and marriage to the foreign entrepreneurs who arrived in Guatemala after independence. Many mestizos who have risen to high public positions in the administration of the coffee republic, and officers of the planter-controlled army who have fulfilled their role as instruments of repression, have benefited from this system of domination.

This system of exploitation to which the rural laborers have been subject cannot be fully explained unless we also take into account the fact that the people who imposed and maintained it were agrarian entrepreneurs interested in making capitalist profits. These entrepreneurs have been supported by powerful North American consortia such as the United Fruit Company, which began to operate in Guatemala at the beginning of this century under the protection of the dictatorship of Manuel Estrada Cabrera. The modern Guatemalan state (the established order now in crisis) was organized in response to the interests of foreign capital concerned with developing the plantation economy, the "developmentalist" sector of the traditional oligarchy, and mestizos interested in coffee cultivation. These groups gave the Guatemalan political and social structure its racial prejudices and conservative character. The capitalist system which emerged in Guatemala can be described as "deformed" because the profits made by the entrepreneurs were obtained through the economic ruin of the country and by means of labor relationships which were basically feudal in nature.

Frustrated Reforms, 1940s

During the Second World War, the United States pressured the Guatemalan government to declare war on Germany and her allies. The agrarian bourgeoisie supported this move because it was interested in gaining control of the valuable German plantations, which in 1939 occupied a third of the best arable land in the country. The expropriation of most of the German properties and the Germans' departure in 1943 still have not been studied as they deserve. Nevertheless, there is no doubt that these events had a profound effect on the stability of the existing system of political and social domination. In the rural areas, many peasants foresaw the possibility of transforming the relations of agrarian labor and property.[38]

In 1944, a period of political agitation began in Guatemala City which reached its high point with the overthrow of the Liberal dictatorship in October of that year. Juan José Arévalo, the candidate of the mestizo middle class which had previously been excluded from political power, ascended to the presidency in 1945. The presidential elections of December 1944 demonstrated that the mestizos (known in Guatemala as *ladinos*) now constituted a political and social force to be reckoned with. Arévalo obtained 82.5 percent of the total vote, while the candidate of the traditional oligarchy, Adrián Recinos, received less than 8 percent. Never again would a Guatemalan president-elect receive such a high percentage of votes (see Table 4.1).

Arévalo's government, which remained in power until 1951, was characterized by its moderate reformism. Partly, this was due to pressures from the traditional oligarchy, which feared the elimination of its privileges, and from the U.S. government which was not at all disposed to accept legislation unfavorable to the interests of the North American concerns operating in the country. Also, the middle class that supported Arévalo (intellectuals, small landholders, artisans, the urban middle sectors) were primarily interested in improving their living conditions and in trying to win some concessions from the dominant groups that traditionally wielded power. They did not wish direct conflict with the dominant class with whom they had a closer affinity than with the peasants. Luis Cardoza y Aragón states that "many of our 'revolutionaries' became frightened and distrusted those who were blazing new trails, and there occurred the classic response of rejecting 'exotic ideas' in order to find nonexistent homegrown solutions."[39]

As a result of this middle class political opportunism, the latifundium managed to survive, and the conditions of poverty, illiteracy, ill-health, and exploitation that reigned in the rural areas remained unchanged. The Agrarian Census of 1950 revealed the extreme concentration of land ownership (see Table 4.2). While 96.4 percent of all rural properties were smaller than 45 hectares and represented only 27.9 percent of the nation's cultivated land, 3.5 percent of the remaining properties made up 72.1 percent. The estates with more than 2,250 hectares, comprising only 1 percent of all properties, included more than a quarter of all Guatemala's cultivable land. This census also revealed that 57 percent of the peasantry owned no land, while 22 estates accounted for 525,000 hectares.

In order to placate the peasants, the middle class government abolished the forcible recruitment of laborers and the Anti-Vagrancy Law. However, in practice, the agents of the estate owners continued to obtain peasants for work on the plantations during harvest time by advancing them a portion of their wages. This system (*enganche*), still exists, and it is not uncommon for many

Table 4.1. Electoral results: 1944–78

Year	Eligible Voters	Votes	Abstention Rate (percent)	Votes for Winning Candidate	Percentage of Eligible Vote for Winning Candidate
1944	310,000	296,200	4.5	255,700	82.5
1950	583,300	407,500	31.1	266,800	45.7
1958	736,400	492,300	33.1	191,000	25.9
1966	944,200	531,300	43.7	209,400	22.2
1970	1,190,500	640,700	46.2	251,100	21.1
1974	1,568,700	727,876	53.6	298,953	19.1
1978	1,785,876	651,817	63.5	269,973	15.1

Source: Adapted from "Erupción Internacional," official publication of the Organización del Pueblo en Armas (ORPA), Guatemala, 1982, p. 8.

Table 4.2. Agricultural census of 1950: number and size of farms

Size of Farm	Number of Farms	Percentage of Farms	Number of Manzanas	Percentage of Manzanas
Less than 5 manzanas	265,629	75.1	478,886	9.0
5 manzanas to 1 caballería[a]	75,485	21.3	1,008,202	18.9
1 to 10 caballerías	6,488	1.9	1,161,803	21.8
10 to 20 caballerías	5,569	1.6	506,188	9.5
20 to 50 caballerías	358	0.1	707,869	13.3
50 to 100 caballerías	104	—	468,070	8.8
100 to 200 caballerías	32	—	280,476	5.3
200 caballerías or more	22	—	714,069	13.4
Total	353,687	100.0	5,325,563	100.0

[a] A caballería is equal to 64 manzanas or 45 hectares.

Source: "Erupción Internacional," official publication of the Organización del Pueblo en Armas (ORPA), Guatemala, 1982, p. 20.

trucks loaded with peasants headed for work on the coast to overturn in mountain ravines due to poor vehicle maintenance.

In 1949 an attempt was made to help the landless peasant through promulgation of the Law of Obligatory Rental. Large landowners were required to rent their unused lands to peasants who owned none. However, the estate owners ignored this law that damaged their interests. In fact, during the seventy-odd years that the estate owners completely controlled the Guatemalan government, they were always able to develop legal mechanisms to protect their land and to ensure themselves access to the labor they needed on a temporary basis without entering into direct confrontation with peasant communities. For example, many estate owners set up so-called *fincas de mozos* where they kept indebted laborers, parceling them out to their plantations as need required. Romeo Lucas García, the president deposed in 1982, was the owner of one of these fincas de mozos and rented his laborers to neighboring landowners at a modest rate.

To assure better administration and control of the workers, the great estates were divided into the headquarters and various annexes that functioned as autonomous production units. The estate owners managed to obtain legislation which permitted peasant unionization *when and if* more than 500 people were employed on a given estate. The Arévalo government collaborated in this maneuver when it promulgated the Labor Code in 1947. However, under pressure from the peasant leaders, the Code was amended in 1948 to stipulate that peasant unions of more than 50 members could be organized when and if two thirds of the union members were literate. Once again, what was given with one hand was taken away with the other since 98 percent of the peasantry was illiterate.

All these cruel jokes created great resentment among the peasants, as well as the objective conditions for change in the countryside. It was believed that such changes might be brought about by Jacobo Arbenz Guzmán, a young army officer who had figured prominently in the overthrow of the Liberal dictatorship and was named Minister of Defense by Arévalo. Arbenz was supported by the more radical groups within the middle class, as well as by the Guatemalan Labor Party (Communist Party). Nevertheless, his own class interests corresponded to those of middle sector groups concerned with promoting the industrialization of the country through import substitution.

Arbenz was elected president of Guatemala and took office on March 15, 1951, at the age of thirty-seven. In one speech he stated that his government would change Guatemala "from a dependent nation with a semicolonial economy into an economically independent country," that he would transform "our backward nation with a predominantly feudal economy into a modern capitalist country," and that he would carry out this transformation in a way that would raise the standard of living "of the masses of the people."[40] To achieve this, he began an agrarian reform program which, while bourgeois in concept, was of great social significance because it aimed at returning large areas of land to the peasantry. The peasants, cultivating these lands with technical assistance and credit from the government, would—it was hoped—improve their living conditions, increase their buying power, and promote the growth of the internal market for industrial products manufactured in Guatemala.

The agrarian reform envisioned the expropriation of land from estates of more than 100 hectares, although the government declared that it would respect those where all the land was efficiently cultivated. The landless peasants would receive plots of up to 20 hectares, either in title or for lifelong use, and would pay for them in yearly installments, without interest and at the rate of 3 to 5 percent of the value of their production. The proprietors were to be compensated with state bonds payable in twenty-five years at 3 percent interest. The value of their lands was to be determined by the assessment made by the estate owners for tax purposes. In 1951, 10,000 hectares owned by the United Fruit Company were intervened to provide a guarantee of back pay due 4,000 dismissed workers. And in 1952, 107 estates formerly owned by Germans were parceled out to the peasantry.

Promulgation of Decree 900 of Agrarian Reform on June 17, 1952 was the first victory of the Guatemalan peasantry in centuries and a solid blow against the established order. The agrarian entrepreneurs declared the reform "unconstitutional"; "the most monstrous confiscatory decree that any government in our history has issued, due to its size and sweep"; and "an attack against our democracy that flows from an economic and political creed that follows Marxist-Stalinist lines." They accused Congress of having passed it "through a slick maneuver, restricting the representatives of the opposition in the exercise of their parliamentary rights, and by means of a climate of pressure and threats intensified by the presence of peasants armed with machetes."[41]

The Agrarian Reform Law went into effect on January 5, 1953, a little more than six months after it was issued. On January 23, the Association of Agrarian Entrepreneurs (AGA) claimed that in some departments of the country "large bands of armed men have invaded several privately owned estates and have marked out plots which they are dividing up among themselves, without any more authority than the whims of whomever is in charge of the invading group."[42] They demanded that the government take immediate measures against these peasant activists.[43]

In view of the fact that the government was providing legal protection for the landless peasantry, the estate owners began a public campaign of defamation and systematic attacks on the Agrarian Reform Law, on the government, and on the president himself. According to AGA, Guatemala's agriculture was "seriously threatened and on the edge of disaster. Day by day there are aggressive attacks of the most primitive kind against landowners and in this series of unspeakable usurpations, there has been more than one bloody clash among the peasants."[44]

The large landowners armed the workers they could rely on and encouraged them to repel the peasant activists with gunfire. They also sought the support of small and medium-sized landholders, organizing what they called "Civic Unions for the Defense of Our Land" in an attempt to unleash civil war in the countryside. They hoped to create such a chaotic situation that the army would carry out a coup d'etat. In pursuit of this goal, they published a manifesto on March 3, 1953 in which they maintained that "effective government is demanded by an honorable citizenry which is directly suffering the consequences of a political jamboree that, not finding enough room in the capital, has spread to the countryside in a greedy and aggressive form."[45] On the fourteenth of the same month, they addressed themselves to President Arbenz, warning him "not to underestimate the climate of rejection among the citizenry of the hasty and capricious application of the Agrarian Reform Law, because this citizenry will not stand by passively when it sees its property on the edge of destruction."[46]

The Arbenz government can be accused of a lack of organization in its land reform efforts, as well as of excessive tolerance of the attacks made on it by the large landowners. Nonetheless, it is necessary to take into account the fact that there was a great diversity of political positions and attitudes among the forces that supported the president and his social reforms. The middle class, which had initially supported him, gradually distanced itself from the revolutionary cause as the influence of the Communists in the worker and peasant organizations increased. The gradual rise in peasant consciousness and its growing assertiveness caused alarm among a large portion of the urban and rural middle sectors. Their fear of the Indian peasantry outweighed their inclination to help in the agrarian reform efforts.

It is true that many Communists had infiltrated Arbenz's government. Nevertheless, their sectarianism greatly limited their influence. Victor Manuel Gutiérrez, the most prestigious of the Communists and the principal leader of the General Confederation of Guatemalan Workers, had drawn up the first agrarian reform proposal, taking the specific conditions of the country into account. But it was not necessary to be a Communist to understand that only an agrarian reform could contribute to the economic and social development of the country. Even the United States government was aware of the need to bring about changes in the forms of landholding in the underdeveloped countries as a means of lessening political and social tensions there.[47]

The resulting peasant agitation in favor of the agrarian reform and the disorganized way in which land occupations took place in some areas was to divide Guatemalans into two apparently irreconcilable camps. On the one side was the poor and landless peasantry, supported by the urban workers and the radicalized nationalist sector of the middle class. On the other side was the agrarian bourgeoisie and the rest of the dominant class dependent on and allied with foreign (especially North American) interests. This bloc allied itself with the North American businesses that were pressuring the U.S. government to take punitive measures against the Arbenz regime. The maneuvers of the United Fruit Company as well as the role of the Central Intelligence Agency in finding a Guatemalan (Colonel Carlos Castillo Armas) to command the armed invasion of the country are well known.[48] They resulted in Arbenz's overthrow in 1954 and in his flight to Mexico City. "And thus, completely disregarding the freedom and the self-determination of the Guatemalan people, the United States added another page to its long history of intervention in Latin American affairs under cover of the highest ideals, while what it basically pursued was the perpetuation of North American economic interests at the expense of the poorest of the Guatemalans."[49]

Prelude to Rebellion

The second dictatorship of the agrarian bourgeoisie (a dictatorship which has lasted to this day) began with the fall of President Arbenz at the beginning of July 1954. Castillo Armas immediately annulled Decree 900, returning to the entrepreneurs the lands which had been confiscated for distribution to the peasantry. More than 9,000 peasant activists were murdered during the first months of the estate owners' triumph, and thousands of peasants were forced to flee to the mountains and to the neighboring countries of Mexico, British Honduras, Honduras, and El Salvador. Thousands of Arbenz supporters sought asylum in foreign embassies, especially in those of Mexico, Costa Rica, and Chile. In the countryside, violence and terror reached such proportions that Castillo Armas's government itself publicly asked the great landowners to cease repressing the peasantry, or they would have no one left to till their lands. The new government and those that followed attempted to neutralize the peasants politically by issuing the so-called Agrarian Statutes which sought to transform the agrarian structure by dividing up the former German plantations confiscated in 1943, as well as by establishing colonies in the jungle regions.

In 1839, the restoration of traditional oligarchic domination was presented as a patriotic effort to preserve the moral and religious values of the Guatemalan people against the subversive anticlericalism of the Liberals. After 1944, the oligarchy tried to hide the defense of its own interests behind the flag of the struggle against communism. As a result, ideological confrontation has been couched in terms of a life and death struggle between the forces of "godless communism" and militant anti-communism, around which the most conservative entrepreneurs, the mestizo middle class landowners linked to the Movement of National Liberation, and army have rallied. Before 1944, Guatemalan officers sympathized with the Nazi ideology which predominated among the German estate owners and the agrarian bourgeoisie. From 1954 until today, thousands of army officers have received military training and political education at United States military bases which has increased their loyalty to so-called Western values.[50]

From 1954 to 1960, Guatemala experienced a period of intense social agitation. After the assassination of Carlos Castillo Armas in 1957, the opposition to the estate owners' dictatorship increased. Many exiles returned to Guatemala from different Latin American countries and renewed their activities aimed at lifting the nation out of the political stagnation into which the oligarchy had led it. The Cuban Revolution in 1959 was a determining factor in the growth of revolutionary consciousness among portions of the middle sectors, such as university and secondary school students. The Cuban Revolution inspired the generation of the 1940s, which after 1960 decided to break with the orthodox leadership of the Communist Party. This generation led the opposition to the dictatorship along the path of armed struggle after overcoming many obstacles, including the prejudices which many members of the radicalized urban middle class felt toward the Indian peasantry.

In November 1960, a military rebellion occurred which at first seemed to be like many others in the convulsive political history of Latin America. It was organized by army officers who wanted to remove the corrupt incumbent president, general Miguel Ydígoras Fuentes. The rebellion was put down quickly and most of the participants were reintegrated into the army; however, a few sought refuge in Honduras and El Salvador. Among these latter were Marco Aurelio Yon Sosa and Luis Augusto Turcios Lima, who decided to continue the struggle against the system of oligarchic domination after establishing contact while in exile with the peasantry. Yon Sosa wrote in 1967:

> In our most difficult days when we were imprisoned in towns in El Salvador and Honduras, we felt so intimately the solidarity of

those poor people dressed in rags and with bare feet who came in great numbers to give us fruit, coffee, food, words of encouragement, and even an occasional 5 centavo coin. This experience, in addition to the attitude of the Guatemalan peasants . . . made us meditate deeply and led us to the conclusion that the behavior of these people was due to the fact that they were trying to win us to their cause. They wanted leaders to stand at the head of their struggle, and they partly achieved their objective, because several of the officers who participated in the revolt seven years ago have embraced the cause of the exploited.[51]

Luis Augusto Turcios Lima arrived at the conclusion that the main lesson to be learned from the counterrevolution of 1954 was that the Guatemalan people could free themselves from the oppression of the estate owners and their national and foreign allies only through armed struggle. This struggle had to be prolonged and anti-imperialist in nature. At a moment when the diversity of positions with regard to the role of the peasantry and urban mass movement divided Guatemala's leftist organizations, Turcios Lima pointed out the path that the revolutionaries had to follow if they were truly ready to conquer or die for their cause:

Guatemala is a semicolonial country in which the peasantry constitutes the immense majority of the population, and where the working class, because of our limited industrial development, cannot carry the burden of national liberation by itself. Our war is essentially a war of the countryside against the city, a war in which the peasantry, with all its strength will be the decisive factor which will permit the seizure of power. On the other hand, our enemy is not only the national Army and the machinery of the bourgeoisie state but primarily Yankee imperialism, against which it is necessary to follow a strategy based on an objective analysis of reality. We can have no illusions about victory in the short run, and even less can we instill that illusion, a product of petty bourgeoisie desperation, in the masses. Imperialism will not abandon its dominions easily. It will take a prolonged war to force it to do so.[52]

In spite of the orientation provided by Turcios Lima, the nation's guerrilla movement is still in the process of acquiring its own personality, a personality it must achieve if it is to be able to overcome the ideological disagreements that have characterized its development during the past twenty years. From 1968 to 1971, the movement was weak due to the blows it suffered at the hands of the army and the U.S.-supported oligarchy's police forces. Turcio Lima himself was killed in 1966. Nevertheless, the second phase of the people's revolutionary war began in 1972 with the establishment of the "Edgar Ibarra" guerrilla force in the Northwest of the country. This group eventually succeeded in transforming itself from an "army in rags" into the Guerrilla Army of the Poor (EGP).

The agrarian bourgeoisie, sensing the vigor of the revolutionary movement, placed the zones of guerrilla operation under military control. However, the results have been counterproductive. The pacification of rural areas led to the formation on February 24, 1979 of a broad opposition front called the Democratic Front against Repression (FDCR). This Front included the National Committee of Syndical Unity (CNUS), the Committee of Peasant Unity (CUC), and various student and mass organizations.[53]

The lower clergy, closely linked to the peasantry since colonial times, have played an important role in the opposition movement. As early as 1960, Clemente Marroquín Rojas, former spokesman for the estate owners and vice-president of Guatemala (1966–70), pointed out that the rural priests were potential enemies of the regime since their doctrine inclined them to become defenders of the peasants.[54] The massacres of peasants perpetrated by the army have evoked strong feelings of compassion among the religious, leading them to identify politically with those struggling for social justice. Many priests have been murdered, while others have left Guatemala in order to publicize the situation that exists in the country; a few have joined the guerrillas as combatants. After centuries spent serving the interests of the powerful, a large sector of the Guatemalan Catholic Church has come to defend the cause of the poor. This is one of the most striking characteristics of the political and social transformation which is currently taking place in Guatemala.

Another phenomenon worth mentioning is the role of the armed forces. In the past twenty years, the military has not only learned modern techniques of counterinsurgency warfare but also has become more demanding vis-à-vis the dominant groups.

Many high-ranking army officers have become prominent members of the dominant class after having enriched themselves in the exercise of power.

Unstable Order

In March 1963, the army carried out a coup against the regime of Ydígoras Fuentes, who they blamed for popular discontent and the crisis situation that existed in the country. This was the first time in the modern history of Guatemala that the estate owners were obliged to share control of the state machinery with a clique of uniformed parvenus. What Edelberto Torres-Rivas has called "the marriage between military men and entrepreneurs through the control of the government" was in fact a shotgun wedding accepted with distaste by the estate owners. They feared that the social agitation which had destabilized the Ydígoras regime might become a people's insurrection capable of destroying the traditional order. The estate owners found themselves obliged to satisfy the political ambitions and the thirst for riches of the senior army officers and this led to tensions between the two groups.

For the oligarchy, the state had been more than merely a source of wealth. But the military governments which have succeeded each other in power since 1966 have been concerned much more narrowly with administering state property and funds to the benefit of a few high functionaries. In addition, the clique of generals who came to power in 1970 attempted to perpetuate itself in power, openly combating the groups within the dominant class that disputed its hegemony. These power struggles destabilized the established order, accelerating its decay and deepening the existing crisis.[55]

In order to prevent the discredited clique of politicians and officers which held power from 1966 to 1982 from retaining control of the state machinery, the agrarian bourgeoisie sponsored another coup on March 23, 1982. They relied on the collaboration of Mario Sandoval Alarcón and Leonel Sisniega Otero, prominent leaders of the Movement of National Liberation, presenting the coup as a movement of the young officers of the army who were anxious to end official corruption and the nation's violence. This coup, and its aftermath, suggests that the contradictions within the governing sectors have reached such an extreme that a change in the tactics of the counterinsurgency war have become absolutely necessary for the estate owners. "The nation needs its military men to return to the tasks for which they were trained," the principal spokesman for the estate owners, Antonio Nájera Saravia, wrote recently. "That is, to do battle against those who want to turn us into another Russian colony like Cuba or Nicaragua."[56]

Guatemala remains a predominantly agrarian nation whose peasant population has not been able to make great advances in its socioeconomic, political, and technical development. In spite of the country's apparent industrial growth in the last twenty years, permanent political instability and the poverty of the majority of its inhabitants have impeded the expansion of the plantation economy, of industry, and of trade. The figures for Gross Domestic Product have plummeted as the insurrectionary war has intensified. The plantation economy, the power base of the traditional oligarchy, has also been battered by the drop in the prices of coffee, cotton, sugar, and meat. A rise in the daily minimum wage on the plantations from $1.50 to $3.20 ruined many medium-sized landholders, already in debt to the banks.

The International Coffee Agreement, according to whose terms the coffee producers can place only half of their yearly crops in Western markets, led to increased stocks of warehoused coffee. Says one observer of the current crisis:

> The banks need repayment and are calling in their loans and since there is no money with which to pay them, the tragic prospect is that of lawsuits, embargos, and the auction of the estates. In addition, several factors, including the circumstances in the banking sector, have lessened our hopes of improving the situation through cotton production. Of 150,000 *manzanas* (a manzana equals 1.75 acres), this year only 40,000 will be planted.[57]

Less land has been committed to growing commercial crops due to low market prices, lack of credit from banking institutions, the poor financial situation of many growers, and the state of civil war that exists in the rural areas. The war not only keeps many temporary laborers from their traditional harvest tasks, but also has caused many estate owners to stay far away from their properties for fear of kidnapping. Violence has reached such a level that it has been proposed that the estate owners be officially declared police authorities.[58]

In the past few years, the country has seen an incredible flight of capital. Rich estate owners, manufacturers, merchants, financiers, and corrupt functionaries have transferred more than two billion dollars out of the country, thus contributing to a greater destabilization of the system and to the ruin of the economy. The government finds it more difficult to obtain financing from the private international banks due to the internal crisis. The external debt grew from 512.2 million dollars in 1978 to more than one billion dollars in 1982. According to one expert, the only real options the present Guatemalan government has to obtain foreign funding for its ambitious development projects are through bilateral assistance from the United States.[59]

As a result of the crisis in public finances and the massive flight of capital, exchange controls were imposed in 1979. These controls have especially affected the merchants and the manufacturers who import foreign products and raw materials, making it impossible for them to pay for their orders and to expand their commercial activity. The devaluation of the quetzal (on a par with the U.S. dollar since 1924) is now likely and would increase inflation, lower the buying power of the population, and increase social tensions.

Prominent businessmen have been kidnapped by the leftist forces and made to pay large ransoms for their release. This has increased the war chests of the revolutionary organizations and has caused many entrepreneurs to emigrate with their capital to the United States or Europe. From there, they direct their nearly bankrupt enterprises entrusted to administrators in Guatemala.

The nation's great tragedy was exemplified by the rise to power in March 1982 of General Efraín Ríos Montt who had evangelistic delusions and was capable of carrying the war of extermination against the Indian peasant population to unpredictable limits. Ríos Montt caused the massacre of more than 10,000 people supposedly involved in the guerrilla movement. He decreed a general amnesty for all the criminals linked to previous governments. He declared a nationwide state of siege in order to give greater latitude to the genocidal actions of the army and police forces. He organized civilian patrols among government collaborators, thus exacerbating the civil war and the hate and division among the Guatemalan people. He established strategic hamlets in which to concentrate peasants who have not yet joined the guerrilla movement. He ordered the general mobilization of the army reserve and expanded military recruitment and training. The fact that Ríos Montt was overthrown on August 8, 1983 by a coup that installed General Oscar Humberto Mejía Flores as the new chief of state will not put an end to these repressive measures. Guatemala marches along the road toward open civil war.

Notes

1. Richard Konetzke, *Colección de documentos para la historia de la formación social de Hispanoamérica, 1493–1810*, Vol. 1 (Madrid: Consejo Superior de Investigaciones Científicas, 1953), p. 34.
2. J. C. Pinto Soria, *Estructura agraria y asentamiento en la Capitanía General de Guatemala*, Vol. 13 (Guatemala: Editorial Universitaria, 1981), pp. 11–12.
3. Konetzke, *Colección de documentos*, Vol. 1, p. 183.
4. Francisco de Solano, *Los mayas del siglo XVIII: Pervivencia y transformación de la sociedad indígena guatemalteca durante la administración borbónica* (Madrid: Ediciónes Cultura Hispánica, 1974), p. 83.
5. The author's personal estimate.
6. Severo Martínez Pelaez, *La patria del criollo: Ensayo de interpretación de la realidad colonial guatemalteca* (San José, Costa Rica: Editorial Universitaria, 1979), p. 83.
7. Konetzke, *Colección de documentos*, Vol. 1, p. 258.
8. Pinto Soria, *Estructura agraria*, p. 20.
9. Ibid., p. 42.
10. Martínez Pelaez, *La patria del criollo*, p. 159.
11. José María Ots Capdequi, *El régimen de la tierra en la América española durante el período colonial* (Santo Domingo: Universidad de Santo Domingo, 1946), pp. 105–17.
12. Pinto Soria, *Estructura agraria*, p. 10.
13. Ibid.
14. Ibid.
15. "Acerca del racismo," *Polemica* (San José, Costa Rica), No. 3 (January-February 1982), p. 66.

16. Cited by J. C. Pinto Soria, *Guatemala en la década de la Independencia* (Guatemala: Editorial Universitaria, 1978), p. 49.
17. Ibid., p. 13.
18. Enrique del Cid Fernández, "Llegada de los primeros alemanes a Guatemala como consecuencia de la colonización belga," mimeo (Guatemala, 1969), p. 3.
19. Archivo General de Centroamérica (AGCA), B1, Ministerio de Gobernación y Justicia (MGJ), Legajo No. 28621, Miguel García Zelaya al Ministerio de Gobernación, November 16, 1868.
20. AGCA, B1, MGJ, Legajo No. 28628, exp. 227, Leandro Quiñónez a Miguel García Granados, November 18, 1871.
21. Pío Casal, "Reseña de la situación general de Guatemala" (Guatemala 1981), p. 30.
22. AGCA, B1, MGJ, Legajo No. 28576, Gregorio Solares al Ministerio de Gobernación, March 4, 1858.
23. AGCA, B1, MGJ, Legajo No. 28593, Joaquín Faye al Ministerio de Gobernación, August 22, 1863.
24. AGCA, B1, MGJ, Legajo No. 28595, Pedro Aju al Ministerio de Gobernación, January 22, 1864.
25. AGCA, B1, MGJ, Legajo No. 28595, Comunidad de San Felipe a Rafael Carrera, February 15, 1864.
26. AGCA, B1, MGJ, Legajo No. 28607, Comunidad de San Felipe a Rafael Carrera, February 27, 1864.
27. AGCA, B1, MGJ, Legajo No. 28604, Comunidad de San Cristóbal Cajcoj a Vicente Cerna, August 20, 1866.
28. Ignacio Solis, *Memorias de la Casa de Moneda de Guatemala y del desarrollo económico del país*, Vol. 3B (Guatemala 1979), p. 911.
29. Chester Lloyd Jones, *Guatemala: Past and Present* (New York: Russell and Russell, 1966), pp. 141–52.
30. J. C. Cambranes, "Desarrollo económico y social de Guatemala, 1868–1885" (Guatemala: Instituto de Investigaciónes Económicas y Sociales, 1975), p. 65.
31. AGCA, B1, MGJ, Legajo No. 28629, exp. 31, Jefe Político de Suchitepéquez al Ministerio de Gobernación, September 1, 1871.
32. AGCA, B1, MGJ, Legajo No. 28630, exp. 14, Emilio López al Jefe Político de Sololá, August 18, 1871.
33. AGCA, B1, MGJ, Legajo No. 28629, exp. 35, Jefe Político de Chimaltenango al Ministerio de Gobernación, August 31, 1871.
34. AGCA, B1, MGJ, Legajo No. 28652, exp. 70, Jefe Político de Quezaltenango al Ministerio de Gobernación, August 25, 1874.
35. AGCA, B1, MGJ, Legajo No. 28652, exp. 70, Hernán Escobar al Jefe Político de Quezaltenango, January 5, 1875.

36. AGCA, B1, MGJ, Legajo No. 28569, Jefe Político de San Marcos al Ministerio de Gobernación, April 3, 1877.
37. Ibid.
38. Information obtained in interviews of agricultural laborers on the "Candelaria Xolhuitz" estate, Nuevo San Carlos, Retalhuleu, December 1979.
39. Luis Cardoza y Aragon, "La revolución guatemalteca de 1944," in *Pensamiento Crítico* (Havana, 1968), pp. 103–23.
40. Cited by *Erupción Internacional* (Guatemala: Organización del Pueblo en Armas, 1982), p. 8.
41. Published in *Centinela de los intereses de Guatemala* (Guatemala: Asociación General de Agricultores, September 1953), pp. 1–7.
42. *Centinela* (January 23, 1953), pp. 7–8.
43. *Centinela* (January 30, 1953), pp. 10–12.
44. *Centinela* (February 17, 1953), pp. 22–25.
45. *Centinela* (March 6, 1953), pp. 32–35.
46. *Centinela* (March 14, 1953), pp. 35–37.
47. *Department of State Bulletin* (September 17, 1951), p. 467, cited by Thomas and Marjorie Melville, *Tierra y poder en Guatemala* (San José, Costa Rica: Editorial Universitaria Centroamericana, 1975), p. 68.
48. See the book by Stephen Schlesinger and Stephen Kinzer, *Bitter Fruit: The Untold Story of the American Coup in Guatemala* (Garden City, N.Y.: Doubleday, 1982).
49. Melville, *Tierra y poder en Guatemala*, p. 97.
50. Guillermo Toriello Garrido, *Guatemala: más de 20 años de traición, 1954–1979* (Guatemala: Editorial Universitaria, 1980), pp. 29 and 39.
51. Marco Aurelio Yon Sosa, "Breves apuntes históricos del Movimiento Revolucionario 13 de noviembre," in *Pensamiento Crítico* (Havana 1968), p. 134.
52. "Carta abierta del comandante Luis Augusto Turcios Lima a la dirección nacional del Movimiento Revolucionario 13 de noviembre," in *Turcios Lima* (Havana: Instituto del Libro, 1969), p. 95.
53. "Llamamiento de FDCR para integrar al Frente Político," in *Polémica* (San José, Costa Rica), No. 1 (September-October 1981), pp. 63–66.
54. Clemente Marroquín Rojas, Editorial in *La Hora* (March 27, 1960). On the role of the Catholic Church in today's Guatemalan political and social reality, see Bruce Johnson Calder, "Crecimiento y cambio de la Iglesia Católica Guatemalteca, 1944–1966" (Guatemala: Semenario de Integración Social Guatemalteca, 1970).
55. "Fríjoles y Fusiles," in *Coyuntura* (San José, Costa Rica), Vol. 1, No. 3 (May 15, 1982).

56. Antonio Najera Saravia, "Desde la montaña," *Prensa Libre* (Guatemala City), June 25, 1982.
57. Ibid.
58. Ibid.
59. "Situación de la Economía guatemalteca," in *Carta Socialista* (San José, Costa Rica), Vol. 1, No. 4 (June 1982).

5

Representative Constitutional Democracy in Costa Rica: Adaptation to Crisis in the Turbulent 1980s

John A. Booth

For three decades Costa Rica has stood alone in Central America as an example of stable, constitutional representative democracy, but enormous internal and external strains now appear to threaten both stability and the nation's constitutional, representative democracy. Is Costa Rica about to become politically more like neighboring Central American states? Can the contemporary institutions of Central America weather the storm of economic crisis, international pressure, political mobilization, and subversion? In seeking an answer to these questions, this chapter explores the historical origins of the system of government of Costa Rica since 1948, and surveys the contemporary political culture and certain structural features of the polity. It also explores critical internal and external economic and political strains that between 1980 and 1983 destabilized Costa Rica somewhat and could intensify. What will befall Costa Rica's political system under such strains?

Introduction: Democracy, Stability, and Political Culture

The distinction between democracy and political stability has been drawn repeatedly, but it merits express attention at the outset of this enterprise. No equation of the two is assumed here, yet a central thrust of this chapter involves the relationship between democracy and stability in Costa Rica.

NICARAGUA
Lago de Nicaragua
CARIBBEAN SEA
INTER-AMERICAN HIGHWAY
La Cruz
ALAJUELA
HEREDIA
Liberia
GUANACASTE
Volcán Arenal
Las Cañas
Villa Quesada
Volcán Poas
Nicoya
San Ramon
GOLFITO DE NICOYA
Puntarenas
Alajuela
Heredia
Atenas
Volcán Irazú
San José
Turrialba
Limón
San Ignacio
Cartago
CARTAGO
LIMÓN
SAN JOSÉ
San Isidro
PANAMA
PACIFIC OCEAN
PUNTARENAS
Palmar Sur
INTER-AMERICAN HIGHWAY
Golfito
GOLFITO DULCE
COSTA RICA
Road
Railroad
0
50 Miles
0
50 Kilometers

Democracy is the participation of citizens in the making and implementation of the public decisions that affect their lives.[1] But there are many different kinds of democracy, a fact often ignored by American political scientists.[2] To be more precise: Costa Rica has had since 1949 a constitutional arrangement best described as a representative, republican government with a comparatively high degree of correspondence between the actual government of the system and the formal political arrangements described in the Constitution. Electoral probity has remained consistently high throughout this period. One may fairly characterize Costa Rica, therefore, as a representative, constitutional democracy. This system of government affords Costa Ricans a degree of participation in public decisions equal to or greater than those in most other Western, liberal, constitutional democracies.[3]

Political stability involves several things, including the presence of public order (the lack of turmoil), and the absence of rapid or abrupt institutional transformations or unscheduled personnel or regime changes. In comparison to neighboring Central American states, Costa Rica has experienced only modest amounts of turmoil in the last thirty years. (Regime changes in Costa Rica since 1949 have been regular, constitutional, and orderly.) In comparison to Latin America as a whole during the same period, the lack of abrupt institutional change in Costa Rica has been notable.

The question addressed here is not whether the Costa Rican political system is good or bad, nor whether the system should continue as it is for some indefinite future. Rather, at issue is how the system came to be as it is now, and whether the stresses and strains to which it is now subjected have the potential to alter significantly the current Costa Rican system through turmoil, sudden institutional transformations, or unexpected regime change. Note that instability in Costa Rica need not diminish the democratic nature of the polity. While the common assumption is that instability in Costa Rica would undermine the extent of democracy, that is not necessarily so. Instability of any of the three sorts (turmoil, sudden institutional change, unscheduled regime changes) might actually increase the amount of democracy in Costa Rica by opening new avenues of participation or by increasing popular influence upon public decisions.

Alternatively, of course, turmoil or sudden institutional or regime change could indeed reduce democracy by diminishing popular influence over public decisions. Since 1905, however, and in particular since 1949, most of the episodes of instability in the Costa Rican system (as well as more ordered change) have brought about expanded popular participation—more democracy—rather than less.

For the purpose of this analysis, it is assumed that any political system is a product of its own history.[4] The interaction of individuals within their material environment and their collective efforts to impose order upon their experience shape the culture of a society and its members. Political culture defines for individuals their public relationships to each other, their interpretations of their shared or public space and roles, the nature of communal decision making, the institutions that govern them, and key aspects of the relation between the public and the private material environments. Political culture may differ among subsets of the society (for example, between elites and masses, classes, racial or religious groups, and so forth). Political culture includes a set of values and related behavior which could be labeled "legitimacy" or perhaps "acceptance" of the extant political arrangements in a society. By whatever label, this attitude of legitimacy or acceptance leads to a behavior of peaceful compliance with public institutions, their incumbents, and their laws and policies.

The stability of political institutions depends upon the firmness with which they become imbedded in the culture of a society through its historical experience. To the extent that existing patterns of expectations, beliefs, and institutions either permit positive satisfaction of key needs or do not alienate major segments of the society, the political culture remains relatively static or evolves very slowly, and thus reinforces or sustains existing institutional arrangements. However, should legitimacy or acceptance of the polity fail (that is, major segments of the society fail to be satisfied or become alienated for whatever reason), the rate of change of culture (overall or within subgroups) can become very rapid, and compliance with (and therefore the strength of) institutions can change suddenly.

The rate and degree of change of political culture and of institutions will likely be in proportion to the number and type of citizens and elites affected, the intensity of their dissatisfactions, the degree of mobilization, and the extent to which dissatisfaction becomes focused on political institutions. There can be many sources of dissatisfaction among members of a society sufficient to bring about important rapid cultural changes and to alter institutions. Among those factors most often identified have figured sudden economic dislocations (rapid growth, high and persistent inflation, depression), rapid shifts in relative status position or experiences among subgroups, or sudden shifts in prospects for power, influence, or survival and safety (war, technological change, personnel changes, etc.). If sufficiently intense and rapid, such factors can cause sudden discrepancies between expectations and reality, frustrating key psychological needs and drives and—if focused upon political values and institutions—the dissolution of cultural supports and even aggressive political behavior vis-à-vis institutions.

The survival of institutions under such pressures depends upon the degree to which elites within them can mobilize resources to diffuse dissatisfaction, remove the underlying causes of dissatisfaction by changing material and social conditions, or lower expectations so as to reduce frustration. The ability of leaders to bring about such changes varies dramatically according to their ability to make decisions, the material resources at their command, their own values and expectations, and the degree of control they exercise over their environment.[5] Juan Linz argues that when a crisis (an insoluble problem) presents itself to a democratic political system and elite and mass dissatisfaction lower legitimacy, a disloyal opposition can mobilize its resources to cause a breakdown and major change in the existing institutional framework or a change in the ruling personnel.

Costa Rica's contemporary political arrangements have deep historical roots, and the political culture of the nation (both among mass public and leaders) provides certain resources that may facilitate the survival of the current system. However, the economic and political problems that Costa Rica now faces, both from within and abroad, are of such magnitude and (in some cases) so outside the control of Costa Ricans that they may greatly accelerate the rate of change of the nation's political culture and decrease the stability of the present institutional arrangement. Indeed, the survival of the current Costa Rican constitutional representative democracy beyond the 1980s seems significantly in doubt. The question of whether new Costa Rican cultural and institutional patterns would enhance or diminish democracy there should this system break down is difficult to foretell.

The History of Costa Rica's Constitutional Democracy[6]

Many observers portray Costa Rica as unique in Latin America because its contemporary representative institutions have evolved from a colonial tradition of egalitarian rural life, civilian rule, equal land distribution, and longstanding electoral probity. Like most myths, this one contains kernels of truth, but they are often misunderstood.

Smaller than West Virginia, Costa Rica is riven by volcanic mountain ranges that rise from hot tropical lowlands. Costa Rican society began and evolved in the elevated intermontane valleys of the nation's center (meseta central), largely isolated from both coasts by the terrain. Not only was Spain's Costa Rican colony isolated, but it also lacked any mineral or agricultural wealth of consequence. Thus Spain attended very little to Costa Rica, the colonists there accumulated few slaves to work in mines, and a scarcity of Indian labor prevented the establishment of large haciendas. Since more land than a family could work by itself was generally wasted in the poor colony, little concentration of land ownership occurred and very little capital accumulated. By the late colonial era nearly all Costa Ricans, regardless of their social standing, had become subsistence farmers.

The relentless economic leveling, however, did not prevent other status differences among colonial Costa Ricans. Noble lineage, race, and ethnicity intertwined to define a status hierarchy topped by a poor but highly self-conscious aristocracy. Participation in formal political institutions during the colonial period was restricted mainly to a political class drawn from the aristocracy. Early liberal and conservative factions emerged within this political class, forerunners of later political parties. Thus, even though the colony's relative economic equality bred egalitarian social values among lower status Costa Ricans, colonial Costa Rica was hardly democratic.

Two things which *did not happen* in colonial Costa Rica—in contrast to most of the rest of Latin America—have contributed to later democracy. First, Costa Rica did not develop a quasifeudalistic hacienda system, in which a white aristocracy controlled highly concentrated landholdings and dominated Indians and black slaves as elements of plantation economic production. Second, the colonial era ended on a note different from much of Latin America because Costa Rica did not have to fight for its independence from Spain. Internal conflict remained low in the early national period and the first several governments were civilian. The aristocracy governed successfully for some time without militarizing itself. A politicized military developed only after Costa Ricans had developed a taste for civilian rule.

The introduction and rapid expansion of coffee cultivation with the opening of the European market in 1845 marked the rapid growth of economic inequality and new social classes. A strong class of coffee planters and importers-exporters evolved, land ownership became increasingly concentrated, and a new class of landless agricultural workers appeared. The social and political aristocracy (now converted into coffee growers) continued to dominate politics, largely excluding the general public. Through much of the nineteenth century, literacy requirements barred all but about 10 percent of the citizenry from voting. Elections for most offices were indirect—those with the franchise voted only in the first round of elections to choose electors (usually from the coffee aristocracy) who in turn chose officeholders. Liberal and conservative elite political factions fought for power using manipulated elections, fraud, and even military force. By mid-century, military institutions had appeared and had begun to take part in the political arena. From 1824 to 1899 the average Costa Rican presidency lasted only 2.4 years, 37 percent of the presidents resigned before completing their terms, and another fifth were deposed by coups d'etat. Over half of the time from 1835 to 1899 Costa Rica was under military rule—the generals in the presidency were almost always coffee aristocrats.

In the late nineteenth century economic change accelerated

Table 5.1. Characteristics of Costa Rican presidencies, 1824–1978*

Characteristic	Period			
	1824–1889	1890–1920	1921–1950	1951–1978
Average years per presidency	2.4	3.4	3.8	4.0
(civilian presidents only)	1.5	3.6	3.8	4.0
(military presidents only)	5.8	2.0	—	—
Percentage of period under military rule	44%	7%	—	—
Percentage of interim presidencies† (not including those due to brief absence of constitutional president)	30%	11%	—	—
Percentage of presidents serving less than one year (excluding interims due to absence)	37%	22%	—	—
Percentage of presidencies ended by resignation	19%	22%	13%	—
Percentage of presidencies ended by coup d'etat	19%	11%	13%	—
Average voter turnout as % of population**	—[a]	14%[b]	15%	29%

†Costa Rica has two kinds of interim presidencies: one during a legal absence of the constitutional president from the country, the other following the untimely ending of a constitutional president's tenure (death, removal, or resignation). This table includes only interim presidencies of the second type, since they indicate instability, whereas the first type does not.

**Computed from Table 5.2.

Notes: [a]Data not available.
[b]Based on elections from 1901–19 only.

*Source: Compiled from Harold H. Bonilla, *Los presidentes*, *Tomo I* and *Tomo II* (San José: Editorial Universidad Estatal a Distancia-Editorial Costa Rica, 1979).

with the construction of a railroad to the Atlantic port of Limón from San José, and with the accompanying cultivation and exportation of bananas. The banana industry absorbed many workers displaced by coffee production, but also bred regional tensions and proved fertile ground for Communist labor organization in the 1930s. Banana cultivation also contributed to spreading Costa Rica's settlement pattern outside of the central meseta region, brought many blacks and Chinese to the nation, and inaugurated an era of racial discrimination. In the late nineteenth century such changes began to spawn some participation in politics by a broader public than before, much of it dissatisfied with the elite's decisions. Mobilized by the church in response to Liberal anticlerical laws, a Catholic party appeared from 1889 to 1891, but was quickly stamped out by repressive measures of the Liberal elite. Somewhat ironically, it was the Liberal dictatorship of the late nineteenth century that laid the foundations for later democratizing transformations of Costa Rican politics by promoting public education.

Growing literacy and an expanding urban middle class in the early twentieth century brought many more Costa Ricans into the political arena. In 1905 a heated election campaign (with over half of the populace now literate) brought Cleto González Vízquez to the presidency on the crest of a large turnout increase over the 1901 election (see Table 5.2). González Vízquez broke with a tradition of decades by tolerating vigorous opposition and by ensuring a free campaign in 1909. This freedom permitted Ricardo Jiménez Oreamuno to win the presidency by appealing for votes to local peasant leaders outside the aristocracy. Once elected, Jiménez Oreamuno secured a constitutional amendment (1913) to institute direct popular election of public officials. These actions by González and Jiménez between 1905 and 1914 broadened the politically active populace outside the aristocracy and persuaded more and more of the general public to vote.

Economic crisis brought on by the impact of World War I led President Alfred González Flores to impose economic reforms, new taxes, and austerity measures. This so frustrated the coffee aristocracy that they promoted yet another coup and two more years of military rule under the Tinoco brothers. The Tinocos, however, were also incapable of solving economic problems; they were very repressive as well. This brought an invasion from

Table 5.2. Election participation in Costa Rica, 1897–1978

Year	Number of Votes[a]	Population Estimate (Booth)[b]	Vote as Percent of Population Booth	Vote as Percent of Population Stone[c]	Turnout (vote as % Registered)
1897	24,065	270,000	8.9	8.8	
1901	35,722	290,000	12.3	11.5	
1905	51,789	315,000	16.4	15.2	
1909	51,623	340,000	15.2	13.6	
1913	64,147	380,000	16.9	15.6	
1919	47,497	425,000	11.2	11.3	
1923	71,543	450,000	15.9	15.6	71.2
1928	70,281	480,000	14.6	14.9	61.4
1932	70,447	550,000	12.8	13.1	64.5
1936	88,324	620,000	14.2	14.9	68.7
1940	108,145	685,000	15.8	15.7	79.0
1944	126,606	740,000	17.1	18.1	83.8
1948	98,941[d]	795,000	12.4	0[e]	57.7
1953	197,489	940,000	21.0	22.4	67.2
1958	229,543	1,160,000	19.8	21.3	64.7
1962	391,406	1,320,000	29.7	29.3	80.9
1966	441,400	1,500,000	29.4	29.6	81.4
1970	562,766	1,780,000	31.6	33.1	83.3
1974					79.9
1978					81.3

Notes:
[a]Source: Samuel Stone, *La dinastía de los conquistadores: La crisis del poder en la Costa Rica contemporánea* (San José: Editorial Universitaria Centroamericana, 1975), pp. 236–37, 569–84.
[b]Population estimate based on graphical point estimation based on census figures for 1864, 1892, 1927, 1950, 1963, and 1973.
[c]From Stone, p. 236. Difference in percentage values between my estimate and Stone's estimate derive from his method of estimating population based on diverse sources. pp. 566–67.
[d]Source: Jacobo Schifter, *La fase oculta de la guerra civil en Costa Rica* (San José: Editorial Universitaria Centroamericana, 1979), p. 81 for 1923–48. Wilburg Jiménez Castro, "Las elecciones," in Chester Zelaya, ed., *Costa Rica Contemporánea, Vol. 1* (San José, Costa Rica: Editorial Costa Rica, 1979), pp. 135–58 for 1953 on.
[e]Stone did not compute this election because the Congress declared it fraudulent.

Nicaragua by exiled Costa Rican elites and popular unrest which together toppled the Tinocos from power. Costa Ricans had rejected the military experiment and expressed a strong preference for civilian, constitutional rule.

During the 1920–50 era, Costa Rica experienced great change because of the increase in the number of organizations and political parties. Among the former, community groups, cooperatives, labor unions, professional and trade associations, school groups, and many other types of associations mobilized many people into the political arena. These groups conveyed a burgeoning array of demands to the political system. One very influential political movement was Jorge Volio's Reformist Party of the 1920s. Volio was a populist, a devout Catholic, a social worker, and a supporter of unions. He both helped pave the way for later cooperation between the church and the Communist unions in the 1940s, and also influenced the social democratic movement that overthrew this church-labor alliance in 1948. The Communist Party was also born during this era and became influential in the banana fields during the depression of the 1930s. Communist success among banana workers helped their unions to spread; the movement reached its peak of political power in 1942–48 as the Confederation of Workers of Costa Rica participated in two administrations. The union activism of the thirties and forties brought about protections for workers, capped by the 1941 Social Security system and the 1943 Labor Code.

Rising popular participation in elections and in demand-making through unions and other economic pressure groups combined with depression economic hardships to form a coalition between coffee aristocrats and Social Christian reformer President Rafael Ángel Calderón Guardia and the Communist Party from 1942 to 1948. Opposition to the Calderón-Communist alliance and to their reformist policies in turn led to the emergence of both conservative and progressive middle-class movements in the early 1940s. Under the leadership of José Figueres Ferrer, these forces eventually unified and adopted strongly anti-Communist yet reformist social democratic policies. Escalating partisan violence after 1946 and an attempted electoral fraud in 1948 prompted a short civil war between the forces of Calderón and the Communists and those of Figueres's National Liberation insurgents.

Victorious, the National Liberation Junta dissolved many unions, outlawed the Communist Party, and enacted a number of economic reforms including nationalization of all banks and a major tax levy on wealth. The Junta ruled for eighteen months, during which the 1871 constitution was revised. It established new mechanisms to guarantee honest elections, abolished the army which had lost the civil war, and gave full political rights to women and blacks. The Liberation leaders in 1949 returned power to the 1948 presidential victor (Otilio Ulate) and transformed their movement into a political party (the National Liberation Party—PLN) whose platform incorporated many of the social reforms of the Calderón era and called for greatly increased governmental participation in the economy.

The victory of the Liberation insurgents and their rise to power represented a definitive change in the political elite, now broadened to include the urban middle sectors. The PLN won the 1953–58 presidency for José Figueres, and has greatly influenced Costa Rican politics ever since. By relinquishing power to the opposition coalition in 1958 the integrity of elections was reinforced. Even though it lost the presidency in several alternate terms, the PLN has retained its control of the Legislative Assembly (except for 1978–82), thus imprinting its vision of a new social and economic order even when "out of power." Under PLN leadership, the government's role in the economy grew greatly through the nationalization of banks, insurance, rails, and utilities among others, and joint public-private financing of many productive enterprises. Many social welfare programs also were implemented to provide medical care, social security, housing subsidies, and other services to middle- and (somewhat less) to lower-class groups.

Since the civil war of 1948, successive governments have continued to appeal to the mass public for support. Electoral turnout has continued to increase and public policy has stimulated other types of participation. A strong tradition of porkbarrel and special interest legislation evolved in the post-1948 Costa Rican system, leading pressure and interest groups to develop high expectations of satisfaction of their demands and thus further encourage intense demand-making. Development programs have promoted popular organizations by the thousands to work for community improvement, health, nutrition, and education—almost all of them making demands upon the state. Vigorous efforts to fragment and to control the union movement, combined with co-optative social welfare and labor policies, neutralized much of the political clout and dissatisfaction of the working class for over two decades. Strongly pro-developmental policies led to the creation of several big-spending autonomous institutions that now represent a substantial problem for the central government.

In sum, though Costa Rica had experienced civilian rule during the nineteenth century, it did not become a firmly established mode until 1950 and strong constitutional institutions have emerged only in the last thirty years. Electoral probity became a widely shared goal in the early twentieth century, but remained often unrealized until the 1950s. Costa Rica's representative constitutional institutions, then, have come to full maturity only in the last three decades and have done so in a period of generally growing prosperity and progress.

Political Culture

Mass and Elite Values and Behaviors[7]

Despite a national myth to the contrary, Costa Rica is a highly participant society. Although Costa Ricans often characterize themselves as uncooperative, individualistic, and difficult to mobilize, they in fact frequently vote, join and take part in organizations, perform electioneering and party activities, engage in communal self-help activities, discuss politics and community affairs, and contact public officials (see table 5.3). They do so at levels higher than many other Third World and Latin American nations, and only slightly lower—if at all—than levels observed in the United States and Europe. Such participation bespeaks the democratic nature of Costa Rican political structure.

In addition to being participatory, Costa Rican political culture has strong egalitarian traits that date from the colonial era when virtually all Costa Ricans were small-scale subsistence farmers. Centuries of fundamental economic equality imbued Costa Rican popular culture with a sense of the fundamental worth of each citizen, regardless of ascribed status. Thus the rural and

Table 5.3. Political activities of Costa Rican family heads (in percentages)*

Type of Activity	Percent
Voting in 1970 election	84
Member of 1 or more voluntary groups	66
Medium level of overall group leadership[a]	66
Medium level of overall attendance at group functions[b]	59
Engaging in 1 or more community improvement projects	56
Member of 2 or more organizations	39
Has contacted 1 or more public officials	31
Talks national politics "from time to time" or more often	30
Member of a political party (past or present)	27
Talks local politics "from time to time" or more often	22
High level of overall group leadership[c]	18
Medium or higher political party function attendance	16
Member of 1 or more community improvement organizations[d]	16
Soliciting aid from municipal executive	13
Soliciting aid from municipal councilman	11
Soliciting aid from Legislative Assembly deputy	10
Soliciting aid from police	9
Soliciting aid from 2 or more public officials[e]	8
High level of political party function attendance[f]	7
Medium level of political party leadership positions[g]	6
Soliciting aid from the President	3 |//
(Number of individuals = 1446)	

[a] A level of leadership achieved by persons who were either officers or presidents of some of the organizations to which they belonged.
[b] An attendance level achieved by persons who attended, on the average, all the organizations to which they belonged at least "from time to time."
[c] Is a president or other officer in nearly all the groups to which he belongs.
[d] Member of a Community Development Association, Junta Progresista, Nutrition Committee, or Social Welfare Committee.
[e] Soliciting aid from at least two of the following: municipal executive, municipal councilman, a legislative assembly deputy, the police, the president, or some other government official.
[f] Attends almost all party functions and activities.
[g] Is at least an official of a local party chapter.
*Source: John A. Booth, "Democracy and Citizen Action in Costa Rica: The Modes and Correlates of Popular Participation in Politics" (Ph.D. dissertation, The University of Texas at Austin, 1975), p. 628.

urban poor today often manifest little reticence about expressing their opinions to those of higher status or greater wealth and influence. The elaborate systems of deferential reference between social classes that exist elsewhere in the Hispanic world because of longstanding semifeudal agrarian traditions do not exist in Costa Rica.

Costa Ricans tend to behave in a democratic fashion in collective settings—painstakingly hearing all points of view and voting on issues to make decisions. Recent surveys have shown that Costa Ricans generally support democratic civil liberties, although they tend to be intolerant of certain types of participation by critics of the political system. Costa Ricans also generally disapprove of participation by "communists" despite a longstanding and active role in the nation's politics by the Popular Vanguard Party and by the left-coalition United People's Party.

Another characteristic of Costa Rican political culture is a general striving toward compromise and consensus. Parties to a dispute tend to seek mutually acceptable solutions in a middle ground rather than to hold uncompromisingly to initial principles or positions, permitting the resolution of differences of opinion and face-saving on both sides of an issue. This practice has often contributed to innovative public policy that has permitted the co-optation of the disgruntled into the system rather than their defeat and exclusion from it. For example, Costa Rica's victorious National Liberation Junta in 1948 retained the Labor Code and social security system established by their opponents before the 1948 civil war, despite the intense criticism leveled at these laws by many of the insurgents' major backers prior to the confict. Other examples of innovative public policies born of compromise between powerful pressures include the successful land reform initiated by the Institute of Land and Colonization (ITCO) in the mid and late 1970s, and the mixed economy as a whole.

Despite Costa Rica's general tradition of peaceful political intercourse, violence has occurred with some frequency. Banana workers under the leadership of Communist unions, residents of the depressed Atlantic zone, and some landless peasants have, when unable to achieve their objectives through other means, employed strikes and confrontations that cause violence. The use of violence (occasionally including limited small arms fire) has on some occasions been premeditated—sometimes instigated by the protestors and sometimes by the police. Violent civil disturbances have occurred in 1979, 1980, 1981, and 1982—in particular in the Atlantic and Pacific banana zones.

Government response to such incidents is generally moderate, unlike neighboring nations. Force has been employed cautiously, and instead common ground is sought for the resolution of the problem. Such moderation has usually defused violence and kept it focused around the original issue rather than spreading it to other issues or groups. Despite the frequency of violent conflict in recent years, the press and politicians have tended to react with concern and with disavowals of violence as acceptable for political discourse. Thus, while violence is not infrequent, it is rarely extolled even by leftist parties and is generally regarded as exceptional and warranting special efforts to resolve its causes.

Terrorist incidents since 1980 have stunned Costa Ricans, although both parties to the 1948 conflict had employed terror. Nevertheless, terrorism has been quite rare in comparison to other Central American societies. Both right and left-wing terrorist groups seem to lack a significant popular base, but are nurtured by international contacts with extremist elements among other Central American revolutionary or counterrevolutionary movements through the exile communities.

Political Resources and Constraints

Considerable political resources are available to the Costa Rican government in comparison to its neighbors in Central America: (1) the absence of a large, politicized armed force frees fiscal resources to address other problems and permits political flexibility; (2) the democratic and constitutional traditions of the last three decades have given legitimate access to public policy formation to an extensive variety of political viewpoints. This has given at least some vested interest in the system to many groups that elsewhere have become not only alienated but actively hostile toward their regimes; (3) the drive for compromise and conciliation have led several administrations to recognize competing claims upon public resources, and to co-opt rather than to suppress intense opposition; and (4) policymaking flexibility and innovativeness have characterized recent Costa Rican administrations, leading to a variety of novel (within the region) institutions and social policies. These patterns of elite behavior tend to enhance the policymaking efficacy of the government, while the lack of armed forces increases effectiveness in problem solving by keeping resources free for social problems.

There are also important constraints upon the government's ability to cope with problems. The executive branch's weakness vis-à-vis the decentralized bureaucracies means that it has been unable effectively to influence them to forestall unwanted policy trends or to control them in times of crisis. Certain of the autonomous agencies are responsible for promoting development (the Institute of Land and Colonization—ITCO; the Institute of Municipal Development—IFAM) or for major public services (the Central Bank; the Costa Rican Social Security System—INSS; the Water and Sewer Service—AyA; the Housing and Urbanization Institute—INVU; the Costa Rican Electrical Institute—ICE; and the Costa Rican Petroleum Refinery—RECOPE). These institutions not only perform critical services for the economy, but they are also typically monopolies occupying strategic positions in the economy, the government, and the nation as a whole. They are, therefore, quite vulnerable to certain kinds of political and economic pressures, especially from their employees' unions. Moreover, the capacity of certain agencies (especially ICE) to acquire debts without regard for the desires of the administration or Assembly has contributed in a significant way to the current economic crisis of Costa Rica. Calls for constitutional reform in Costa Rica often mention a need to curtail the great autonomy of these entities, especially in matters of credit and borrowing policy.

Despite freedom from the burden of an armed force, Costa Rica is further constrained by the fact that it is not a wealthy society and has relatively limited resources. Since coffee and bananas are important sources of public revenue (directly through export taxes and indirectly through income taxes on workers and earners in these sectors) the government is vulnerable to sudden revenue declines in response to international price changes, changes in value shifts, and labor conflicts. A final constraint derives from the fact that the tradition of co-optation and conciliation has led most administrations and Assemblies to give in, at least partially, to special interest demands rather than to refuse such pressures. The resultant habit of "saying yes" of Costa Rican governments has recently made difficult the formulation and implementation of austerity programs.

State and Economy

The writings of José Figueres in the 1940s foreshadowed the economic philosophy of the National Liberation Junta and the party to which it gave birth. The basic economic premise which has shaped the development of the Costa Rican economy since then is that unfettered capitalism causes socioeconomic dislocations and inequalities that produce social ills and unrest. The solution to these tendencies is to constrain the free market through government involvement (both by public ownership and by regulation) in order to redistribute income sufficiently to improve the living standard of the poor, and to protect the national patrimony. Since 1948 the Costa Rican government has, then, greatly expanded its role in the economy; it currently accounts for 60 percent of GNP. Among public sector industries are banking, insurance, most public utilities, petroleum refining, railways, ports, and some urban mass transit. The government has also entered joint ventures with private investors and given special tax concessions in efforts to promote developmental objectives. In addition, the Costa Rican government extensively regulates the private economy with rules affecting exports and imports, agricultural production, environmental protection, public health and welfare, and consumer prices. Examples of the comparative advantage Costa Ricans have enjoyed over other Central Americans because of such policies may be found in table 5.4. Costa Rica's lower military expenditures and higher education and health spending have dramatically raised the quality of life for its citizens.

Despite such extensive government involvement in the economy, private enterprise still flourishes in Costa Rica. Many public officials in the PLN and other parties have business interests which have survived or prospered even while public involvement in the economy has grown. Criticism of the Costa Rican mixed economy from the right often now focuses on the stifling weight of the government's bureaucracy upon productive individuals

Table 5.4. Selected social indicators for Costa Rica and other countries*

Index	Costa Rica	Nicaragua	El Salvador	Guatemala	Honduras	Mexico	United States
Physical quality of life, 1974	87	53	67	53	50	75	96
Death rate among children 1–4 yrs.	4.0	18.4	14.5	30.0	20.0	10.6	
Inhabitants per physician	1804	2014	5101	4498	4085	1726	569
Daily caloric intake (DCI) as % of average daily requirement (ADR) (2,025 calories/day), 1974	117	117	81	83	89	121	167
Percent of 1977 central government budget spent on							
a. education	33	13	23	16	19		
b. health	4	12	11	11	12		
c. education plus health	37	25	34	27	31		
Life expectancy at birth:							
males	61.9	51.2	56.6	48.3	62.1	62.8	68.7
females	64.8	54.6	60.4	49.7	55.0	66.6	76.5
Percent of all deaths from intestinal diseases	5.4	18.7	15.6	18.9	15.3	12.7	0.1
Percent of Gross Domestic Product for military expenditures	0.5	1.5	1.7	0.8	1.7	0.7	6.1

*Source: John A. Booth, *The End and the Beginning: The Nicaraguan Revolution* (Boulder, Colo.: Westview Press, 1982).

and firms, and on the restrictions imposed upon initiative by excessive regulation. In contrast, criticism from the left notes persistent and growing socioeconomic inequality, and the misdirection of social services and benefits away from the most needy poor and toward the middle sector supporters of the major political parties and toward public employees.

Political Parties[10]

Although Costa Rica's multimember districting and proportional representation encourage the survival of small parties, only two groups effectively vie for the presidency—the Partido de Liberación Nacional (National Liberation Party—PLN) and the Unidad (Unity) opposition coalition that forms for most elections. The PLN is the largest party. Founded in 1951 by José Figueres from his 1948 revolutionary movement, Liberación is a highly organized, permanent party organization of social democratic ideology advocating social guarantees and a mixed economy. President Luis Alberto Monge Álvarez, the PLN presidential nominee in 1982, won a resounding 58 percent of the national vote, and the PLN won 33 of 57 seats in the Legislative Assembly. One problem now evident in the PLN is the degree to which its founders from the revolution (Figueres, Orlich, Oduber, and Monge) continue to dominate the organization. New talent from a younger generation has until recently been largely excluded from presidential bids and most ministerial posts.

The main opposition party, the Unity Party, is in reality a changing coalition of several parties that has successfully contested the PLN in 1958, 1966, and 1978. In its most recent variant the united opposition elected president Rodrigo Carazo Odio in 1978. Carazo, however, was unable to forge a stable majority coalition in the Legislative Assembly in which the PLN had lost its outright majority for the first time. The defection of some of his allies early in his term cost Carazo his legislative majority and resulted in a paralyzing internal stalemate within the Assembly as well as a standoff between the administration and the disunited opposition parties in the legislative branch.

Another significant party group is the leftist coalition known as the Partido Pueblo Unido (United People's Party—PPU) consisting of the pro-Soviet Popular Vanguard (Communist) Party, the Socialist Party, and the People's Revolutionary Party. Electoral support for the left comes predominantly from the Gulf Coast banana regions around Golfito, from San José's working class neighborhoods, and from some intellectuals and students. The growth of support for the left had been slow but steady in recent years; but even though in the February 1982 election left voting declined, the PPU coalition won four seats in the Legislative Assembly, an increase of one. The United People's Party and its constituent parties maintain close ties to the labor movement and have advocated and supported recent strikes. Despite unrest in 1982 in the banana zones and organization of rural and urban squatter movements since then, the left coalition is generally moderate, its demands reformist rather than revolutionary.

Pressure Groups and Demand-Making[11]

Costa Rica is a society distinguished by its large number of formal organizations, the Costa Ricans take part in many groups, and through those groups make demands of the government. The tendency to organize is not new in Costa Rica, but well established since community improvement groups and unions first appeared in the 1880s. A 1973 representative national sample survey found that Costa Rican family heads reported a mean of 1.52 organization memberships each.[12] Two-thirds of the sample reported having held office in some group, and about 60 percent attended with medium frequency. About 56 percent reported having engaged in at least one project to improve their communities, an activity that frequently brought people into contact with public officials.

Costa Rica abounds with organizations of a variety limited only by human imagination. While not all organizations make demands upon the government, many of them do. In particular business and producer groups, unions, cooperatives, and self-help groups such as community development and health/welfare groups constantly bring demands to the government.

The Costa Rican government has a lengthy tradition of responding favorably to pressure group initiatives of many sorts. A 1973 survey of community organizations and their projects nationwide found that a substantial majority of those projects received some form of outside assistance, usually from the national or municipal government.[13]

The demand-making process followed by Costa Rican organizations generally involves initial contacts with the competent agency or official through regular channels followed by appeal to other agencies or to higher authority if unsuccessful. If various initiatives fail to produce results, the demands are sometimes escalated through confrontational tactics such as demonstrations, small acts of civil disobedience, consumer or employee strikes. The government generally responds to such confrontations with study and compromise to defuse the conflict. Heavy-handed repression of demand-making has been relatively rare in Costa Rica, even when the demands are made through confrontation.

Among the more powerful pressure/interest groups is organized labor. Labor has been fragmented since the 1948 defeat of the Communist-Calderón alliance and has been restrained by a restrictive labor code. Most of the nation's unions are unaffiliated—about 40 percent of the organized work force. There are three major confederations of unions. The Christian Democratic Federation (CTC) has about 4 percent of the organized work force. The Social-Democratic, ORIT-affiliated Costa Rican Democratic Workers Confederation (CCTD), has about 16 percent of the organized workers. Its splinter federation (CATD) has another 8 percent. These unions' leaders are linked to the Liberation Party. Public employees and skilled workers comprise key elements of this segment, which generally presses moderate, wage- and job-oriented demands. The third major confederation, the Communist-dominated General Confederation of Workers (CGT), and several other Communist-led unions united in 1980 to form the Unitary Confederation of Workers (CUT), which controls up to a third of the nation's organized workers. The major base of CUT is among banana workers, with some public employee affiliates (such as the relatively small National Public Employees Association—ANEP). The CGT and its CUT successor have been very militant and were responsible for a large proportion of the 1981–82 strikes, some of which led to violence. Calls for sympathy strikes from other unions, however, even within the CGT/CUT, have proven largely unsuccessful. However, strikes that threaten major productive sectors (in particular, banana and dock workers) usually bring government mediation. Wage gains in such economically strategic areas have been quite high.

Other important unions are those representing such public employees as teachers (National Educators Association—ANDE; National Secondary Teachers Association—APSE), and employees of the electrical generation/telephone system, ICE, the Ministry of Public Works, and health workers. Given their strategic position vis-à-vis important (even critical) services, these unions' demands often influence the government. During the summer of 1980, a threat that ANDE and several other public employees' unions might strike because of promised but unpaid wage raises led the president to invoke emergency powers to raise taxes by decree. In August of 1983, a similar crisis developed with teachers, bank employees, health workers, and refinery workers pressing for major wage increases. Such organizations have been key agents in pressing middle sector demands upon the Costa Rican government, and in shaping policy to favor the middle classes.

Another class of pressure groups is the associations (colleges) or professionals which are more widespread than in the United States. These organizations act as important vehicles representing middle sector interests in Costa Rican politics.

Business/pressure groups are numerous, and several of them exercise great influence over economic policy. Representing management and with links to the Council of the Americas, the Costa Rican Management Association (ACOGE) presses for economic revitalization (especially through export-oriented new investment) and development. ACOGE has put forward a national economic plan in response to the current economic crisis, one element of which is an extensive foreign aid proposal for the region. An older, more conservative probusiness group is ANFE, the National Association for the Promotion of Enterprise. The Chamber of Commerce, Chamber of Industries, and National Union of Chambers represent private capital at large. While the commercial and industrial chambers often differ on specific economic policies, they strongly support business interests in general, and oppose greater public intervention in the economy.

In general, business interests loom large in policy making in Costa Rica—entrepreneurs contribute to political candidates, and business organizations often lobby effectively in the legislative, executive, and regulative arenas. The inability of the probusiness Carazo government to promote private sector growth or effectively to regulate the economy intensely disappointed such leaders, and generally alienated business from his administration. The Monge administration has been more receptive to business initiatives and positions than previous PLN governments.

In summary, Costa Rica has numerous clearly articulated and heavily involved pressure groups making demands upon the government and in some cases even competing for power. Although overt interclass competition for influence and benefits has not been common in Costa Rica since 1950, there already exist effective political organizations representing lower-class, middle-class, and bourgeois interests. Because the last three decades have been relatively prosperous, these mobilized interests have all been favored (to varying degrees) by the growing Costa Rican government. The economic crisis that began in 1980–81, however, markedly reduced the size of the pie that could be divided among them. The crisis has sharply reduced the living standards of middle-class and working-class Costa Ricans, a change with the potential to undermine political consensus, spark turmoil, and sharpen class conflict as these groups struggle over fewer and fewer resources. Growing, and more clearly defined, class conflict could well be a critical problem for the Costa Rican political system in the 1980s.

Policy Problems Facing Costa Rica in the 1980s

Various and severe problems now confront Costa Rican public policy makers. The following discussion itemizes some of these difficulties, with special attention to those problems that might alter Costa Rica's current representative, democratic institutional framework.

Internal conflict, governmental instability, and popular unrest originate in the psychological motivation of individuals and groups. Social and economic conditions, like those afflicting Costa Rica in the early 1980s, seriously threaten many people's basic needs and expectations. Such conditions, especially if they should develop very rapidly, could well produce frustrations capable of changing political culture and causing political turmoil. Governments with resources, adaptive capacity, and the ability to respond to turmoil with moderation would have greater likelihood of coping with social problems before they undermined their own sustaining consensus than would rigid, resource-poor, or repressive governments.

The problems outlined below include some of the very thorny issues Costa Rican policy makers wrestled with in the early 1980s. Many of these problems were serious sources of popular frustration, or they threatened the resources and adaptive capacity of the government.

Economic Problems[14]

Costa Rica entered the 1980s with several external economic problems. First, Costa Rica was highly vulnerable to the price fluctuations of its two major exports (coffee and bananas) and to the price of imported oil. Moreover, Costa Rica was importing great quantities of consumer durables and food, and it had established a very high level of external indebtedness by both the public and private sectors. In the late 1970s, Costa Rican export revenues plummeted as coffee and banana prices fell. Revenues thus became insufficient to balance foreign purchases of ever more expensive oil and the massive consumer-goods diet of Costa Ricans. The government borrowed heavily to finance imports, but heavy interest payments and capital flight due to regional turmoil caused dollar reserves to run out in 1980. This precipitated a crisis of the *colón*, which on the free internal market fell from 9:1 to 60:1 to the dollar. The government defaulted on numerous loans, and the private sector could not import raw materials and replacement parts, thus causing a severe recession, layoffs, and growing unemployment.

President Carazo rejected the draconian terms demanded by the International Monetary Fund to help resolve this crisis, but in 1982 the Monge government agreed to the IMF's conditions. The $2.5 billion debt was rescheduled, and economic policy was revised in order to facilitate debt repayment. This permitted new credits to allow the continued acquisition of essential imports. With these changes the *colón* recovered strength and stabilized at 43:1 to the dollar.

The fall in the *colón* sharply curtailed spending on foreign consumer goods and fuel and helped conserve the outflow of dollars for essential import items. This, plus declining world oil prices in 1982, contributed to a positive balance of trade for that year. The Monge administration also proposed programs to promote nontraditional exports and more domestically generated fuel and food in order to reduce national vulnerability to coffee and banana price fluctuations, to banana strikes, and to energy prices. After one year in office, however, progress toward implementing such programs had been very modest.

Reorganization of the debt in 1982 permitted continued food and energy imports, thus avoiding a general economic collapse. However, in 1983 Costa Rica still needed several things to recover from its crisis: continued foreign-development aid on concessionary terms, new export markets, and the development of nontraditional export products. Though no long-run solution to national problems, the 1983 increases in coffee and banana prices assisted Costa Rica's balance of payments and bought some time for the government's new economic programs. Perhaps most critically, Costa Rica badly needed a return of peace and stability in Central America. This would permit the resumption of lost commerce with the region, could attract both foreign and domestic capital back into the country, and would help tourism recover. However, given the trajectory of international events since 1981, prospects for a significant short-run decline in tensions and turmoil in Central America during the mid-1980s appeared very limited.

Several internal economic problems bedeviled the Costa Rican government in the early 1980s. Costa Rica's large bureaucracy had grown rapidly in the Carazo administration, outstripping the generation of government revenue. Public deficits were financed with external borrowing, while the government sought to implement tax reforms and import restrictions. But a legislative stalemate and fierce private sector opposition to tax reforms blocked efforts to increase revenues, so that the government could not meet salary increases promised to many public employees in 1979. Only the threat of a broad public employees strike in 1980 permitted Carazo to use emergency powers to decree tax increases, thus forestalling the strike. Following the 1980 devaluation of the *colón*, consumer imports declined, but inflation soared to about 150 percent within two years. Despite modest wage increases, labor dissatisfaction again escalated to the point that, as this went to press in late 1983, the Monge government confronted a broad challenge from public sector unions much like what Monge had faced in 1980.

Costa Rica's social democratic tradition of subsidies for key consumer goods and services had long moderated the impact of inflation on the working classes. The 1982 IMF accord, however, required that the government end such deficit-creating subsidies. The impact of this policy was to undermine the living standards and health of broad sectors of Costa Rican society and to generate turmoil. For example, in mid-1983 thousands of Costa Ricans blocked every major artery in San José to protest a doubling of electricity rates. The government backed down before the public ire, so that ICE was once again operating at a loss and ballooning the national deficit. The Monge administration largely ignored the critical need for agrarian reform to relieve the plight of the rural poor, preferring instead to stimulate export-oriented production by the largeholding sector. This policy caused domestic food production to stay far below demand and accelerated both the migration of the rural poor to the cities and urban and agrarian squatter movements.

Observers of the Costa Rican economic and political scene agreed that as of 1983 the Monge administration still needed to reduce the number of public employees, to begin an aggressive agrarian reform, to maintain austere wage policies, and to generate new tax revenues. Although prospects for the implementation of such policies had appeared fairly good in 1982, by mid-1983 performance had been lackluster and observers had become increasingly pessimistic about the government's chances for success. One problem with the development strategy and public welfare and subsidies policies was that it represented a sharp break with Liberación's social democratic tradition. It therefore had great potential for taxing the intellectual resources of the PLN, for alienating lower class supporters who expected more social welfare programs than the government could deliver, and for sharpening conflict within the government.

Political Problems[15]

By 1983 the political consensus supporting the Costa Rican political system appeared to be eroding due to the severe depression that began in 1981 and to poor governmental performance in solving economic problems. The 58 percent landslide for Monge in 1982 represented a strong mandate for a party widely believed capable of delivering needed reforms. But after a year of tolerance of the new government's slow start on addressing national problems, signs of impatience had begun to appear.

The severity of the depression's impact on most Costa Ricans (a sharp and palpable decline in living standards) introduced a large gap between what many had come to expect during the 1970s and new and unpleasantly deteriorated circumstances. This appears to have frustrated many Costa Ricans. Turmoil increased in 1983, including numerous demonstrations, protests, strikes, threats of strikes, and land invasions. Terrorism at home and rising concern about political instability in Central America also troubled Costa Rica. Emulation of radical revolutionary and counterrevolutionary movements from elsewhere in Central America apparently accounted for several incidents of terrorism in the early 1980s. The need to combat such terrorism raised the demand for additional police and military forces which were both expensive and represented some threat to Costa Rica's generally excellent human rights record. Several incidents of rights abuses by police—albeit minor in comparison to those common in other Central American states—began to surface after 1980.

The expanded strength of the labor left (CUT/CGT) and the general dissatisfaction of Costa Rican organized labor with rapidly rising prices and declining real wages raised the specter of major strikes that could severely damage banana exports or impair the government's and autonomous agencies' delivery of public services. Though organized labor remained more divided than unified, most of the public sector remained vulnerable to strikes. Moreover, the Atlantic zone continued to be mired in its structural depression and subject to the longstanding social and political strains that always threaten renewed turmoil there.

The National Liberation Party in the early 1980s manifested internal strains that could easily erode its ability to rule effectively. A growing rift between older leaders (dominant) and younger activists (excluded from key ministerial positions and from the presidential candidacy) risked defections among ambitious and talented younger Liberaciónistas. Former president Daniel Oduber's (1974–78) campaign for constitutional reform that would permit reelection of past presidents appeared particularly prone to inflame generational conflict. The PLN in 1983 also suffered strains between the Monge apparatus and other influential and economically powerful elements. Several top administration officials were pursuing their own electoral goals for 1986 and reportedly ignoring their policy responsibilities. These strains and poor PLN policy performance had become so obvious by mid-1983 that the party's community leaders had begun to organize and to lead demonstrations against the government. Such circumstances suggested that a breakdown of the PLN remained a possibility.

Costa Rica confronted several grotesquely complex foreign policy problems as it entered the 1980s. Militarily powerful Nicaragua had moved considerably to the left of what most Costa Ricans had hoped. Nicaraguan exiles were fighting their battles with the Sandinistas from Costa Rican territory, provoking border incidents, diplomatic problems, and violence in northern cantons. Honduras's struggle to institutionalize representative rule after over a decade of military rule appeared to be failing by 1983 as that country became the spear point of U.S. military policy in Central America. The Guatemalan and Salvadoran regimes remained both highly abusive of human rights and severely challenged by leftist insurgents. The United States loomed over the region with the apparently growing threat of a large-scale military intervention. The initiative of the Contadora Group to promote a political settlement of the various conflicts in Central America was receiving little but rhetorical support from the United States and the Group was threatened from within by severe strains.

Most Costa Ricans would undoubtedly prefer that other Central American governments (whether right- or left-leaning) be both truly democratic and friendly rather than otherwise. During 1978–79 Costa Rica abandoned its traditionally noninterventionist foreign policy and openly assisted the Nicaraguan insurgents against the Somoza regime. Although President Carazo soon repented such support, his government was unable to stop arms smuggling into El Salvador (largely because most of it was conducted by security officials). Consequently, Costa Rica's diplomatic credibility in Central America and its relations with El Salvador and Guatemala suffered. Costa Rica's pact with Honduras and El Salvador to form the Central American Democratic Community was intended, in part, to redress these errors and to symbolize a new commitment to blocking further leftist successes. The Monge administration took an even stronger anticommunist line than had Carazo, a policy extending to tolerating considerable organization and military activity by emergent anti-Sandinista Nicaraguan groups. Despite Costa Rican efforts (largely cosmetic) to control such *contra* activity and to proclaim its neutrality, the situation soon led to serious problems as beleaguered Nicaragua's military buildup accelerated.

In 1980 Costa Rica itself began to suffer an upswing in subversion from abroad, in particular by reputed agents of Cuba and the Soviet Union who encouraged labor unrest. Many political exiles (especially Nicaraguans) have used Costa Rica as a base from which to overthrow neighboring governments. They too contributed to subversion through their influence upon Costa Rican radicals (both leftists and rightists), a factor which has sharply increased political terrorism since 1980. Costa Rica also suffered violations of its sovereignty and constitutional order at the hands of foreign powers in recent years. Among such incidents have been the suborning of the police by foreign agents to arrange illegal deportations in order to avoid time-consuming extraditions, and the arrival or intrusion of foreign military units without the requisite legislative approval. Such incidents (involving the United States, Nicaragua, France, and others) have aroused internal controversy and have weakened Costa Ricans' own sense of the dependability of their constitutional order.

From 1970 to 1980 Costa Rican foreign policy took a course much more independent of the United States than in the two previous decades. This independence included disagreement with the United States over the Nicaraguan insurrection, and increased links to the socialist bloc, to oil suppliers Mexico and Venezuela, and to Europe. However, since 1980, growing apprehension about spreading instability in Central America has created great cross pressures for Costa Rica. Mexico recognized the Salvadoran insurgents while Venezuela denounced them. Economic and political needs clamored for diversity of relations and trading partners, while the United States appeared bent on reasserting its dominance over Central America. Responding to its own concerns and to changing U.S. foreign policy, Costa Rica in 1981 adopted a stance supporting the government of El Salvador, and signed a pact with El Salvador and Honduras to form the Central American Democratic Community to "promote democratic values" and to "create a climate of security."

Despite the trouble to the north, many Costa Rican policy makers greatly feared the consequences of an overt invasion/occupation elsewhere in Central America by the United States (or its surrogates) lest it strengthen the radical left both in the region and within Costa Rica. The perceived risks to both the Costa Rican economy and political consensus from a wider conflict—a flood of refugees, a greatly strengthened left, further loss of trade, tourism, and investment, or expansion of the army—were highly unpalatable to most Costa Rican policy makers. Indeed, refugee problems and increased military expenditures were causing budget difficulties by mid-1983.

Prospects for the solution of these political problems were mixed. Could Monge mobilize sufficient support to force austerity on the powerful middle-class pressure groups and unions and simultaneously soften inflation's blow on the lower classes? Or would Monge's conservative shift in economic policy amount to a "Chileanization" of the economy that benefited wealthy and middle sectors at the cost of the poor? Because of the power of the private sector and middle-class pressure groups within the current system, imposing some austerity upon the PLN's main constituency and redistributing state services to the poor was proving quite difficult as the Monge administration approached its halfway mark.

Prospects for increased attention from the United States and other economically and politically important allies (Mexico, Venezuela) which also value Costa Rican representative democracy seemed better by 1983 than in previous years. The institutional strength and flexibility of the Costa Rican government and its experience in handling dissent with moderation prepare it generally well for coping with even more unrest and subversion than at present without destroying patterned attitudes and behaviors that sustain the present system. If the Monge government should eventually implement further reforms to stabilize the political and economic situations, Costa Rica's democratic political culture could well survive its current strains.

On the negative side, however, were several grave prospects: One political by-product of continued economic austerity policies and perhaps a new devaluation was likely to be greater unrest and increased class conflict. If reforms should favor the lower classes while middle-class interests were not attended to, middle-class mobilization in defense of middle-class interests could occur—as it did in Chile in 1973. If, however, benefits should continue to flow more to the powerful middle sectors, lower-class unrest spurred on by union and party dissidents would undoubtedly rise. As noted, there was evidence by late 1983 that such middle- and lower-class unrest was already building. The government therefore had a difficult course to chart between pressing need and political expediency—in a declining sum game. Should government response to leftist labor militancy prove too heavy-handed, further consolidation and increased militancy of the now divided lower-class parts of the labor movement could easily occur. This would jeopardize needed reforms, the capacity of the government itself to function, and general political stability.

Political conditions elsewhere in Central America showed little promise of improving. Further turmoil on the isthmus would keep up the flow of hungry and politicized refugees/exiles into a Costa Rica in economic recession and already unsettled by subversion and terrorism. Perhaps the most menacing unknown was the prospect of an overt military intervention in El Salvador and/or Nicaragua by the United States, by some other unilateral actor, by other Central American nations, or by an OAS force. Should there be a prolonged occupation or operations by ground forces (lasting more than a few months), the resultant strains upon Costa Rica (popular unrest, labor protests, opinion polarization, increased need for repression of dissent, mobilization for a possible defense of national territory, refugee and exile influx, arms trafficking, and further massive disruption of foreign commerce in the area) could shatter current institutional arrangements. Under such multiple and severe strains, popular frustration would rise, class polarization would develop and intensify, and the rate of change of political culture would accelerate immensely.

Conclusion

It appeared highly likely in mid-1983 that one of the more important variables controlling the future of Costa Rica's current institutional arrangements was the possibility of a military invasion or occupation of some other Central American countries by hemispheric anti-communist forces. Irrespective of its effects upon the target country, such an event—especially if prolonged—would likely aggravate Costa Rica's economic and political strains so greatly as to alter significantly the chances for the survival of representative democracy there. Should no such invasion/occupation occur, the Monge-PLN government would have more time and opportunity to improve its performance on reforms, austerity measures, and curtailments of public services. Emphasis on economic stimulation and development could eventually move the economy out of its doldrums. By thus reducing internal strains, economic recovery would help Costa Rican political institutions survive the turbulent 1980s.

The other critical set of variables includes economic recovery and government policy performance. A weak recovery, continued depression, or continued poor policy performance by the Monge administration would leave unemployment at high levels, prolong the weakness of the *colón*, and keep imported inflation at high levels. Organized labor would thus continue to press for protection, the goals of middle- and lower-class unions and groups would continue to conflict sharply, and the depressed Atlantic zone would continue to be a tinderbox. Such conditions would most likely gradually increase the electoral strength and mass base of the parties of the left and of the CUT/CGT labor confederation. Anti-intervention versus anticommunist sympathies would intensify, polarizing the population and weakening support for democratic institutions. Increased subversion and terrorism and a further radicalization of the Costa Rican left would be likely consequences of invasion/occupation elsewhere in the region. Government efforts to control such activities could, if not very carefully managed, begin to erode human rights guarantees.

At that point, any of three possibilities could develop, depending upon unpredictable conditions. First, a collapse of the government could result in a takeover of power by the highly mobilized labor and political left. In such a coalition anti-American and Marxist-Leninist ideologies could play an important role. Such a government could be expected to promote extensive redistributive policies and to be far more sympathetic toward Nicaragua and other Central American insurgents than has previously been the case in Costa Rica. Second, such conditions could also result in a coup by moderate elements within the PLN with the goal of forestalling a leftist or rightist takeover and remaking the political system. A third alternative would be a coup by rightist elements. While Costa Rica seemed unlikely to become either a Nicaragua or a Chile, a substantial militarization of the nation would be likely under each of the latter alternatives.

Since the social environment out of which these alternatives would develop would be one of great turmoil, popular mobilization, and violence, the restoration of order by any such new regime would likely involve a substantial setback for human rights. The degree of democracy under a new regime is difficult to predict but rarely have violent transformations of a polity led quickly to the establishment of peaceful, participatory institutions. Changes in the political culture are difficult to predict. On the one hand, much of the turmoil and institutional change Costa Rica has undergone in the twentieth century has increased the amount of democracy present in the polity. It is possible that equal or greater opportunities for popular participation might emerge in the aftermath of a social and political breakdown. The past record should not tempt us, however, to trust facilely that current Costa Rican democratic values could restore democracy later should the current system collapse. The sad histories of Chile and Uruguay reveal how quickly and easily a militarily powerful new regime can crush democratic behavior so effectively that values do not matter. Costa Rica's lack of armed forces provides some encouragement along these lines, but the turmoil in Central America, internal unrest, or U.S. pressure could push Costa Rica toward militarizing.

Notes

1. See, for example, Carl Cohen, *Democracy* (New York: The Free Press, 1973).
2. For an example equating democracy with pluralism-elitism, see Juan Linz, *The Breakdown of Democratic Regimes*, Vol. 1: *Crisis, Breakdown, and Reequilibration* (Baltimore: The Johns Hopkins University Press, 1978), pp. 5–8. To Linz, democracy means nation-states that have Liberal constitutions and are elite-dominated, plural, representative, and have open election of leaders and extensive civil rights.
3. Costa Rica closely resembles Linz's "competitive democracy" and Gary Wynia's "democratic game." See Linz, op. cit., and Gary Wynia, *The Politics of Latin American Development* (Cambridge: Cambridge University Press, 1978).
4. For the purposes of this chapter, I propose here a brief general theory of institutional breakdown. There are considerable similarities to Juan Linz's model of breakdown of democracy and Gary Wynia's treatment of instability of the democratic game in Latin America. I believe, however, that the model has broader applicability than to explain the transformation of constitutional, representative democracy to a post-democratic state (Linz's objective). I prefer the broader approach because I prefer not to assume that a major institutional transformation in Costa Rica would necessarily imply a disappearance of democracy. The degree of democracy in Costa Rica *could be enhanced* by a breakdown of the current system and its replacement with one that affords greater opportunity for popular participation. To illustrate, the Costa Rican civil war of 1948 was a system breakdown that brought about *more democracy,* not less.
5. Linz usefully distinguishes between efficacy (the ability to make needed decisions) and effectiveness (the ability to solve problems by implementing policy). Linz, op. cit., pp. 18–24.
6. The historical material is drawn from a plethora of sources including Carlos Araya Pochet, ed., *Historia económica de Costa Rica, 1950–1970* (San José: Editorial Fernández Arce, 1976); James Backer, *La iglesia y el sindicalismo en Costa Rica* (San José: Editorial Costa Rica, 1978); John Patrick Bell, *Crisis in Costa Rica: The Revolution of 1948* (Austin: The University of Texas Press, 1971); Mavis Hiltunen de Biesanz, Richard Biesanz, and Karen Zubris de Biesanz, *Los costarricenses* (San José: Editorial Universidad Estatal a Distancia, 1979); Mitchell A. Seligson, *Peasants of Costa Rica and the Development of Agrarian Capitalism* (Madison: The University of Wisconsin Press, 1980); and Samuel Stone, *La dinastía de los conquistadores: La crisis del poder en la Costa Rica contemporánea* (San José: Editorial de la

Universidad de Costa Rica—Editorial Universitaria Centroaméricana, 1975); Ricardo Blanco Segura, *Monseñor Sanabria: apuntes biográficos* (San José: Editorial Costa Rica, 1971); Ciro F. S. Cardoso and Héctor Pérez Brignoli, *Centro América y la economía occidental (1520–1930)* (San José: Editorial de la Universidad de Costa Rica, 1977); and Chester Zelaya, et al., *Democracia en Costa Rica? Cinco opiniónes polémicas* (San José: Editorial Universidad Estatal a Distancia, 1978).

7. For material on Costa Rican political culture, see Biesanz, et al., op. cit.; John A. Booth, "Are Latin Americans Politically Rational? Citizen Participation and Democracy in Costa Rica," in John A. Booth and Mitchell A. Seligson, eds., *Political Participation in Latin America*, Vol. 1: *Citizen and State* (New York: Holmes and Meier, 1978); and Seligson and Booth, "Structure and Levels of Political Participation In Costa Rica: Comparing Peasants and City Dwellers," in Seligson and Booth, *Political Participation in Latin America*, Vol. 2: *Politics and the Poor* (New York: Holmes and Meier, 1979).

8. See, for example, Santiago Ruiz Granadinos, ed., *Entidades públicas descentralizadas del istmo centroamericano* (San José: Banco Interamericano de Desarrollo-Instituto Centroamericano de Administración Pública, 1979).

9. Wynia, op. cit.

10. See Burt H. English, *Liberación Nacional in Costa Rica: The Development of a Political Party in a Transitional Society* (Gainesville: University of Florida Press, 1971); and Biesanz, et al., op. cit.

11. John A. Booth and Mitchell A. Seligson, "Peasants as Activists: A Reevaluation of Political Participation in the Countryside," *Comparative Political Studies* 12 (April 1979); and Seligson and Booth, "Structure and Levels of Political Participation," op. cit.

12. John A. Booth, "Democracy and Citizen Action in Costa Rica: The Modes and Correlates of Popular Participation in Politics" (Ph.D. dissertation, The University of Texas at Austin, 1975).

13. Booth and Seligson, "Peasants as Activists," op. cit.

14. Oscar Arias Sánchez, *Nuevos rumbos para el desarrollo costarricense* (San José: Editorial Universitaria Centroamericana, 1979).

15. Arias Sánchez, op. cit.

6

Honduras: The Burden of Survival in Central America

James A. Morris

The Setting

The Republic of Honduras sits astride the middle of the Central American isthmus. Touching the shores of the Atlantic on the north and the Pacific on the south, the country is twice as long from east to west as it is between these oceans. Its Atlantic shoreline of over 600 kilometers is four times that of the Gulf of Fonseca, the country's opening to the Pacific. The North Coast region has thus been geographically and historically oriented outward toward the Caribbean basin.

Honduras is the second largest country in Central America with 112,088 square kilometers of mountainous land interspersed with highland valleys and once-navigable rivers. There are large expanses of pine, hardwood, and broadleaf forests. With an estimated 4.1 million population in 1983, the ratio of people to land is relatively low for Central America—nearly 36 persons per square kilometer. The country can be divided into three general zones—western, central, and eastern. The western zone is mostly mountainous and borders on Guatemala and El Salvador. Historically, this subregion has been the most populous though it makes up only about a fifth of the national territory. It was the southernmost limit of the Mayan civilization and is where the descendants of indigenous peoples—the Lencas—have lived since the conquest by the Spanish.[1] The original Spanish settlers migrated to the cooler highlands to escape the disease ridden and torrid climate of the tropical lowlands along the northern coast.

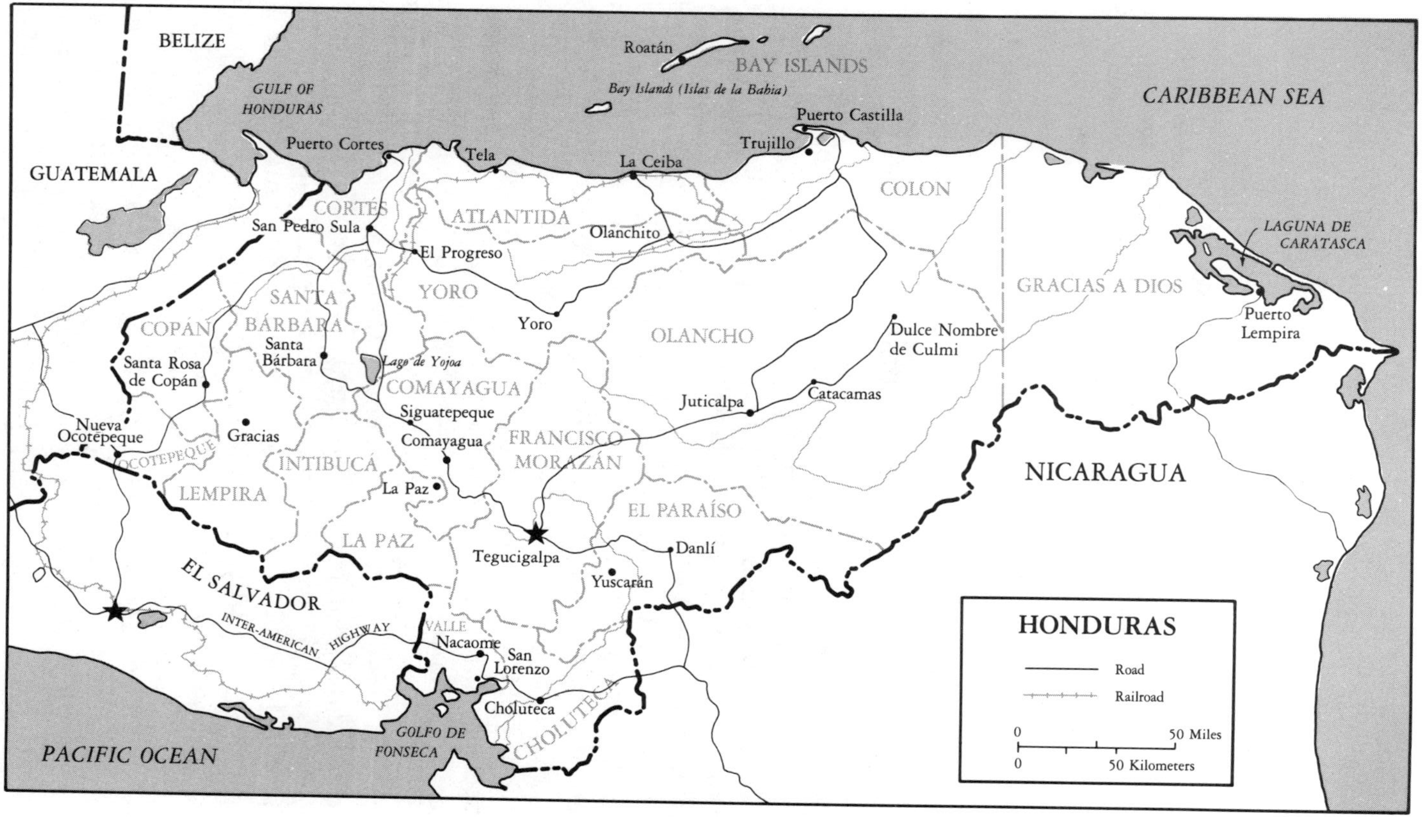
HONDURAS
Road
Railroad
0
50 Miles
0
50 Kilometers
CARIBBEAN SEA
PACIFIC OCEAN
GULF OF HONDURAS
GOLFO DE FONSECA
LAGUNA DE CARATASCA
BELIZE
GUATEMALA
EL SALVADOR
NICARAGUA
BAY ISLANDS
Bay Islands (Islas de la Bahia)
Roatán
Puerto Castilla
Trujillo
La Ceiba
Tela
Puerto Cortes
San Pedro Sula
El Progreso
Olanchito
Yoro
Santa Bárbara
Lago de Yojoa
Santa Rosa de Copán
Gracias
Nueva Ocotepeque
Siguatepeque
Comayagua
La Paz
Tegucigalpa
Yuscarán
Danlí
Juticalpa
Catacamas
Dulce Nombre de Culmi
Puerto Lempira
Nacaome
San Lorenzo
Choluteca
INTER-AMERICAN HIGHWAY
CORTÉS
ATLANTIDA
COLON
GRACIAS A DIOS
SANTA BÁRBARA
YORO
OLANCHO
COPÁN
COMAYAGUA
FRANCISCO MORAZÁN
OCOTEPEQUE
INTIBUCÁ
LEMPIRA
LA PAZ
EL PARAÍSO
VALLE
CHOLUTECA

After 1900, a generalized eastward migration pattern developed and combined with more recent urbanization trends to make the central zone the most populous. Today, much of the population is concentrated in the upland capital city of Tegucigalpa and in San Pedro Sula, the industrial and commercial city located near the North Coast.[2] This central region includes the more urbanized departments, most industry, and is often called the corridor of development.[3] Extending from north to south is a trans-isthmian depression, a series of river and interior mountain valleys. Through this transverse valley, major highways run south from Puerto Cortés and San Pedro Sula to Tegucigalpa and finally to Choluteca.

The three departments of Olancho, Colón, and Gracias a Dios make up the eastern zone, encompassing nearly 45 percent of the national territory. This is the least populated and most isolated region and contains virgin pine forests, unexploited minerals, and natural pasture lands. Few roads penetrate its rugged mountain ranges or extend on to the Mosquitia—the flat coastal lowlands of the far northeast near the border with Nicaragua. Distinct in geography, culture, and history is the department of the Bay Islands (Islas de la Bahía) located off the northern coast near La Ceiba. The British marooned descendants of Negro-Indians (Black Caribs) on these islands prior to the 1800s. The Caribs migrated to the mainland after the Spanish arrived. Not until 1859 was a treaty negotiated with the British that gave Honduras sovereignty over the islands.

Much of Honduras is a jumble of intersecting mountain ranges with no distinct orientation. The higher mountains rise up to nearly 2,900 meters in the western region and average between 1,500 and 2,000 meters in the central portion of the country. Along the 600 kilometer North Coast is a flat strip of alluvial soils through which several rivers meander. It is this littoral and the river valleys where the most fertile agricultural lands are found. Including natural and permanent pastures, about a third of Honduras can be considered arable, but only about 15 to 20 percent of the national territory is actually exploited for agriculture. In contrast to the neighboring republics, Honduras is not covered with layers of volcanic ash since the axis of the Central American volcanic chain skirts the southern limits of the country.

Economic development in Honduras has been hindered by isolation and the inaccessibility of most of the countryside. Many areas are still reached only on foot or by horseback. The rugged topography makes road construction difficult and expensive. Though there are more than 14,000 kilometers of roads, just four decades ago there were only 1,600 kilometers—including all-weather and seasonal routes. The principal highway between Tegucigalpa and the North Coast city of San Pedro Sula was first completed in the 1940s and paved only in 1970. There are scarcely 1,000 kilometers of railways, and since their development was left to the foreign-owned fruit companies, the lines are concentrated in the North and do little to connect this region with the mountainous interior. Tegucigalpa suffers the distinction of being the only Central American capital without rail service.

About 90 percent of the Honduran people are considered to be *mestizo*. The remaining 10 percent are ethnically and racially divided between several Indian cultures, a Black population, and Caucasians. Most of the native population—descendants of the Lenca culture—live in the western departments of Lempira, Intibuca, and La Paz. Isolated groups are found in Santa Bárbara, Yoro, Copán, and in the far northeastern forests of Olancho and Colón. The Black population is composed of two elements—the *morenos*, descendants of the Black Caribs; and Antillean Negroes imported as laborers from Belize, Cayman Islands, and Jamaica.[4]

Another distinguishable ethnic group is the descendants of Eastern Mediterranean immigrants who came between 1900 and 1910. Many Hondurans ascribe to these *árabes* sinister qualities of clannishness and opportunism. Arriving with few resources, the árabes quickly took advantage of the North Coast commercial development that had been neglected by other Hondurans. Social barriers have dropped rapidly, intermarriage is common, and the Levantine community is now thoroughly involved in domestic politics.

Most Hondurans are Catholic, although until the 1960s the church seldom had a decisive historical impact. After independence in 1838, tithes were reduced or eliminated. In the late nineteenth century, Liberal reforms further restricted privileges, legally separated church and state, and revoked the Concordat with the Vatican. With little income or real estate, the Honduran church has been poor and the shortage of priests chronic.[5]

The class structure follows the Central American pattern of a small urban-rural elite, nascent middle and working classes, and a large rural peasantry. Honduras, however, never developed a landowning aristocracy that had a solid foothold in the national economy.[6] Rather, control of the nation's resources fell to foreign investors. The foreign-owned enterprises and the national government became the means of upward mobility. Contemporary elites include both the traditional landowning families of long-established reputation, and the more recently arrived industrial-commercial-financial entrepreneurs concentrated in Tegucigalpa, San Pedro Sula, La Ceiba, Choluteca, and other urban centers. The cities and towns encompass a growing middle sector—commercial and skilled service workers, professionals, technicians, bankers, and educators. The working classes are both urban and semi-rural. Industrial, manufacturing, and government employees are for the most part located in the cities. However, the largest bloc of organized workers are the banana workers of the Tela Railroad Company (United Brands) and the Standard Fruit and Steamship Company (Castle and Cook).

Of the 4.1 million people in Honduras, between 60 and 65 percent live and work in rural areas. The peasant farmer has traditionally been relegated to the fringes of the economy and participated in politics only through the local political bosses. Almost 80 percent of the rural lower classes consist of traditional subsistence farm families whose lack of access to credit, health, and educational services account for much of the poverty indicated by global statistics. The urban lower classes are growing due to migration from the countryside and from small towns to larger cities. Even though living in hillside slums with inadequate housing or services, most of the urban poor regard their plight as temporary and seek opportunities not present in rural Honduras.

While most of the population labors in subsistence agriculture, more than three-quarters of all Honduran export income is derived from commercial-agribusiness operations. The economic impact of the banana industry has recently been reduced in relative terms, falling from 60 percent of exports in 1960 to around 28 percent in the 1980s. Commodities such as coffee, wood, beef, and minerals compete now for export markets. The original investments of the banana companies (1900–1930) have been diversified into manufacturing, chemicals, and stockraising.

In structural terms, the Honduran economy is export dependent for its foreign exchange and for a substantial portion of its gross domestic product. The agrarian nature of the economy and reliance on exports of primary products was established early in Honduran history. Mining and cattleraising initially determined land use patterns. After 1880, Liberal reform governments encouraged the acquisition of private holdings, and provided import and tax concessions which went mostly to foreign investors. It was under this protective Liberal umbrella that mining interests and later the large foreign-owned banana companies came to Honduras.[7] The production of bananas and their export created subsidiary service and manufacturing industries, primarily along the North Coast. The long-term result was the creation of a relatively dynamic economic enclave which traded with the United States and Europe. This outward orientation and the localized nature of infrastructure development led to the formation of a dual economy—a modern capitalist export sector, embedded in but not integrated with the traditional latifundia (ranching) and minifundia (subsistence farming) structure of interior Honduras.

It was not until after World War II that social and economic changes breached divisions between the modern enclave society and the relatively backward precapitalistic economy. Economic diversification increased demand for commodities, and newly available international credit helped to stimulate industrial growth and revitalized the agribusiness-commercial sector. Economic expansion accelerated during the 1950s and on into the mid-1960s. As agriculture became more commercialized, land use patterns were affected which in turn changed the traditional relations between peasant and rural landlord. Landless farmers were evicted from formerly idle private lands, the cost of renting small parcels rose, and in some cases, ranchers illegally appropriated national lands for their own use.[8]

During the early 1960s, industrial production was contributing 13 percent of Honduran exports. Growth was rapid at first, but stabilized near the end of the decade. Limited infrastructure, an underskilled labor force, and a relatively inexperienced entrepreneurial class were principal reasons for the slower rate of expansion. The bulk of Honduran industry consists of sugar refining, flour milling, textile production, beverage and food processing, and light consumer goods. Secondary production includes chemicals, plastics, petroleum derivatives and cement. By the end of the 1980s, it is expected that the long-envisioned pulp and paper mill will be operating in Olancho.

Political History

After the United Provinces of Central America collapsed in 1838, Honduras struggled throughout most of the nineteenth century to establish a workable governmental system. As an independent republic, life was difficult and there was little in the way of resources, leadership, or institutions upon which to base a solid national identity. The rugged mountainous topography and the absence of major communication routes conspired to isolate Honduras from the rest of Central America, and to separate regions from one another. Moreover, there were few if any significant international contacts whether through trade, commerce, or migration. Most Hondurans were engaged in subsistence agricultural production regardless of whether their farms were small or large.

Mining of the country's mineral wealth (silver, gold, lead, zinc) ebbed and flowed in accordance with market prices, levels of investment, and the exhaustion of ore deposits. Coffee did not become a major crop as it did in Costa Rica, Nicaragua, El Salvador, or Guatemala, in part because small and medium sized holdings dominated the land tenure patterns in the highlands of central western Honduras.[9] Most farmers were required to work their own plots and since cultivation and harvest periods were common to all, there were scarcely adequate labor supplies. Coffee required heavy labor during harvest periods. Moreover, the system of roads and transport was inadequate so that coffee that might have been delivered to seaports would have cost more than the same product from other Central American republics. A coffee elite did not develop in Honduras during the middle to late nineteenth century. Instead it was not until after World War II that infrastructure development, credit facilities, and world market prices combined to make coffee a leading export crop.

Governments and self-styled politicians rose and fell in a confusing sequence of fraudulent elections, civil revolts, and international intervention. The domestic base for political stability in Honduras was undermined by regionalism. *Caudillos* established personal networks of loyal followers. Communication among the widely scattered settlements was difficult at best. In the absence of any well-established national authority, the style of political conflict pitted regional caudillos against one another with few rules other than the survival of the strongest, the most cunning, or in some cases, those who were able to enlist the support of neighboring governments.

During the late 1870s and early 1880s, some resolution of the conservative-liberal struggle that prevailed in most of Central America was achieved. The era of Liberal reforms which lasted until the 1940s introduced the principle of positivism, separation of church and state, and the concept that the state should directly support conditions favorable to free enterprise. These principles were first introduced by President Marco Aurelio Soto (1876–83).[10] Government leaders desired to transform the traditional economic structures and create a dynamic, more diverse economy. New legislation replaced the old Spanish colonial laws. Efforts were made to expand the country's export capacity, raise investment capital, and liberalize the state's role in promoting economic growth and development. Internal tariffs and customs duties were suppressed. New authority enabled the national government to collect taxes and revenue with more success. Roads, seaports, and public works projects were initiated as well as telegraph and telephone systems. Hondurans were encouraged to acquire lands offered for sale by the state. Tax exemptions were given to agriculturalists and liberal concessions made to foreign investors. The most important concessions were those granted by the state to foreign-owned enterprises along the North Coast where the banana industry flourished after 1900.

From the turn of the century until the early 1930s, banana cultivation reigned supreme within the Honduran economy and not surprisingly played a central role in the nation's political dynamics. Bananas accounted for as much as 80 percent of export revenue. In 1930, Honduras was the world's leading exporter of bananas, shipping over one-third of the global supply. By the 1950s, the proportion of export revenue earned from bananas dropped to approximately 50 percent and by the 1980s had dropped further to between 25 and 28 percent as coffee, fresh beef, lumber and minerals successfully competed for market shares.

As the major economic resources of the nation came under foreign control and influence, Honduran political elites accommodated their interests to the needs of United Fruit, Standard Fruit, the Cuyamel Fruit Company, and other solidly entrenched foreign investors such as the New York–Honduras Rosario Mining Company.[11] For many professional and technical occupations, working for the companies directly or acting as consultants became important means of social mobility. The nation's resources were tied up in large landed estates or controlled by the large plantations along the fertile northern littoral. The wealth and opportunity offered by the foreign companies was matched only by that present within the Honduran government itself.

The concessions made by the government to foreign investors, though perhaps compromising latitude of action and control, did result in ever-increasing revenues for Honduran administrations. Capturing control over the government then became an attractive goal for the various political factions. To gain control over the state apparatus provided access to wealth, patronage, and personal advancement. No unified social class emerged in Honduras that had a firm grasp on any other solid economic base.

Gradually, two loosely constructed political alliances evolved from the chaotic legacy of the nineteenth century. Under the persistent leadership of Dr. Policarpo Bonilla (president 1894–99), the Liberal Party of Honduras (PLH) was formed and was able to govern intermittently until 1932. Dissidents and more conservative Liberals eventually grew tired of internal party struggles and moved to organize the National Party of Honduras (PNH) in 1916. During the 1920s, Nationalist followers unsuccessfully rebelled against the Liberal administrations. Finally, an experienced, strong-willed caudillo emerged to lead the National Party into power through fair elections in 1932. In the next two decades under General Tiburcio Carías Andino, the PNH became a highly disciplined, well-integrated political organization.

Carías utilized networks of personal loyalty, patronage, and at times coercion to extend government authority to most parts of the nation. He maintained close ties with the large fruit companies whose objectives were to create and maintain political conditions that would help preserve their economic interests. By linking the social and economic welfare of Honduran elites to their activities, the long-term goals of the banana companies would be more assured. In turn, Carías and his Nationalist followers would be supported in their retention of political power. Dominating the executive and the legislative branches, the Carías government was able to maintain itself in power without the benefit of elections. *Continuismo,* the practice of extending terms of office through legal maneuvers, kept Carías at the helm of the Honduran government from 1932 until 1949.

The era of Carías was the first lengthy period of political stability achieved in Honduras since its independence from Spain in 1821. It was a time of national consolidation, centralization of the state, and imposed authority. Though a measure of political discipline was achieved, the legacy of the Carías era was a dubious one in that the nation was ill prepared to meet the challenges of modernization and social change after World War II.

Honduras has experienced a rapid transition over the past three decades. Economic diversity and social differentiation began to foster a realignment of social relations, and the development of these new forces eventually challenged the traditional political elites that had coalesced around the Liberal and National parties. Demands for wider political participation by new groups, the rise of a modern professionalized military, and intra-elite competition were paralleled by significant growth in the national government as it assumed a leading role in development of infrastructure and economic planning.

With the retirement of Carías in 1949, Hondurans were faced with the task of electing new leaders—a process they had not engaged in for more than sixteen years. The long-exiled Liberal Party failed to mount a successful challenge and the designated successor to Carías, Juan Manuel Gálvez, assumed office in 1949 with over 80 percent of the national vote. Gálvez modernized the government bureaucracy and liberalized the political and social climate. Near the end of his term, he was confronted with a massive strike of banana workers that threatened to spread throughout the nation. After nearly three months of tension, workers gained the right to organize and became a decisive element in Honduran politics.

This new political role for labor was exercised during the next two national elections which favored the Liberal Party and its leader Dr. Ramón Villeda Morales. The Liberals carried 48 percent of the popular vote in the 1954 elections, but since the required absolute majority had not been obtained, the selection of the president was constitutionally delegated to the National Congress. The refusal of the badly split National Party to attend the Congress and the overall confusion permitted Vice-President Julio Lozano Díaz to declare himself president in accordance with provisions contained in the 1936 Constitution.

Lozano's zealous attempt to continue in power was cut short as disillusioned National and Liberal political factions invited the military to step in. For more than a year (1956–57), a military junta exercised governmental authority, pledging to return power to civilian hands via open and honest elections. Villeda Morales and his Liberal followers then swept into power, winning all eighteen departments in the 1957 constituent assembly elections (see Table 6.1).

The Liberal interlude brought significant reforms—labor legislation, social security, and the 1962 Agrarian Reform Law. Honduras officially became part of the Central American Common Market in 1960. Even so, the Villeda Morales government was buffeted by pressures for broad social change and by the resistance of traditional elites. Patterns of caudillo politics remained to plague the administration with revolt and conspirational political deals undermining Liberal policies. Attempts to bolster the government through the creation of a Civil Guard posed a threat to the increasingly powerful Honduran armed forces. As tensions arose within the political system, the military led by Air Force Colonel Oswaldo López Arellano brought down the Liberal government in late 1963.

Colonel López Arellano enlisted the shrewd and experienced National Party stalwart, Ricardo Zúñiga, as his major civilian political ally. Liberal politicians were sent into exile for the time being, labor and peasant activism was controlled, and the expanding state bureaucracy was filled with National Party supporters. Colonel (and later General) López Arellano was elected president of the Republic in 1965. The Liberals gained minority representation in the National Congress, but the Nationals controlled the legislature, the judiciary, and the bureaucracy. The

Table 6.1. National elections in Honduras, 1954–81

Year	Liberal Party	National Party	Third Parties**	Total Voters	Registered Voters
1954	122,312 (47.9%)[a]	79,648 (31.2%)[a]	53,241 (20.9%)[a]	255,231	NA
1956*	41,724 (10.1%)	2,003 (0.5%)	370,318 (89.4%)	414,045	NA
1957*	209,109 (61.5%)	101,274 (29.8%)	29,489 (8.7%)	339,872 (65.1%)[b]	522,359
1965*	272,062 (44.2%)	335,726 (49.3%)	—	614,696 (75.4%)	815,261
1971	269,989 (44.4%)	299,807 (49.3%)	—	608,342 (67.5%)	900,658
1980*	495,768 (49.4%)	423,642 (42.2%)	35,044 (3.5%)	1,003,470 (81.3%)	1,233,756
1981	636,392 (52.4%)	491,089 (40.4%)	48,582 (4.0%)	1,214,735 (80.7%)	1,504,658

*Constituent Assembly elections.
**1954, MNR; 1956, PUN; 1957, MNR; 1980, PINU; 1981, PINU and PDCH.
[a]Percentage of total voters.
[b]Percentage of registered voters.
Sources: 1954, *El Cronista* (20 October 1954); 1956, Anderson in Needler; 1957, *El Día* (23 September 1957); 1965, 1971, Consejo Nacional de Elecciónes; 1980, 1981, Tribunal Nacional de Elecciónes.

president with Zúñiga as his secretary made most policy decisions.

The civil-military alliance enhanced and aided the emergence of the Honduran military as a major force in Honduran politics. Relations between the military and the Nationals were traditionally close due to family contacts between the civilian elite and the officer corps. Access to increased state funding and the growing institutional identity also aided the consolidation of the military as an autonomous entity.[12] The era of López Arellano ushered in what was to be more than two decades of military rule, whether direct or indirect.

López Arellano's first term (1965–71) was punctuated by conservative policies and economic stagnation. The newly emerged commercial and industrial classes grew perturbed. Their view was that the government was inept and many bureaucrats corrupt. As world market demands increased the local commercialization of agriculture, rural unrest increased with peasants occupying both private lands and public lands that had been illegally acquired by large estate owners. This cycle of tension was interrupted by the 1969 border war with El Salvador and a hurricane later that year. Soon after, however, pressures to institute aggressive development policies and minimal reforms were resumed by progressive political groups.

Potential conflict appeared likely as the constitutionally mandated national elections approached in 1971. Progressive private sector organizations from the North Coast in alliance with some labor and peasant groups struck a last-minute bargain with General López Arellano. The Liberal and National parties were called upon to share power and act in concert to solve the nation's development problems.[13]

The ensuing National Unity Plan, or Pacto, was reluctantly accepted by the parties. The Nationals won the 1971 elections and control of the congress, with Ramón Ernesto Cruz becoming president. However, Ricardo Zúñiga was appointed Minister of Interior and Justice. From this post, he was able to control most government policies and influence the bureaucracy. The Pacto Government (1971–72) failed to act decisively, or implement even minimal reforms. General López, with the support of the progressive and popular sectors, returned to power in late 1972, this time as a reformist leader.

The December coup initiated a decade of direct rule by the military. López was succeeded by Colonel Juan Alberto Melgar Castro in 1975, who was followed in turn by Colonel Policarpo Paz García in 1978. With each change in leadership, the regime became less reformist and more developmentalist. Social peace and political order were deemed necessary to attract international public and private capital to Honduras to finance state-led development programs. The Liberal and National parties were temporarily cast aside as younger military officers and technocrats proceeded to implement emergency decrees that allowed the state to assume a more aggressive role in national development.

But pressures to broaden the political process and eventually

Table 6.2. Chief executives and changes of government in Honduras, 1932–82

Tiburcio Carías Andino (1933–49)	Elections	30 October 1932
	New Constitution	1936
	Term Extended	1939
Juan Manuel Gálvez (1949–54)	Elections	11 October 1948
Julio Lozano Díaz (1954–56)	Elections	10 October 1954
	Elections	7 October 1956
Military Triumvirate (1956–57)	Golpe	21 October 1956
Ramón Villeda Morales (1957–63)	Elections	21 September 1957
Col. Oswaldo López Arellano (1963–65)	Golpe	3 October 1963
Gen. Oswaldo López Arellano (1965–71)	Elections	12 February 1965
Ramón Ernesto Cruz (1971–72)	Elections	28 March 1971
Gen. Oswaldo López Arellano (1972–75)	Golpe	4 December 1972
Gen. Juan Alberto Melgar Castro (1975–78)	Autogolpe	22 April 1975
Gen. Policarpo Paz García (1978–80)	Autogolpe	7 August 1978
Gen. Policarpo Paz García (1980–82)	Elections	20 April 1980
Roberto Suazo Córdova (1982–86)	Elections	29 November 1981

return the reins of government to civilian hands reappeared. Conservatives called for a return to constitutional rule. Since the historical parties had held a monopoly on electoral competition, this was a natural course to follow. New political movements such as the Innovation and Unity Party (PINU) and the Christian Democrats (PDCH) sought legal recognition and felt that open and honest elections were reasonable means to demonstrate the growing support that they claimed. The conservative policies of the military governors, combined with blatant corruption (both military and civilian) and a stagnating economy during the late 1970s, caused disaffection among elements of the peasant sector and organized labor.

Such domestic unrest was underscored as the Nicaraguan Sandinistas toppled the Somoza regime in 1979. National constituent assembly elections were held in 1980 in partial response to United States encouragement of democratic alternatives to change in Central America. The military governors reluctantly carried on as the Liberal Party won control of the Assembly, despite predictions that the National Party (in alliance with the armed forces) would assure themselves victory at the polls.

During the term of the Constituent Assembly (July 1980–January 1982) General Paz García maintained the military's predominance by ensuring his selection as provisional president. This transitional administration, preoccupied with the tasks of revising the electoral law and devising a new constitution, was heavily influenced by the military, and attempts to investigate corruption were easily thwarted.

In January 1982, the Liberal Party leader, Dr. Roberto Suazo Córdova assumed the presidency after resoundingly defeating the Nationals in the elections of November 1981. The Liberals won almost 53 percent of the popular vote, 14 out of 18 departments, and 61 percent of the local municipal councils. Although the military governors had formally retreated from the halls of government, the balance of political power remained with the armed forces. Conscious of political realities, the newly-elected president and the Liberal controlled National Congress ratified Colonel Gustavo Alvarez Martínez, commander of the Public Security Force (FUSEP), as head of the armed forces. Barely four months later, Alvarez was promoted to brigadier general. The general then consolidated his control over the nation's military forces by reducing the size and functions of the Superior Council of the Armed Forces (CONSUFFAA) and isolating his closest rivals in the high command.

Nature of the Crisis

The political struggle in Honduras during the 1980s and beyond will center around the clash between new sociopolitical forces and traditional elites. The stakes involved in the competition among conservative ranching interests, newer commercial and financial elites, and the popular sectors include control over resources of the state. To this end, labor unions, peasant groups, and progressive elements of the small middle class have demanded greater political representation and pressed for economic reforms. Political change is inevitable if Hondurans are to accommodate new groups, make strides toward economic development, and devise institutions that will facilitate national integration.

Periods of political uncertainty since 1950 have been bridged by interludes of military rule. The erosion of traditional social relations, outmoded political institutions controlled by caudillos, and economic stagnation gradually created a political void. The old guard elite's control over the national government and maintenance of the status quo was preserved in part through military intervention. Under pressures of widening political participation the Honduran regime has survived through a unique combination of cultural and social attributes, although signs of repression appeared as the Central American crisis unfolded. Even so, the "hardening" of the Honduran political system during the latter 1970s was sporadic and uneven, and cannot be compared with that of neighboring regimes. A certain degree of political stability under military rule, similar to that attained during the Carías era, was achieved. And measurable progress was made in the country's economic development.

Regardless, the Honduran polity is vulnerable to both domestic and external challenges. New groups seeking access to the political process place in doubt the capacity of contemporary political institutions, and a potential crisis of legitimacy has resulted. The low absolute level of national development, dependency on agricultural exports, and fluctuating world market prices expose Honduras to external political influences and economic policy made by both public and private international financial institutions. Currents of revolution in Central America and the fragility of regimes in Guatemala and El Salvador add to the woes of Honduras.

Political Aspects

In predominantly rural Honduras, traditional elites have governed the nation and regulated political participation through the long-established Liberal and National parties. Both parties included ranchers, workers, and peasants among their loyal rank-and-file. However, there are significant differences in the pattern of political support. The strength of the more conservative Nationals tends to reside in the rural, less-developed regions of the country. The Liberals, governing for less than ten of the past fifty years, are more factionalized. But the PLH has been able to hold on to its urban, working-class, and more progressive support base, winning impressive electoral victories in 1980 and 1981.

The PNH dominated Honduran politics beginning in 1932 when the party's caudillo, Tiburcio Carías Andino, assumed the presidency. After World War II, new political sectors emerged to push for significant but non-revolutionary changes. The nationwide labor strike of 1954 was a major turning point, and the reappearance of the PLH under Villeda Morales in 1957 temporarily opened the political system. In 1963, Nationalist political factions recaptured power in alliance with the reorganized armed forces. Intra-elite divisions and the lack of unity among new political participants left a political vacuum that was eventually filled by the military. After the mid-1960s, the military acquired a self-interest in power and economic opportunity, a pattern not unlike that of the traditional elites whose focal point was control of the government.

Honduras was undergoing a classic set of modernization problems with old institutions undermined by change and increasing demands being made to open up the political process. Political fragmentation was aggravated as power was dispersed among the anachronistic political parties, new interest groups, and the military.[14] The new interest groups failed to merge their sectoral interests into or with a particular political movement. Instead, electoral participation was still dominated by the traditional political apparatus. The traditional parties have endured despite retrograde structures and visions. Old-line political bosses still plead their case in the villages and hamlets. Control over the electoral machinery enabled conservatives—for the most part the PNH with ties to the armed forces, but Liberals as well—to inhibit official competition by new parties. Failing that, direct manipulation at the polls and violence against voters by party-sponsored groups such as the Mancha Brava increased political tensions and undermined legitimacy.

The return to civilian rule in 1982 under Liberal President Suazo Córdova raised hopes and expectations. Disillusionment returned to haunt the administration and infect the body politic as familiar patterns of caudillo politics and military rule soon reappeared. General Alvarez's rise, and Suazo Córdova's enthusiastic support of the armed forces confirmed what most Hondurans suspected or already believed—that real power still resided with the military.[15] National Party representatives refused to attend the presidential inaugural; and later on the party threatened to withdraw its deputies from the National Congress. The PNH, stunned by two decisive losses, now had to cope with internal factions that were either dissatisfied with the party's traditional mold or ready to challenge Ricardo Zúñiga who had controlled the fortunes of the Nationalists for nearly two decades. The left wing of the Liberal Party, ALIPO, though forming an important part of the Liberal's political support base, was not significantly included within the Suazo government. Dissatisfaction surfaced as ALIPO itself divided into subfactions in 1983.

Factional competition, the government's difficulty in acquiring confidence vis-à-vis the military, and the inability of the Nationalists to function as a loyal opposition distracted the regime. The Liberal administration was challenged by peasants, militant sectors of organized labor, and a nationwide strike of teachers. Most of the demands were economic, but implicit was the ongoing quest for inclusion and participation in the society and polity well beyond the electoral process. Serious economic and development problems, though not ignored, were not addressed properly. At least this was the public's perception as reflected in the daily press. Signs of official corruption persisted despite Suazo's campaign theme of "revolution, work, and honesty." As economic conditions deteriorated further, external pressures upon Honduras exacerbated the country's social and political tensions.

Crime rates rose with kidnappings and bank robberies becoming more widespread; and dramatic incidents of terrorism became more frequent. The discovery of clandestine graves outside Tegucigalpa shocked public sensibilities. Signs of official repression, which had appeared early in 1980, began to develop ominous patterns. Arbitrary arrests and detentions rose with questions about individuals and leaders who had "disappeared."

Economic Aspects

These political difficulties were grounded upon an unstable base of economic growth and development. Poverty and daily hardships are part of Honduran life. The economic downturn at the beginning of the 1980s was costly to the small middle sector and impacted severely upon the working classes. Inflation and scarcity of basic grains raised the cost of food. The difference between the contemporary era and the 1950s is that the poor workers and rural peasants have since attained some degree of political awareness. Access to the media, a leadership cadre, and network of organizations are new elements within the political system. Peasant associations, cooperatives, and slum-dweller organizations serve to activate the poor.

Social and economic indicators provide an idea of the immensity of the problem facing the Honduran regime. Literacy rates are increasing but still only 60 percent of the population is considered functionally literate. From 60 to 70 percent of the economically active population work in agriculture and most are involved in subsistence cultivation, sharecropping, or as migrant farm workers. Infant mortality rates in Honduras are the highest in Central America and studies suggest that up to 90 percent of the children less than five years of age suffer to some extent from malnutrition.[16] Schools, health facilities, and similar social services have increased, but delivery of those services has been hampered by the lack of skilled technicians and administrative inefficiencies. While these services are more available in urban areas, the rate of urbanization has accelerated, placing greater burdens on the government.

Many of the country's natural resources have yet to be exploited. Inaccessibility of remote areas, mountainous terrain and antiquated forms of land use have presented formidable obstacles to national development. With the exception of banana cultivation and other export crops, only a small portion of the nation's agricultural output utilizes modern production techniques. Numerous farmers still produce barely enough to feed their families and perhaps a small surplus to exchange for other goods. Subsistence levels of production are maintained because most small plots (minifundia) are located on marginal lands that are not amenable to mechanization or more efficient cultivation. In addition, most credit facilities are not designed to aid the marginal farmer or landless peasant. Cooperatives and other types of associative production units have been successful; but cooperatives are often skeleton organizations and members resist change, or are unable to make the initial sacrifices in order to acquire extra capital.

The large landed estates of the interior highland valleys have also tended to produce at subsistence levels. The hacienda economy, primarily based on stockraising and some crops, is a form of extensive production. Historically, the rancher produced little more than was required to support the hacienda. Thus, large expanses of land were utilized inefficiently. After World War II, market demand and urban growth induced changes as cattle production was increased to take advantage of export opportunities. Cotton, sugarcane, and other cash crops were cultivated and in some cases supplanted basic grain production. The agricultural economy has a dual nature: the subsistence aspect of the traditional forms (hacienda-minifundia) contrasted with a modern export-oriented sector. Because of this dual system, much of the arable land in Honduras (15 to 30 percent of the total national territory) is underutilized.

Agricultural exports are crucial to the Honduran economy, providing the ability to pay for import needs, finance investments, and support the government's national development efforts. The small industrial sector is highly dependent on imported raw materials, equipment, and technology. The costs of crude petroleum have translated into higher fuel prices for individual households as well as for enterprises and transportation services.

Honduran export income varies in accordance with international market prices and levels of production. Silver, lead, zinc, and other metal/mineral prices are determined by world market forces. Similarly, prices of coffee, meat, and fruit fluctuate in response to international supply and demand. Production levels are often affected by weather and seasonal crop failures. The Honduran North Coast is subject to hurricanes. In 1974, Hurricane Fifi devastated thousands of hectares in banana and other crops. High winds toppled the banana stalks, and flooding in the aftermath of torrential rains left much land underwater or heavily eroded. Plant disease can wreak havoc with the medium-sized farms of coffee producers. Sometimes Honduras is subject to periods of drought, and with few lands under irrigation, a delayed or short rainy season leaves the nation's small farmers and peasants in a precarious position.

The rising costs of petroleum imports during the 1970s, falling prices for traditional exports, and increased public sector investments contributed to government budget deficits. Development programs have pushed international borrowing to new limits as extensive credits have been required for ambitious undertakings such as the El Cajón dam and the Olancho forestry project. Higher foreign debt, inflation, world credit shortages, and declining terms of trade have shaken the Honduran economy.

External Aspects

Economic dependency and short-term economic crises weaken the Honduran regime and frustrate efforts at national development. To this structural facet of dependency is added the regional crisis of conflict and revolution within Central America. Historically, Honduras has been vulnerable to outside interference. Often the domestic political balance has been tipped by rebels or political factions supported by Guatemalan or Nicaraguan leaders.

Honduras is at once a landbridge and sanctuary within Central America. Many problems have been created with the flow of refugees from Nicaragua, El Salvador, and Guatemala. The location of Honduras and its porous, isolated frontiers leave the country open to infiltration by subversive elements. Thus, both revolutionary forces and defenders of the *ancien régime* in Central America have a stake in what happens in the country.

More than 40,000 people have sought refuge in Honduras. For the most part, they have fled the violence of rebellion and counterinsurgency campaigns. Many refugees from El Salvador have lived in camps since 1979. Thousands of Miskitu Indians crossed into northeastern Honduras in 1982 when the Sandinistas attempted to extend their control into the historically isolated Nicaraguan province of Zelaya. Members of Somoza's defunct National Guard and other anti-Sandinista elements have made forays into Nicaragua from Honduras. The resulting clashes between Sandinistas and anti-Sandinistas have kept tensions high along the Honduran-Nicaraguan border.

The geopolitics of regional violence in Central America has dragged Honduras unwillingly into the fray. During 1981 and 1982, terrorism and insurgent actions intruded upon the relatively tranquil political environment. In May 1982, insurgents captured a SAHSA airliner and held its passengers for several days. In July, the capital city lapsed into darkness when the electrical grid was heavily damaged by explosives. In September of the same year, one hundred business leaders attending an economic conference in San Pedro Sula were held hostage for eight days. Bombs have exploded outside buildings housing U.S. owned corporations. Attacks were made upon the U.S. Embassy and military advisors. Honduran authorities have uncovered various "safe houses," arms caches, and clandestine radio stations.

Most of the terrorist activity has been claimed by the Lorenzo Zelaya Brigade of the Popular Revolutionary Forces and the "Cinchoneros," an armed wing of the Popular Liberation Movement. The strategy, tactics, equipment, and personnel involved strongly indicated that El Salvador's revolutionary front, the FMLN, had been assisting Honduran dissidents and leftists. It is also believed that the Sandinista government of Nicaragua had encouraged terror and disruption in Honduras.

Revolutionary forces, whether emanating from Cuba or from among indigenous elements in Central America, had for some time utilized Honduran territory as a means to supply arms and provide logistical support. It was thus to be expected that Hon-

Table 6.3. U.S. aid to Honduras, 1979–84 (millions of dollars)

	FY 1979	FY 1980	FY 1981	FY 1982	FY 1983	FY 1984*
Economic**	29.1	53.1	36.4	80.6	99.6	86.2
Military	2.3	3.9	8.9	31.3	37.3	41.0
Total	31.4	57.0	45.3	111.9	136.9	127.2

*Proposed
**Includes Economic Support Funds
Sources: *U.S. Overseas Loans and Grants;* Obligations and Loan Authorizations, July 1, 1945–September 30, 1981; WOLA, *Occasional Paper #2* (May 1982); *Country Reports on Human Rights, Practices for 1982,* Committee on Foreign Relations, U.S. Senate and Committee on Foreign Affairs, U.S. House—Joint Committee Report, 98th Congr., 1st sess. (February 1983); Committee on Foreign Relations, U.S. Senate, "The Situation in Honduras," 97th Congr., 2nd sess. (December 1982); and WOLA, *Washington in Focus,* Vol. 1, No. 2 (14 October 1983), p. 4.

duras would eventually gain the full attention of the region's insurgents. Such attention came with the temporary lull in the Salvadoran conflict early in 1982 and the growing insecurity of the Nicaraguan regime. Collaboration of Honduran security forces with El Salvador along the western frontier, an apparent tolerance of anti-Sandinista groups on Honduran soil, and the expanding role of the U.S. military caused revolutionary forces to turn toward Honduras. An attempt was made to accelerate the demise of the Suazo government, stimulate official repression, and widen the regional conflict.

U.S. foreign policy must be considered as another external aspect of the Honduran crisis. The principal objective of that policy has been to enhance the regime's opportunity for survival. The United States has supplied bilateral military sales credits and provided military advisors. Monies have been allocated to expand three military airstrips. Port facilities are being constructed on both the northern and southern coasts; and joint exercises, although held annually, were greatly expanded in 1982 and 1983 (see Table 6.3). Earlier, the Reagan administration approved a diverse plan of covert operations directed at Nicaragua said to cost more than $19 million. The plan included support funneled to the various anti-Sandinista groups freely operating on Honduran territory.[17]

The original intent of U.S. policy was to insulate Honduras from the regional violence. But the objectives evolved more toward increasing the pressure upon the Sandinista government in Nicaragua. The impact (if not the intent) of this policy was to reinforce the already dominant position of the Honduran armed forces within the constellation of domestic political actors. To some degree, the role forced upon Honduras by regional geopolitics as well as by U.S. policy focused the attention of the insurgents upon the country.

It is still questionable whether Honduras has developed the institutional capacity to maintain domestic social and political peace. The long-term impact of external forces is likely to erode the ability of the regime to implement socioeconomic reforms and to promote political compromise between progressive and traditional sectors. The Honduran "oasis" has become a magnet for regional conflict, and the crisis atmosphere has disrupted the tranquil environment within which domestic problems might be effectively managed.

Fundamentally, the Honduran crisis is one of a regime searching for a workable, contemporary institutional arrangement. The issues of political and social participation and integration of the polity remain key problems for future governments. Beginning with the 1980s, political uncertainty had been exacerbated by economic deterioration and the dynamics of revolutionary change in Central America. Short-term and long-term economic crises heightened political tensions, making the government's task even more complex. At the same time, the fragmentation of political power, excessively partisan competition, and new signs of violence hindered the formation of a constructive political consensus. Conflict between traditional elite sectors and the more numerous politically awakened middle classes, workers, and peasants has yet to be resolved. A solution to the Honduran crisis lies in devising a domestic political consensus that will facilitate institution-building, manage conflict, promote national integration, and enhance the legitimacy of Honduran governments.

Adaptation and Survival

Honduras has muddled through internal political crises, weathered the worst storms of its dependent export economy, and resisted the more acerbative forces generated by the Central American crisis. Despite obvious weaknesses, the country has demonstrated an ability to avoid conflict such as unfolded in Nicaragua, El Salvador, and Guatemala. Honduran society is less polarized than that of its neighboring republics. This is explained in part by a less pronounced degree of social stratification. The distance between upper and lower classes is also reduced because Hondurans continue to talk to one another. Distinct political sectors differ on a wide range of issues, yet they are able to fashion agreements and understandings. The personal level of communication, the intimacy of the society, and to some extent the overlapping relations of economic, social, and family ties facilitate a common ground and some perspective of mutual benefit.

Another factor influencing adaptation is the success of both traditional and more recently formed institutions (including the military) in diffusing political tensions. Reducing the possibilities of conflict has not always been intentional nor driven by altruistic motives. At times, external pressures, most often from the United States, have been the impetus behind socioeconomic reforms or decisions to hold fair and open elections. The result of occasional but incomplete reforms has been an imposed political order achieved through repression of radical activity in combination with orthodox patterns of political participation.

Political Aspects of Adaptation

The armed forces of Honduras became the repository of political power as the consensus of traditional elites dissolved in the post–World War II era. New civilian political sectors have yet to develop sufficient influence to mount a successful challenge. During the 1950s and 1960s, erosion of traditional social relations contributed to the formation of horizontal class-based or sectoral relations in the form of new political alliances and interest group organizations. From just a few nationally organized groups, a plethora of business associations appeared.[18] The emergence of class consciousness and new perspectives, coupled with the development of national organizational ties, was instrumental in the rise of an active peasant movement.

However, inexperience and divisions within various sectors inhibited the building of solid political bases. Though the range and number of groups and associations is significant, and though demands are made directly to government agencies, the new sectors that emerged over the past three decades have failed to translate their interests into a viable political movement.

Without any direct political challenge, the historical two-party system has endured. Despite anachronistic practices and retrograde visions, it is the Liberal and National parties that attract most voters and retain their respective bases of political support. The parties claim adherents among the landed elites, urban sectors, and the poorer rural classes. In some respects, this multiclass profile lends an air of similarity to the two parties. Both the PLH and the PNH have sought to preserve their interests by maintaining the ongoing regime and avoiding drastic transformation of social and economic structures.

But socioeconomic change along with differing political experiences have created some important distinctions between the parties.[19] While multiclass support has been maintained, the core of the National Party support is to be found in the less-developed regions where political bossism lingers. The PNH, the party of the caudillos and creature of the wily General Carías, sits upon the classical structure of personalist political leadership. This traditional structure, however, is beginning to disappear as more people migrate to the towns and cities. More rural workers have become migratory and thus the control that local political leaders have had over their economic welfare has been diluted. Also contributing to the difficulties of the National Party was the shrewd but secretive style of Ricardo Zúñiga, a style that conveyed the image of intrigue and corruption associated with the PNH.

After the solid electoral defeats in 1980 and 1981, latent demands for change surfaced within the National Party. For years members of Zúñiga's inner circle had bided their time. Younger party stalwarts chafed at the less-than-democratic internal politics of the PNH. The electoral losses triggered calls for new leadership and launched several factions as they fought for control over provincial executive committees.[20]

The very existence of factions within the PNH is significant in that it might eventually lead to internal party reforms and perhaps sensitize party leaders to national issues. On the other hand, the factions were organized to support strong political personalities; and the dialogues, temporary alliances, and criticisms were woven together by self-seeking interests of leaders and rank and file alike. Meanwhile, enlightened debate about the evolving economic, political, and international crises remained dramatically absent.

The Liberal Party, despite being out of power for most of the past fifty years and despite chronic factionalism, has constructed an image of comparative rectitude, openness, and reformism. Its political base was reestablished during the 1950s among the emerging urban middle sectors and the organized labor movement. By retaining the voting allegiance of its left wing—the Popular Liberal Alliance (ALIPO)—the PLH has been able to broaden its urban support base. In addition, the coffee growers with medium sized holdings have joined the Liberals as an important voting bloc. If current trends continue, the PLH should further benefit from expanding urbanization and heightened political awareness.

The historical parties have survived partly because their followers have been bound to them through traditional social ties and networks of personal loyalty. These relations have deteriorated under pressure of social mobilization and modernization. But party loyalties have endured even though peasants, workers, and urban middle class groups have developed other organizational ties and often communicate to the government through their own separate channels. The parties, of course, have maintained an electoral system that works in their favor by restricting official recognition of new political parties, manipulating registration of voters, as well as by controlling the casting and tallying of the actual votes. The simultaneous election of national and local officials also tends to support straight party voting.

The irony of the current Honduran situation is that these so-called retrograde institutions (the historical parties) may be one of the keys to survival and adaptation. Lingering traditional values and modes of political interaction have served to maintain communication patterns throughout the country. Similarly, the multiclass nature of party adherence helps preserve amicable relationships among the various social strata. Elites associated with the PLH and PNH have resisted change and have been unable to deal adequately with problems of national development. Nevertheless, there exists within these traditional structures the basis for institutions that might eventually function to integrate the polity.

Meanwhile, the military governors have imposed order and political stability. Even with the return of government to civilian hands, the armed forces retain power and still function with strong praetorian overtones, influencing who actually governs and what kind of policies are implemented. An important characteristic affecting the military's ability to govern has been its newness as an institution.[21] The Honduran armed forces reached a status of professionalism only during the late 1950s. Thus as an institution, the military in Honduras has few, if any, historical commitments to traditional political elites as do their counterparts in El Salvador and Guatemala.

Regardless, the military has maintained a conservative bias, insisting on order and social peace. Originally, ties to the polity were through the National Party. But as the armed forces became more professionalized, an institutional identity was formed. The trauma of the 1969 war with El Salvador, explosive rural conditions, and the abject failure of the traditional elites to manage domestic crisis stimulated the armed forces to review their own capabilities and to revise the military's national role. National security and national development converged and the military shifted its role perception from that of an occasional political arbiter toward broader involvement in political and economic affairs. This new professionalism eventually led the armed forces to assume power and govern directly for a decade.

Besides diffusion of tensions through progressive legislation, dialogue, and some socioeconomic reforms, the national elections that returned government to civilians in 1982 were another facet of Honduran adaptation to crisis. Rising popular dissatisfaction paralleled the military government's turn toward more conservative policies. Elites within the ostracized political parties were impatient. And after the sudden collapse of the Somoza dynasty, the United States encouraged the return to constitutional rule. The elections themselves were characterized by multiparty competition and high-level voter participation in what were termed "civic fiestas."[23] Positive expectations were derived from the process, as Hondurans sensed that their elections, national debates, and constituent assembly contrasted starkly with the escalating regional violence.

By the 1980s, the Honduran polity had survived several social and political crises. Political institutions remain fragile, although the regime and society have demonstrated remarkable flexibility. Military factions persist but do not threaten the institutional integrity of the armed forces. There is also factionalism within both of the historical political parties. Impatience reigns among the ranks of labor, teachers, and peasant organizations, yet all continue to accept "dialogue" as the significant and desired means of communication and conflict resolution. Even so, as economic conditions worsen, external pressures threaten to undermine the legitimacy of the regime.

External Aid and Adaptation

Honduras is vulnerable to outside economic influences because of the nation's dependence on exports and sources of external financial development aid. Nevertheless, the country remains relatively tranquil in large part because of continued positive support from the United States and multilateral agencies. Officially, the United States has been involved in financing development of the country's infrastructure. It is also a principal source of private sector investment. Over the past few decades, considerable technical assistance has been made to both the private and public sectors.

Bilateral aid programs have involved projects such as construction of farm-to-market roads, completion of the 1974 census, construction of rural schools, and housing for rural schoolteachers. Also, rural development has been stressed with extensive assistance for agrarian and other producer cooperatives. Since 1946, U.S. aid programs have delivered an estimated $281 million. Allocations of economic development aid for fiscal year 1980 were $53.6 million. Requests for fiscal year 1983 were over $60 million.[24]

Even more dramatic has been the steep rise in military aid and foreign military sales since 1979 (see Figure 6.1). In part, the

Figure 6.1. U.S. aid to Honduras, 1979–84

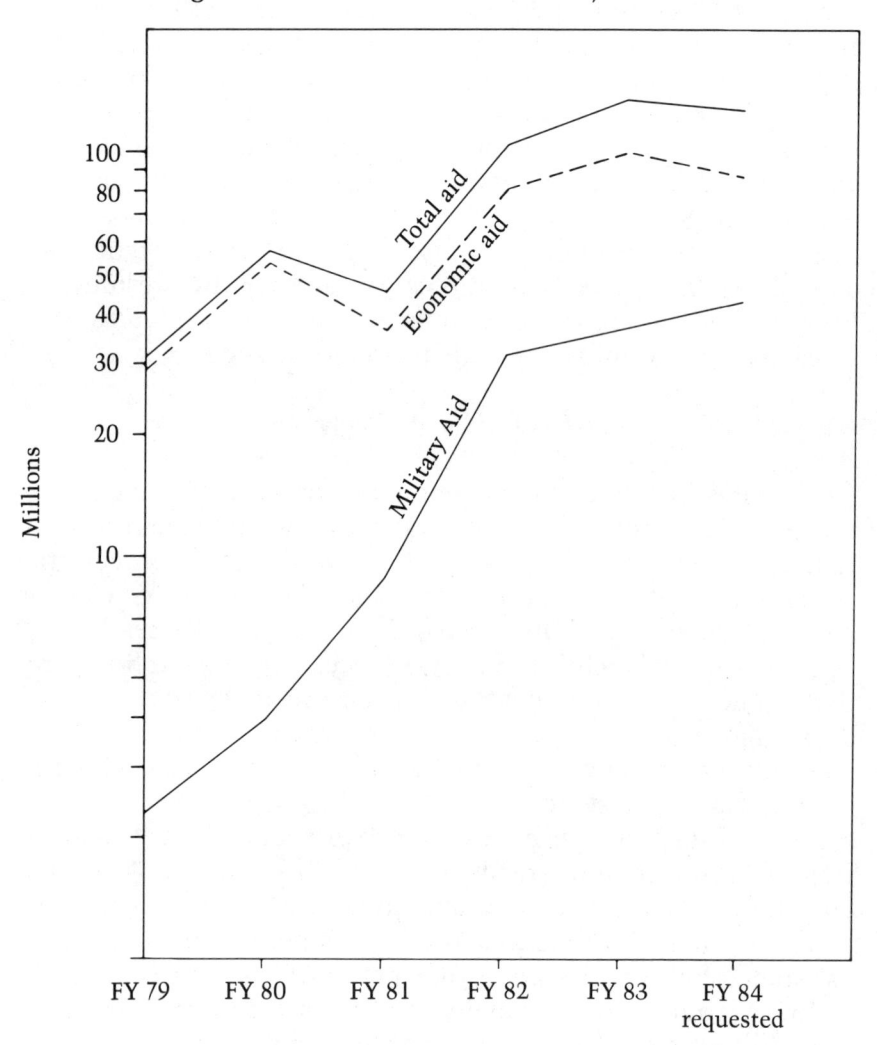

increase in military aid may be viewed as a reward to the Honduran armed forces for maintaining a relatively decent human rights record and for returning formal power to civilians. More important was the leftward drift of the Nicaraguan regime and the possibility of other Central American governments following the example of the Sandinista revolutionary government. Military aid levels jumped from $2.3 million in 1979 to nearly $32 million in 1982. The fiscal year 1984 request was $41 million. In addition, $21 million was authorized for airfield construction; and ten helicopters on loan for a year were formally turned over to the Honduran armed forces. These totals did not include other discretionary funding of allotments contemplated in the Caribbean Basin Initiative. Even so, they helped to place Honduras near the top of the list among Latin American military aid recipients.

Bilateral aid from the United States is important for the course of Honduran national development. But economic and military aid can and do affect political development. For example, increased resources given to the government make control of state institutions more attractive for political elites as well as military governors. U.S. military aid and credits may strengthen the capability of the Honduran armed forces but they also fortify the power of the military as an independent political force. In competition for control over the state, civilian political factions are often at a disadvantage.[25] As the military exercises its control, whether directly as governors or behind the scenes, it can assure preservation of its resources and position of political power.

Another source of external economic assistance was the Mexican-Venezuelan oil facility agreement signed in Costa Rica on August 3, 1980. Honduras imports all of its crude petroleum and prior to 1980 most came from Venezuela. Under the facility agreement, Honduras and other Caribbean basin countries were guaranteed supplies from Mexico and Venezuela. Pressures upon import costs were relieved through discounts of 30 percent, which were accomplished through long-term, low-interest loans. Some problems have been alleviated; however, it remains to be seen whether long-term debt servicing can be maintained. The key will be how freed monetary resources (that is, oil savings and loans) are reinvested in the economy. If funds are used merely to balance domestic budgetary shortfalls or finance nonessential imports, the Mexican-Venezuelan oil facility would only delay a serious economic crisis which could be fatal to the current regime.

In the face of declining export income, capital flight, and rising budget deficits, the Liberal administration of Suazo Cordova was forced to implement economic austerity measures. Tentative agreements with the International Monetary Fund were linked to such measures. The number of public employees was reduced. Despite a potentially explosive confrontation with the United Teacher's Movement (FUM) in mid-1982, Suazo Cordova stood firm against granting wholesale pay increases. The defense budget was frozen at the previous year's level, although this was done in the context of U.S. military assistance programs. An increase in municipal bus fares was accomplished, thereby relieving the central government of certain transportation subsidies.

These were necessary short-term measures that helped Honduras weather cyclical market and investment patterns. But the long-term needs of infrastructure and capital investment, economic diversification, and the perennial issues of agrarian reform remained. External help would be needed, but only the Hondurans would be able to fashion and implement policies of structural change and national development. It was problematical, however, whether pressures from outside the country would provide such time and space to adapt.

Adaptation within the Context of the Regional Crisis

Honduras faces considerable difficulties associated with the spreading regional crisis. The flow of refugees from Nicaragua, El Salvador, and Guatemala may total more than 50,000 by 1984. Attendant pressures upon government resources and disruption of local economies are just two facets of the refugee problem, but they point out the importance of international assistance to relieve the plight of the refugees and reduce the burden on Honduran society. The refugee situation has also become highly politicized as both radical leftists and counterrevolutionary Somocistas utilize Honduran territory for their own purposes. The tendency is to move Honduras closer to direct involvement in the Central American crisis. There has been evidence of complicity by Honduran military units in preventing the escape of

Salvadorans fleeing the rebels or their own government's armed forces. The Salvadoran army has made incursions into Honduran territory in pursuit of suspected guerrillas, in some instances entering the refugee camps in search of their victims.

In 1981-82, the Honduran armed forces adopted a more aggressive national defense posture. Along the border with El Salvador, its strategy was to hinder guerrilla operations, especially as they relied on Honduran territory or those still-disputed zones called *bolsones* to avoid direct contact with Salvadoran troops. A batallion was transferred to the Mosquitía region near Puerto Lempira. Construction began on two naval bases (on the northern coast at Puerto Castilla and in the Caratasca lagoon). And authorities tolerated, or perhaps had lost control of, the anti-Sandinista forces in southern and northeastern Honduras. These groups, encouraged by covert U.S. support, harassed the Sandinista regime. Relations between Honduras and Nicaragua suffered, but meetings between each country's military officers helped maintain communications along the border. Occasionally, diplomatic channels were used to reassure each government of its "nonintervention."

Some sectors within the Suazo government sought to defuse the regional danger by "internationalizing the peace." A plan presented early in 1982 urged a reduction in military forces and armaments, respect for the territory of all Central American states, and establishment of a continuous regional dialogue. In October, nine Caribbean basin countries met in San José to create a Forum for Peace and Democracy. Not invited was Nicaragua, nor were Mexico or Venezuela represented at the meeting. The effort to mobilize world opinion against Nicaragua was paralleled by the domestic mobilization of Hondurans in support of "peace."

Geopolitical pressures upon Honduras have increased as insurgents in El Salvador and the Nicaraguan regime have reacted to actual and perceived threats. Subversive probes into Honduras were designed in part to frustrate the government's task of maintaining social order and public tranquility. Honduran leaders had to counter these threats without reacting to terrorism in a way that would alienate the populace and polarize the polity. Leading Honduras into the vortex of regional violence would further destroy its economic resource base, shatter the investment climate, and endanger the political order. However, if Honduras were attacked (for example, by Nicaragua), nationalistic feelings would unite the country in its self-defense. In either case, the most likely result would be an abrupt return to military rule.

The return to military rule would occur in a context of revolutionary change and conservative reaction. It would represent a Honduran failure to adapt to its current crisis and to recognize the underlying attitudinal and structural changes taking place in the region. It would also represent a failure to recognize the growing disconformity between the nation's social bases and its governing institutions. In effect, embroilment in the regional violence would perpetuate the pattern of intervention in which the Central American states have participated since their independence from Spain. It would suffocate the fragile process of civic and political evolution in Honduras with domestic political gains being sacrificed upon an altar of regional conflict.

Conclusions

Throughout the 1980s and beyond, Honduras will face problems of long-term development and integration of its political system. Domestic tensions will have to be managed in such a manner that demands for reform and participation are either met or moderated over the long haul. Part of the solution will involve inclusion of new groups in the political process. Elimination of public corruption and restraints on government "sponsored" violence are critical if regime legitimacy is to be maintained. Even more difficult will be the problem of achieving economic development.

Honduras, with a relatively homogeneous society and a polity that has not yet developed unbridgeable cleavages, should be able to adapt to domestic change. External assistance and support are crucial aspects of this process, although certainly not sufficient in themselves. Involvement in the Central American conflict, whether as a counterrevolutionary platform or through spillover from its neighbors' internal conflicts, would hamper the process of adaptation and almost certainly would endanger the survival of the regime. The dilemma is that more direct involvement by Hondurans may be inevitable.

Regime performance, alleviation of the stress engendered by

economic dependency, and institutional development are necessary aspects of reducing vulnerability to external pressures. The flexibility of the society and its ability to avoid the excesses of political polarization give Honduras an advantage in the quest for survival. But the context of prerevolutionary conditions in Central America and the tendency to internationalize regional tensions have narrowed the regime's options and timing for achieving these goals.

Notes

1. See Richard N. Adams, *Cultural Surveys of Panama–Nicaragua–Guatemala–El Salvador–Honduras* (Washington, D.C.: Pan American Sanitary Bureau, 1957), pp. 607ff.
2. See Guillermo Molina Chocano, "Población, estructura productiva y migraciónes internas en Honduras (1950–1960)," *Estudios Sociales Centroamericanos* 4, No. 12 (September-December 1975), pp. 9–39.
3. Howard I. Blutstein et al., *Area Handbook for Honduras* (Washington, D.C.: American University, 1971), p. 58ff.
4. See Nancy L. González-Solien, *Black Carib Household Structure: A Study of Migration and Modernization* (Seattle: University of Washington Press, 1969).
5. See Gene Alan Mueller, "The Church in Poverty: Bishops, Bourbons, and Titles in Spanish Honduras, 1700–1821" (Ph.D. dissertation, University of Kansas, 1981); and Robert Anthony White, "Structural Factors in Rural Development: The Church and Peasant in Honduras" (Ph.D. dissertation, Cornell University, 1977).
6. Cf. Guillermo Molina Chocano, *Estado Liberal y desarrollo capitalista en Honduras* (Tegucigalpa, D.C.: Banco Central de Honduras, 1976); and Antonio Murga Frassinetti, *Enclave y sociedad en Honduras* (Tegucigalpa, D.C.: Universidad Nacional Autónoma de Honduras, 1970).
7. Kenneth V. Finney, "Rosario and the Election of 1887: The Political Economy of Mining in Honduras," *Hispanic American Historical Review* 59, No. 1 (February 1979), pp. 81–107; and Vilma Lainez and Víctor Meza, "El enclave bananero el la historia de Honduras," *Estudios Sociales Centroamericanos* 2, No. 5 (May-August 1973), pp. 115–56.
8. See Robert Anthony White, op. cit.; and his *The Adult Education Program of Acción Cultural Hondureña: An Evaluation of the Rural Development Potential of the Radio School Movement in Honduras*, Part I (St. Louis: St. Louis University, 1982).
9. See Ciro F. S. Cardoso and Hector Pérez Brignoli, *Centro América*

y la economía occidental (1520–1930) (San José: Editorial de la Universidad de Costa Rica, 1977), *passim.*

10. See Reina Valenzuela and Mario Argueta, *Marco Aurelio Soto: Reforma Liberal de 1876* (Tegucigalpa: Banco Central de Honduras, 1976).

11. See Mario Posas and Rafael del Cid, *La construcción del sector público y del estado nacional en Honduras, 1876–1979* (San José: EDUCA, 1981); and Edward Boatman-Guillán, "The Political Role of the United Fruit Company, 1890–1950" (draft of Ph.D. dissertation, Johns Hopkins University, 1982).

12. Steve C. Ropp, "The Honduran Army in the Sociopolitical Evolution of the Honduran State," *The Americas* 30, No. 4 (April 1974).

13. See James A. Morris, *The Honduran Plan Político de Unidad Nacional, 1971–1972: Its Origins and Demise* (Occasional Paper, Center for Inter-American Studies, University of Texas at El Paso, 1975).

14. See the works by Rafael Leiva Vivas, *Un país en Honduras* (Tegucigalpa, D.C.: Imprenta Calderón, 1969); and *Vacío político, crisis general y alternativas al desarrollo* (n.p., 1975).

15. In November 1982, just ten months after the 1982 Constitution took effect, the Honduran military high command proposed constitutional amendments which apparently would transfer the power of commander-in-chief from the president of the republic to the head of the armed forces. Debate focused on whether the changes were mere formalities or whether the civilian president would be further estranged from authority over the armed forces.

16. U.S. Agency for International Development, *Honduras: Country Development Strategy, 1982* (Washington, D.C., January 1980), pp. 2–3; also see CONSUPLANE, *Desarrollo y aprovechamiento de los recursos humanos* (Tegucigalpa, D.C., June 1980).

17. See the *Washington Post* (February 22; March 10; August 8; and August 15, 1982); *Central American Report 9*, No. 33 (August 27, 1982); *Latin American Weekly Report* (November 2, 1982); and "A Secret War for Nicaragua," *Newsweek* (November 8, 1982).

18. James A. Morris and Steve C. Ropp, "Corporatism and Dependent Development: A Honduran Case Study," *Latin American Research Review* 12, No. 2 (Summer 1977), pp. 27–63.

19. See James A. Morris, "Honduran Elections and Party Support" (Central American Working Group Paper, New Mexico State University, June 1982); and Ernesto Paz Aguilar, "Breve análisis de las elecciónes 1981," *Alcaraván* No. 11 (February 1982), pp. 2–7.

20. The Movement for Change and Unity (MUC) was led by Mario Rivera López and others who had long been under the shadow of Zúñiga. This "officialist" movement was challenged by former chief of

state, retired general Melgar Castro. The November 1982 National Party internal elections were preceded by living room strategy sessions, demonstrations of the Melgaristas, and politics conducted via the nation's broadcast and print media. Ricardo Zúñiga's influence, however, was not to be diverted easily. The Melgarista movement was shut out as Zúñiga persuaded his closest rivals not to openly break ranks. The National Party's central executive committee remained in the hands of longtime Zúñiga associates.

21. See José Z. García, "Origins of Repressiveness and Moderation in the Militaries of El Salvador and Honduras" (Paper presented at the Western Political Science Association, San Diego, California, March 25, 1982).

22. See Leticia S. Salamon, *Militarismo y reformismo en Honduras* (Tegucigalpa, D.C.: Editorial Guaymuras, 1982), passim; and Mario Posas and Rafael del Cid, "Honduras: Los límites del reformismo castrense (1972–1979)," *Revista Mexicana de Sociología* 42, No. 2 (April-June 1981), pp. 35–36.

23. See Neale J. Pearson, "The 1980 and 1981 Honduran Elections: Manifestations of Critical Realignment of Political Participation and Power" (Paper presented at the Rocky Mountain Council on Latin American Studies, Glendale, Arizona, March 1982).

24. Figures from U.S. Agency for International Development, *U.S. Overseas Loans and Grants and Assistance from International Organizations: Obligations and Loan Authorizations, July 1, 1945–September 30, 1981* (Washington, D.C., 1982), p. 51; and Brad Roberts, "The Countries of Central America: A Primer," Report No. 82-47f, Congressional Research Service (Washington, D.C., March 18, 1982), p. 4. Also see Washington Office on Latin America (WOLA), "U.S. Assistance to Latin America: Profound Reorientations" (Occasional Paper No. 2, Washington, D.C., May 1982); and WOLA, *Washington in Focus* I, No. 2 (October 14, 1983), p. 4.

25. Cf., Gabriel Marcella, "Security Assistance Revisted: How to Win Friends and Not Lose Influence," *Parameters* 12, No. 4 (December 1982), pp. 43–52, especially p. 47.

7

Leadership and Political Transformation in Panama: Two Levels of Regime Crisis

Steve C. Ropp

Introduction

Panama has traditionally been classified as a South American nation rather than as part of Central America. This was because the Isthmus's historical ties were first to Peru through trade and later, during the nineteenth century, to Colombia through political incorporation. Yet there are compelling reasons to consider Panama part of Central America. Geographically, it seems to fit better as an independent nation with the small countries of the region. Also, during the nineteenth and twentieth centuries, construction of a railroad and later a canal across the Isthmus increased both Panamanian commerce with and impact on Central America. For example, construction of the trans-Isthmian railroad by U.S. entrepreneurs in the 1850s opened up new areas of development along Central America's Pacific shore to commercial agricultural crops such as coffee.[1]

Today, Panama also shares with its Central American neighbors many of the crisis conditions that have afflicted the region during the late 1970s and early 1980s. Regardless of the historical factors that have tied the Isthmus to South America, the current reality is one in which Panama's political destiny and stability are perceived as intimately linked to resolution of the problems plaguing Central America. With the collapse of the Somoza dynasty in 1979 and the increasing violence in El Salvador and Guatemala, Panama remained buffered only by the neighboring state of Costa Rica. Growing economic and political difficulties in the "Switzerland of Central America" suggest that it may soon

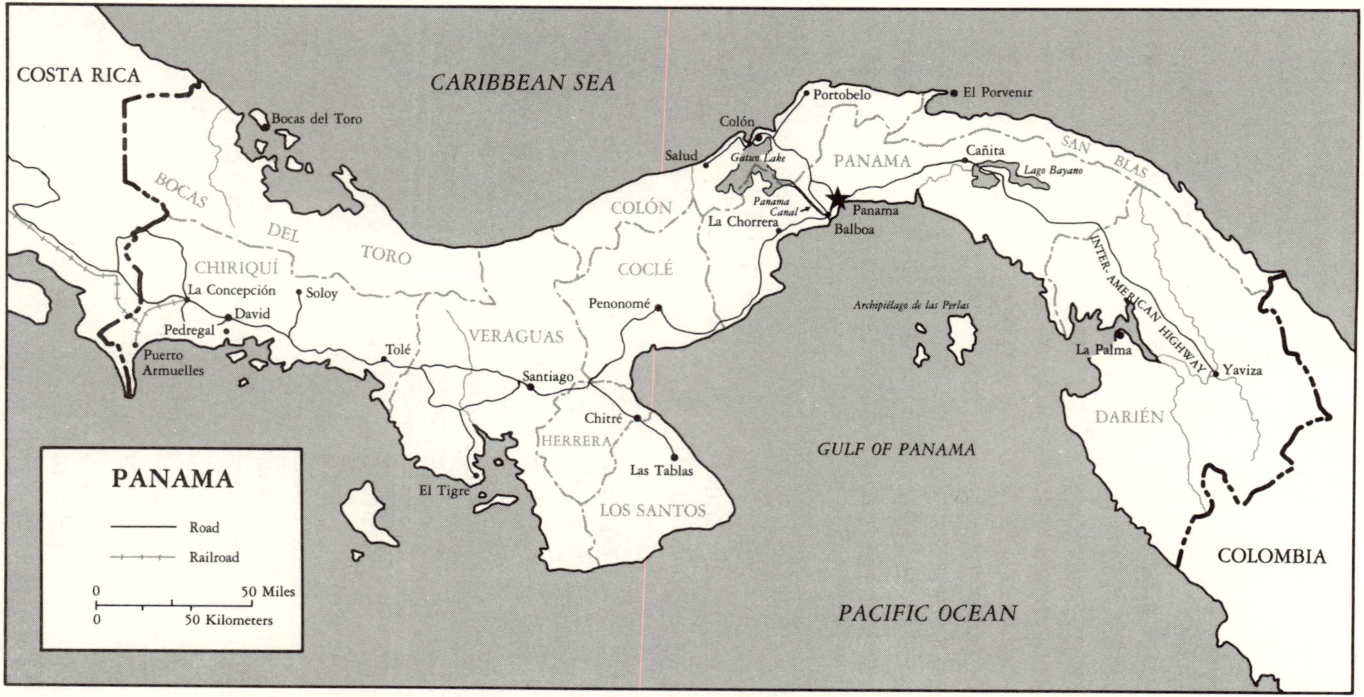

PANAMA
Road
Railroad
0
50 Miles
0
50 Kilometers
COSTA RICA
CARIBBEAN SEA
PACIFIC OCEAN
GULF OF PANAMA
COLOMBIA
BOCAS DEL TORO
CHIRIQUÍ
VERAGUAS
HERRERA
LOS SANTOS
COCLÉ
COLÓN
PANAMA
SAN BLAS
DARIÉN
Bocas del Toro
La Concepción
David
Pedregal
Puerto Armuelles
Soloy
Tolé
El Tigre
Santiago
Chitré
Las Tablas
Penonomé
Salud
Colón
Gatun Lake
Panama Canal
La Chorrera
Portobelo
Panama
Balboa
El Porvenir
Cañita
Lago Bayano
Archipiélago de las Perlas
INTER-AMERICAN HIGHWAY
La Palma
Yaviza

be Panama's turn to become more directly involved in the crisis sweeping the region.

Whether Panama will eventually be swept up in this broader Central American crisis is difficult to say. To assess such likelihood, it is first necessary to examine the ways in which Panama's situation is similar to and different from the prevailing situation in other Central American countries. Each country has its unique history and contemporary set of problems which must be understood in order to make such a judgment. This chapter will begin with a brief description of Panama and its people followed by some historical perspective on political crises in the country. Then, the regime established by General Omar Torrijos, which has governed Panama since 1968, will be examined to determine why it was able to survive for so long. Finally, an assessment will be made of the role that external actors such as the United States government and multinational corporations are likely to play in the process of survival and adaptation.

The Country and Its People

The Republic of Panama is an S-shaped country that joins North and South America. It is bounded on the north by the Atlantic Ocean and on the south by the Pacific. To the west lies Costa Rica and to the east Colombia. The total area of the Republic is 77,082 square kilometers, making it approximately the size of West Virginia. In defiance of our common-sense perceptions, the Isthmus runs generally from east to west. The southern Pacific littoral is considerably longer than the northern Atlantic one since it includes the Azuero Peninsula that extends some distance into the ocean.

Panama's dominant topographical feature is a relatively low mountain chain that runs from the Costa Rican border to Colombia. Although these mountains are not imposing by Central American standards, there are a number of peaks near Costa Rica over 3,000 meters in height. The relatively low elevation of the Isthmus and its narrow waist (only approximately 48 kilometers along the Panama Canal) are important geographical features in that they have historically facilitated travel between the Atlantic and Pacific oceans.

Panama has a tropical climate with accompanying high humidity and heavy rainfall. Rainfall has historically played a major role in determining where people lived and worked. The Atlantic side of the Isthmus (to the north of the central highlands) receives an average of 130 inches per year. For this reason, it is lightly populated except around United Brand's banana plantations near the Costa Rican border and in Colón at the Atlantic terminus of the canal. Rainfall to the south of the central highlands averages only 68 inches annually. Consequently, the national population clusters in the major cities and farming areas bordering the Pacific littoral.

The Pacific side of the Isthmus contains a wide belt of fertile volcanic soil. The combination of fertile soil and a longer dry season historically made the central provinces of Herrera, Coclé, Los Santos, and Veraguas a magnet for agricultural activity. Today, these provinces are dotted with small farms and increasingly attract large-scale agro-commercial enterprises. It is here also that many of Panama's farming and marketing towns are located.

General patterns of agricultural activity in Panama have been heavily influenced by geographic and climatic conditions. The humid lowlands along the Atlantic and parts of the Pacific coast lend themselves to banana production, and it is here that the large plantations of United Brands are located. In the central provinces, where a longer dry season encourages a variety of agricultural pursuits, cattle ranches prevail along with areas of sugar cane, rice, corn, and bean cultivation. The slopes of the central highlands, particularly in Chiriquí and Coclé provinces, have proved suitable for coffee production. However, coffee does not predominate to the extent that it does in various other Central American republics.

The development of Panama's transportation network has also been heavily influenced by geography and climatic conditions. Panama's waist is traversed by both a railroad and a canal, reflecting the historical and contemporary international importance of this transit route. The humid lowlands to the east of Panama City and toward the Colombian border have proven inhospitable to human habitation, and major road networks have yet to be built. Most of Panama's road network (7,800 kilometers with 2,500 kilometers paved) lies to the west of Panama City and connects the canal transit area with the agricultural towns of the interior. Given the inaccessibility of many mountainous and lowland areas, particularly along the Atlantic coast, the air transportation system has been highly developed.

Panama's total national population in 1980 was approximately 1.8 million. The average annual rate of growth dropped from 3.0 percent during the 1960s to 2.1 percent during the 1970s.[2] Because of the historical and contemporary importance of the transit area and canal, the majority of the people are concentrated in and around Panama City and Colón. This leaves much of the interior lightly populated. While the post–World War II period witnessed the rapid growth of agro-industrial activities, there are still many peasants engaged in subsistence agriculture on state-owned land.

Panama contains a number of distinct racial and ethnic groups. While exact figures are not available, it is estimated that the population is 70 percent *mestizo*, 13 percent black, 10 percent white, 6 percent Indian and 1 percent Oriental/Levantine. Mestizo cattlemen and subsistence farmers predominate in the central provinces while the Indian population is concentrated in tribal reserves and contiguous areas at the polar extremes of the Isthmus. Both the white and black population are closely associated with the historical development of the transit area as will be detailed below.

Panama today is a developed country by Central American standards. The per capital gross domestic product in 1980 was $1,917 although this figure masks major inequalities. Generally speaking, the farther one is away from the concentration of wealth and opportunity around the canal, the less income one can expect to receive. The national population is 80 percent literate and life expectancy is seventy years.[3]

Another important component of the Panamanian demographic scene is the Canal Area (formerly referred to as the Canal Zone). The Canal Area is a 1,432 square kilometer strip of territory running through the middle of the Republic. Approximately two-fifths of the Canal Area is covered by the waters of Gatun Lake, which was formed when the Chagres River was dammed during canal construction. The Canal Zone was created after ratification of the Hay–Bunau-Varilla Treaty in 1903, which granted the United States permanent powers as if it were sovereign. In 1978, a new treaty was ratified which gave Panama full sovereignty within the Zone and control over operation and administration of the canal in the year 2000.

The population of the Canal Area currently is approximately 40,000 U.S. citizens and 4,400 Panamanians. Of the U.S. citizens, some 28,000 are servicemen and their dependents. Although the Canal Area is now officially under Panamanian jurisdiction, it remains distinct in terms of its population and degree of U.S. influence.

Historical Perspective on Political Crises in Panama

Historically, Panama's major political crises have almost always been the result of the intended and unintended effects of foreign penetration. During the nineteenth and early twentieth centuries, the United States and France engaged in monumental efforts to upgrade the Isthmian transit route through the construction of a railroad and later a canal. These construction efforts altered the relationship between classes and regions in Panama in such a way as to create crises of national participation. To understand the nature of these crises, it is first necessary to examine the Panamanian class and social structure as it existed in the mid-nineteenth century.

During the colonial period, Panamanian politics came to be dominated by an urban creole elite residing primarily in Panama City at the Pacific terminus of the overland transit route from Peru to Spain. This elite was small, closed, and occupied a rather tenuous economic position. Its primary sources of capitalization were commerce in the transit area and services as second-echelon functionaries within the colonial bureaucracy. As for the Isthmian interior, it was sparsely populated because of the marginal quality of the land and the lack of an Indian labor force that could be pressed into servitude.

When the interior was settled, it was by a class of poverty-stricken creoles that had been driven from Panama City by the economic depression that struck the Isthmus during the eighteenth century when the port monopoly was terminated. Lacking funds and a supply of labor, they turned to cattle raising, which required only cheap, readily available land. This class of small cattle ranchers became isolated and gradually turned both inward and away from the urban transit zone. When commercial contact was restored with the transit zone during the 1850s as a result of the increased demand for beef, the rural cattlemen found themselves in a subordinate and dependent position. The stage had gradually been set for political conflicts between the urban commercial groups and this rural class.[4]

Termination of the port monopoly seriously affected commerce in Panama City and the commercial class there only managed to survive during the first half of the nineteenth century by supplying the Colombian garrison troops.[5] However, when U.S. businessmen constructed a railroad across the Isthmus in the 1850s, commerce markedly increased. More importantly, workers began to be imported into the transit area in increasing numbers. This trend was accelerated further with the French and later U.S. canal-building efforts. The majority of the workers who came to the transit zone were blacks from Jamaica and Barbados.

It was this influx of new workers who could not identify either racially or culturally with Panama's elites or masses that created the first major crisis in Panamanian politics. While the transit working class of the colonial period had always been predominantly black, this class during the colonial period learned Spanish and gradually through the years became culturally assimilated. However, the urban elite became seriously concerned when the urban masses were greatly augmented by workers without such cultural ties. The Haitian experience of the early nineteenth century—where a white French elite had been overthrown—served as an early object lesson. Such concern increased markedly during the 1860s and 1870s when Colombia established a federal system that bolstered the power and influence of black politicians. This crisis, one of participation for the black urban masses and of control for the urban elite, was eventually resolved in favor of the elite. It was resolved in 1903 when the elite decided to accept the protection of the United States for their newly independent republic. The elite gained the benefit of free trade after separation from Colombia without risking the loss of domestic control.

Unfortunately, in resolving this crisis of control, a new political problem was created. When the urban commercial elite aligned itself closely with the United States after independence in 1903, it created for itself an exclusive relationship with the Canal Zone enclave that antagonized excluded groups in society. The most important of these groups was the rural cattlemen and small landholders who felt that the urban commercial elite had sold out to the United States and, worse yet, had not included them. These feelings of exclusion were exacerbated by the fact that the rural landowning class had come to see itself as superior to the mixture of races in the transit area.

During the 1920s, the Panamanian government began to experience serious financial problems and control of the country's fiscal system passed to the United States. The Panamanian mestizo professional class was particularly resentful of the fact that they were excluded from the few bureaucratic jobs that remained after fiscal belt tightening. Many key positions were held by U.S. citizens; for example, the superintendent of the largest hospital in Panama City was a U.S. Army major.

The result of these perceptions of exclusion, particularly on the part of the mestizo professionals who had migrated to Panama City to make their fortune, was the formation of a new political group on August 19, 1923. Community Action was formed to wage the battle for political and economic participation and also to raise national consciousness concerning what was perceived as the denigration of national Hispanic culture. To quote from an early communique, Community Action sought to

> animate the sentiments of our national identity, conserving our traditions, strengthening ourselves through a practical morality, imposing our language and our customs, dignifying this type of sons of the Isthmus as opposed to the diversity of races that clash and confuse things here.[6]

In the 1930s, Harmodio and Arnulfo Arias emerged as leaders of this highly nationalistic movement that sought admission to the enclave relationships by denouncing them. While the leadership came from the professional class, the mass base included day workers and skilled laborers in the canal's terminal cities (Panama City and Colón). These workers were mestizos and blacks of Hispanic cultural background who were being seriously threatened by the importation and retention by Canal Zone authorities of workers from the Antilles. Not only did they have to compete for jobs with these workers (many of whom had the advantage of speaking English) but they had to compete for housing. This was an extremely frustrating and explosive situation, given the higher wages prevailing in the Zone.

This major crisis of political participation peaked during the 1940s when Arnulfo Arias was elected president of the republic and promulgated a new constitution, which contained discriminatory provisions against Antillean blacks. Arias's aim was to disenfranchise this class of workers and eventually to have them repatriated to their home islands. Since the United States was also a target of Arias's attacks, Canal Zone authorities assisted in having him removed from office in 1941. While political power temporarily gravitated back into the hands of the urban commercial elite, Arias's shadow always hovered nearby. He returned to the presidency in 1949 and again in 1968, being removed quickly from office on both occasions. As for resolution of this crisis of participation, demographic changes in the transit area and changes in treaty relations eventually blurred the lines of conflict.[7]

Paralleling this crisis of group participation was another of institutional participation. After the 1903 Revolution, the Panamanian army was disbanded since it was viewed as posing a threat both to the commercial elite and to the United States. Gradually, the armed forces began to reemerge as a political force, particularly during the 1930s when the Arias brothers controlled the political system. By the late 1940s, José Antonio Remón had increased the influence of the National Police to the point that as commandant he was a man to be reckoned with in politics.

During the 1950s, the police force, which had been converted into a national guard, consolidated its institutional position. While there was no major crisis associated with admission of the Guard's leadership to the inner political circles, it was definitely a watershed and the urban elite gave in grudgingly. They were afraid that the participation of the police in politics might affect the image of the politicians. They would have preferred to have kept the police at arm's length so that there was someone other than the politicians to blame when force was used to keep the masses in line. But police leaders, who wanted their military status and prestige increased, were not willing to play along.

Historically, crisis conditions in Panamanian politics have also been the product of numerous other factors. However, Panama seems rather unique in the Central American region in the extent to which past political crises have resulted from the high degree of foreign penetration. During the late nineteenth and early twentieth centuries, the urban commercial elite was forced to rely on the United States as a counterweight to the lower classes that had been augmented by non–Spanish-speaking blacks during the years of canal construction. The formation of this close working relationship in turn led to the exclusion and increasing resentment not only of the Spanish-speaking black masses but of rural mestizos. This resentment led to a thirty-year period of political turmoil in which the forces led by Arnulfo Arias clashed with the commercial elite in close alliance with the United States.

Structural Conditions and Crisis: Panama Compared with Other Central American Countries

Contemporary Panama exhibits many of the structural features generally associated in the literature on social change with violence and possible revolution. Although the total population is the smallest in Central America (1,187,000) and the rate of population growth the lowest (2.1 percent annually between 1970 and 1980), there has been increased pressure on the land and a mass movement of people from rural areas to the cities.[8] As elsewhere in Central America, the period after 1950 saw the emergence of large-scale commercial agriculture. Panama had traditionally been a nation with many subsistence farmers who practiced slash-and-burn agriculture on lands owned by the state. The extension of activities such as large-scale commercial cattle grazing and sugar cane production reduced the fertile forest acreage that could be productively used for subsistence farming; peasants were forced to use land before it had lain fallow for a sufficient period of time. Production of traditional subsistence farming crops dropped dramatically: corn declined 19.7 percent between 1950 and 1978 and bean by 40.7 percent.[9]

The movement of Panamanians into major urban areas has

been even more dramatic than that which took place in other Central American countries. The urban population increased from 36 percent of the total in 1950 to 48 percent by 1970. Historically, Panama had always been more highly urbanized than its Central American neighbors due to the importance of activities in the transit zone. Continued rapid economic growth of this area during the post–World War II years led to Panama City's emergence as a major urban center. By 1970, its share of the total national population was as great as that of Argentina's leading city, Buenos Aires. Census data for 1980 shows that the two provinces which enclose the transit zone now contain fully 54 percent of the national population.[10]

Most of the half-million people who left their rural home provinces during the post–World War II decades migrated to the rapidly growing squatter settlements around Panama City. While the older slums were concentrated near the border of the former Canal Zone, more recent settlements are located far from the center of town where the ready availability of land has made for lower population densities. While conditions in these squatter settlements are far from ideal, successive governments during the post-war period did manage to extend basic services. In Panama City, 96 percent of the residents have access to potable water and 67 percent have electricity. Ownership of the land is often a problem as squatters have frequently occupied private property. In areas where the government owned the land, programs have been established so that squatters may eventually purchase their lots.[11]

The increased urbanization which has taken place in Panama has been accompanied by a moderately paced process of industrialization. This process was rather unique in that it responded primarily to developments in the Canal Zone and in changing treaty relations with the United States rather than to domestic or regional market conditions. The origins of Panamanian industrialization can be traced back to World War II when the Canal Zone work force rapidly expanded. Disruption of global supply routes and construction activity in the Zone led to considerable expansion of industrial activity. Industrial development was further spurred during the 1950s when a new treaty was negotiated with the United States allowing for higher wages for Canal Zone employees.

The political effect of industrialization was to encourage the development of urban organized labor. The number of unions grew from three in 1945 to sixteen in 1955 and sixty by 1965. During the 1960s, the number of workers employed in the manufacturing sector doubled from 24,000 to 47,000. As elsewhere in Central America, these workers were increasingly active politically although still rather closely controlled by their respective governments. The bifurcation of the labor movement into a work force employed in the Canal Zone and another employed in Panama's manufacturing sector slowed the growth of labor unity.[12]

Although Panama is similar to other Central American countries with regard to factors such as increased land pressure and rapid urban migration, there are significant differences. For one thing, land pressure is not nearly as intense as in countries such as El Salvador. The return of large amounts of private land to the federal government in 1903 put the government in a position to assure land distribution if necessary. Also, the traditional pattern of subsistence slash-and-burn farming on state-owned land has not led to widespread calls for private ownership.

Another major difference is the nature of Panama's export economy. While Panama relies on a few primary export products as a source of national export earnings, it is the only country in the region that is not heavily reliant on coffee. To the extent that arguments about the effect of coffee production on export earnings, the economy, or on the political structure enter into an evaluation of crisis conditions, Panama clearly falls into a different category. Panama's major export is petroleum derivatives, which it sells to ships transiting the canal. Bananas, which were formerly a key export crop, have declined rapidly as a source of export earnings (see Table 7.1).

Panama is also distinguished from other Central American countries in the degree to which exports are important as a source of foreign earnings. Panamanian supplies of goods and services to the Canal Area are not counted as exports, yet volume regularly exceeds that of formally declared export products.[13] For example, in 1977 Panama's exports totalled $235 million while the net value of goods and services supplied to the Canal Zone was $238 million. An important feature of this uncounted foreign trade is that it consists largely of services for which there has been a rather steady value and market. The large service com-

Table 7.1. Contribution of selected primary export products to the total value of merchandise exports: 1975–79 (percent)

Country	Coffee	Bananas	Sugar
Costa Rica	31.1	16.7	3.2
El Salvador	52.5	—*	5.2
Guatemala	38.5	2.3	8.5
Honduras	28.0	22.9	1.1
Nicaragua	24.7	0.9	5.8
Panama	2.0	21.3	9.4

*Data not available.
Source: Inter-American Development Bank, *Economic and Social Progress in Latin America: 1980–81 Report* (Washington, D.C.: Inter-American Development Bank, 1981), pp. 447–48.

ponent in Panama's real export earnings lends a measure of stability to the economy not found in the coffee-exporting countries in the Central American region.

During the 1960s and 1970s, the Panamanian central government and autonomous agencies expanded rapidly as was the case throughout most of South and Central America. The salaried work force of the central government increased from 23,884 in 1960 to 54,823 by 1975.[14] Employees of autonomous and semiautonomous agencies grew from 4,973 to 29,929 over the same period. The growth of the public sector was paralleled by a rapid rise in the public debt, particularly during the 1970s. During this same period, the Panamanian economy began to experience the effects of oil price increases and stagflation. While the rate of inflation has not generally been as high as elsewhere in Central America, given Panama's ties to the U.S. dollar, there have been increasing pressures exerted on both the public sector and society (see Table 7.2).

The 1968 Coup and the Structure of the Resulting Regime

Before assessing the specific features of the current Panamanian regime that may affect its ability to adapt to crisis condi-

Table 7.2. Inflation, growth of the Gross Domestic Product, and growth of Gross Domestic Investment: 1960–80 (percent)

	1960–70	1970–80
Average annual rate of inflation	1.6	7.4
Average annual growth rate of the Gross Domestic Product	7.8	4.0
Average annual growth rate of Gross Domestic Investment	12.4	1.1

Source: The World Bank, *World Development Report: 1982* (New York: Oxford University Press, 1982), pp. 110–17.

tions, it is first necessary to discuss its general nature. In 1968, a military coup occurred that overthrew the government of President Arnulfo Arias. Rather than returning power to civilians, the National Guard promulgated a new constitution that designated Torrijos Maximum Leader of the Revolution. From that time until his death in 1981, Torrijos's influence was such that the structure of power in Panama was generally referred to as the "Torrijos regime."

But was the Torrijos regime fundamentally different from its predecessors in structural terms? It has been argued that the military coup that occurred in 1968 did not really alter the relationship between political institutions and the underlying structure of economic power. Panamanian scholar Guillermo Castro Herrera believes that the Torrijos years spanned a period during which one particular form of dependent capitalism was merely transformed into another.[15] He does suggest that the "dominant bloc" (urban commercial elite) lost some control during this period, but maintains that the military government was primarily a reflection of the same coalition that had controlled the political and economic system since 1903.

While one can certainly argue that the Torrijos regime reflected continuity with the past along a number of important dimensions, this regime was also new in several respects. First, the formal rules that specified the relationships between the main political institutions were altered. Prior to the 1968 coup, the 1946 Constitution gave the president, as commander-in-chief of the National Guard, the power to appoint and remove Guard personnel. The 1972 Constitution eliminated these provisions. Furthermore, Article 2 of the 1972 Constitution stated that all government agencies should act in "harmonic collaboration" with the National Guard. This article formalized a central and ongoing deliberative role for the armed forces in Panamanian politics.

Another change in the rules governing the relationships between political institutions occurred with the elimination of political parties. Traditional groups such as the Liberals, Panameñistas, and Republicans were allowed no formal participation until 1978 when the 1972 Constitution was revised. The old National Assembly associated with the influence of the traditional parties was abolished and replaced with an Assembly of Corregimientos. This new Assembly contained 505 members elected from the small subdistricts into which Panama had been divided during colonial times. When political parties were revived in 1978, it was through a carefully controlled process in which 30,000 members were required before recognition by the government.

Here, the break with past patterns of institutional relations was somewhat less dramatic than in the case of legalizing military participation in politics. The tradition of controlling the number of political parties through fluctuating membership requirements can be dated back to the presidency of José Antonio Remón in the 1950s. Remón was a military officer who treated the traditional parties as pawns, and created one of his own as a personal vehicle for maintaining power. However, General Torrijos went a step farther in formally banning all party activity for a period of ten years.

That the Torrijos regime was in certain structural ways fundamentally new seems apparent. However, it remains a difficult regime to classify with the existing typologies. Most helpful in this regard is the classification scheme proposed by Guillermo O'Donnell. In an important book published in 1973, O'Donnell argued that political regimes in the Southern Cone countries (Argentina, Brazil, Chile) progressed through three distinct stages (regime types) associated with three levels of economic development. When their economies were dominated by agricultural exports, traditional oligarchies whose fortunes were based on these exports governed. During the 1930s, the emergence of new industrial elites and organized labor led to the ascendancy of populist leaders and associated regimes that reflected these new urban interests. The third type of regime emerged during the 1960s and 1970s with the increasing production of consumer durable and capital goods. These so-called bureaucratic-authoritarian regimes gave the armed forces a central role in ensuring political stability and guaranteeing further economic growth in collaboration with the multinational corporations.[16] Increasingly, the masses and organized labor who had been included in the political process under populist leaders were excluded from participation.

Panamanian governments from 1960 to 1968 reflected traditional oligarchic tendencies in that there was minimal participation by the popular sector and the regime was run by and for the elite. A major difference from the conception of traditional oligarchic regimes in O'Donnell's typology is that the Panamanian oligarchy was not economically reliant on primary exports but rather on the supply of goods and services to the Canal Zone and within the transit area. O'Donnell's populist regime, with its emphasis on the incorporation of new industrial elites, partially fits the later years of the Liberal period (1964–68) and the early years of Torrijos's rule. It is no coincidence that populist members of the Liberal Party, who were increasingly frustrated with the slow pace of reform during the 1960s, emerged as Torrijos's allies during the early years of his ascendancy. The problem of regime periodization and classification is thus complicated by the fact that populist features seem to span two different periods with regard to regime organization and structure.

During the later Torrijos years (1976–81), the incorporating populism of the post-1964 period was replaced by excluding tendencies but certainly not exclusion of the bureaucratic-authoritarian variety that O'Donnell associates with the deepening of dependent industrialization. In Panama, the excluding tendencies were associated with growing economic difficulties and the deepening—not of industrial processes—but of developments in the service sector. The initial phase of import substitution ended by the early 1970s and was superseded by a rapid expansion of services such as banking and warehousing that were linked (as in the case of industrial expansion in the Southern Cone) to the Latin American activities of multinational corporations. Panama quickly developed into an offshore banking center with assets of $35 billion by 1980. The Colón Free Zone at the Atlantic terminus of the Canal is now second only to Hong Kong in terms of volume of goods handled (see Figure 7.1).

This rapid expansion of the service sector since the early 1970s raises the question of the links between the economic structure and the political regime. If the regime is still basically populist (even though more exclusive), it may be increasingly "out of phase" with this economic structure and a candidate for replacement. The possibility of regime replacement due to success in transforming the economy will be addressed in the conclusions of the chapter.

Leadership and Regime Crisis

By the time of his death in 1981, Omar Torrijos had become one of the most long-tenured political leaders in all of Latin America. Although the regime was threatened on occasion by economic and social unrest, it was able to weather these crises with relative ease. Some Latin American military regimes survived during the 1960s and 1970s by changing course and military leadership in the process; examples include Brazil, Peru, and Honduras. The remarkable thing about the Panamanian case is that rather substantial swings and turns in policy took place under the continued leadership of one man.

Studies of political leadership have not been in vogue in the field of political science during recent decades although a number of well-known scholars have produced major contributions.[17] Glenn Paige has suggested several reasons why this has been the case. There is a bias in democratic societies against the idea that leaders should matter as much or more than followers. There has also been an accompanying bias within the social sciences stressing variants of deterministic thinking (for example, the economic determinism of Karl Marx, the evolutionary determinism of Charles Darwin, or the psychological determinism of Sigmund Freud).[18] This deterministic bent within the social sciences has been particularly prevalent in the field of Latin Amer-

Figure 7.1. Gross Domestic Product at market prices by branch of activity: 1950–77 (millions of 1960 dollars)

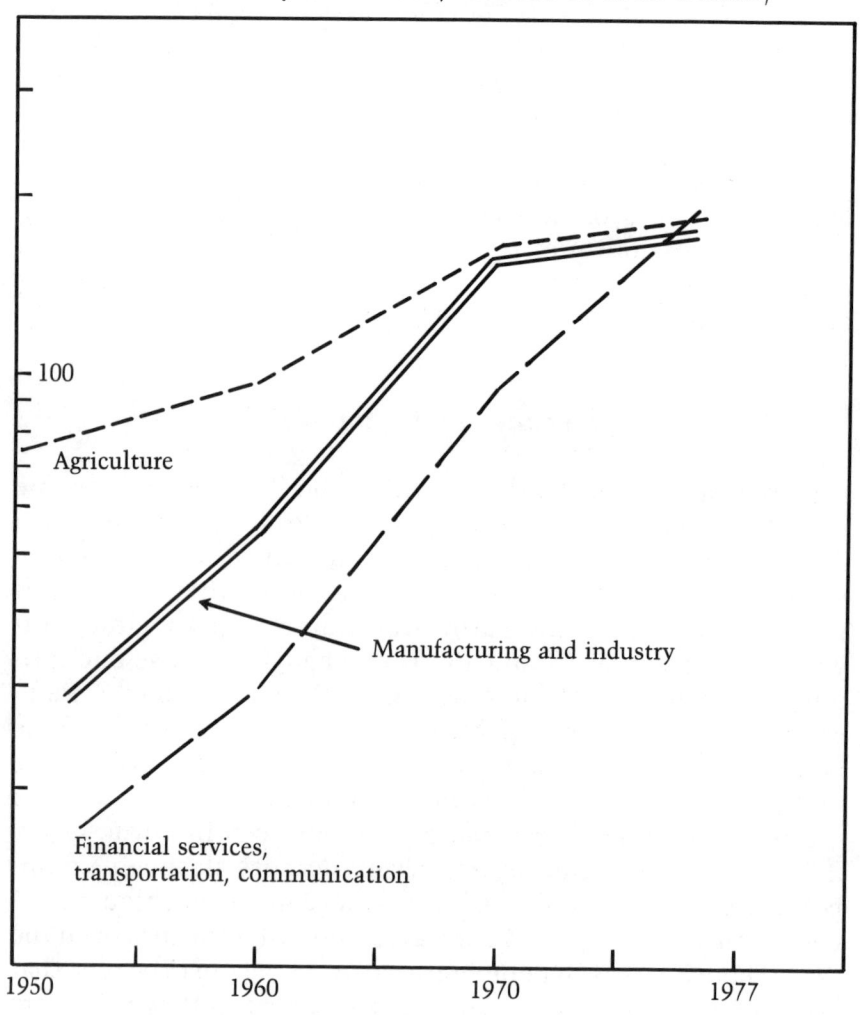

Source: Calculated from Dirección de Estadística y Censo, Contraloría General de la República, *Indicadores economicos y sociales de Panamá: 1968–1977*, September, 1978, p. 5; and Thomas E. Weil, et al., *Area Handbook for Panama* (Washington, D.C.: U.S. Government Printing Office, 1972), p. 248.

ican studies because of the influence among both traditionalists and behavioralists of Marxist thought. It is strange indeed given the historical importance in Latin America of the *caudillo*.[19]

Omar Torrijos was frequently pictured in the United States and Panama as a clever country bumpkin who spent most of his spare time in a hammock, drinking heavily. This image obscures the fact that political survival for such an extended period of time required attention to the day-to-day details of controlling both the government and the National Guard. Torrijos's control of the government was maintained by placing minor political figures and personal friends in ministerial positions and replacing or rotating them regularly. The average tenure for a minister between 1968 and 1980 was 2.2 years. The average for a minister of the interior, a critical position for national political control, was only 1.3 years. Within the National Guard, Torrijos as commander-in-chief maintained direct lines of authority to all military units. He controlled all seven infantry rifle companies and stationed two of these companies, in effect his own private army, at Río Hato a short distance from Panama City. No officer assignments were made, even at the lieutenant level, without the express approval of the General. In addition, he spent a considerable amount of time keeping in touch with the troops through regular field marches and informal talks. Members of the General Staff shared in high-level responsibilities but there was seldom any question after 1970 as to who controlled the National Guard.[20]

Within the broader society, Torrijos's leadership skills were demonstrated by his ability to construct temporary coalitions consisting of unlikely elements and to restructure these coalitions with changing times. The Torrijos years can be divided into three distinct periods in this regard. The period from the coup in 1968 until 1972 was one of ad hoc coalition building. The political challenge was to find a mixed base of support that could serve two partially antagonistic purposes: 1) lend minimal legitimacy to Torrijos and the National Guard as governors, and 2) not antagonize U.S. officials to the point that they would support a countercoup. It was during this period that Torrijos reached out both to the domestic Left and to U.S. banks and multinational corporations.

During the second period (1972–76), Torrijos institutionalized regime relationships with various support groups through the formal provisions of the 1972 Constitution. Having excluded the traditional political parties, he gave himself extraordinary powers for six years through Article 277 of the Constitution. The president became a figurehead with all appointive and policy-making power concentrated in the hands of the Maximum Leader. Distributional policies during these years tilted in the direction of favored peasant groups and the organized working class.

The third period lasted from 1976 until Torrijos's death. It was characterized by growing economic difficulties stemming from stagnation in import substitution, a rapid growth in the national debt, and private sector unwillingness to invest heavily in the Panamanian economy. During this period, Torrijos and the Guard reevaluated the merits of a direct and sustained military role in politics. Constitutional amendments were adopted in 1978 that facilitated an eventual return to civilian government by way of direct presidential elections scheduled for 1984. The coalition upon which the regime relied for support during this period was increasingly drawn from the Right, with the gradual marginalization of both favored peasant groups and organized labor. Lines of communication were opened with the private sector and elements from this sector were included in the new official Revolutionary Democratic Party (PRD) formed in 1978.

It is difficult to estimate the degree to which the Torrijos regime managed to establish its political legitimacy during these three periods. Certainly the regime "survived" and was able to adapt to changing economic and political circumstances. However, it is less clear that it ever developed a base of active support as opposed to passive acceptance due to lack of perceived alternatives. While public opinion polls are not available to document this point, the mass apathy displayed when Torrijos died supports such a conclusion.

Although calling his government revolutionary, General Torrijos did not make extensive use of revolutionary antecedents as a legitimizing device—as was the case for example in Mexico, Cuba, and Peru. To the extent that the regime made reference to such antecedents, they were asserted to be found in the popular Liberalism of the late nineteenth and early twentieth centuries. The regime was portrayed as the inheritor of mass popular instincts that had been crushed in 1903 by the alliance between urban elites and the United States. Yet the effort to draw on these sources of historical legitimacy were intermittent and half-hearted.

Regime legitimacy was also linked to Torrijos himself and the National Guard. The Guard was portrayed as being led by a new generation of officers concerned with national development.

> The seed sown at Punta del Este in 1960 by John F. Kennedy has borne fruit in the creation of a new generation of young men, well prepared professionals with good intentions, that speak, think, and live the language of development, and who little by little are occupying key decision-making positions in Latin American countries. I consider myself to be a product of this crop.[21]

Perhaps more important than the attempt to derive legitimacy from a modernizing image was the portrayal of Torrijos and the men who surrounded him as true "sons of the people." Torrijos consistently used the metaphor of the family to describe Panamanian society. Within this family, he and his rustic military cronies were portrayed as "bastards," challenging the governing credentials derived from blood lines of the urban commercial elite.

> Gentlemen, the only criticism that the legalists of this country have [of our military leaders] is that they are illegitimate children of the nation. Illegitimate children, okay, but I always remember the parable that says it is often the illegitimate son who serves the honor of the family, the same honor that the illegitimate sons originally tarnished.[22]

At the symbolic level, the regime relied primarily on this image of illegitimacy to derive mass support. It was an appealing approach for Torrijos who was himself a rather uncomplicated product of rural Panama. Torrijos had all the instincts of the marginalized rural middle sectors who had no respect for the urban commercial elites that they traditionally had served through institutions such as the National Guard. The "legitimacy of illegitimacy" may have also had popular appeal by providing a feeling of unity and confronting open elite disdain for the "mongrelized" masses and the high national rate of birth out of wedlock.

In spite of this veneer of legitimizing symbolism, it seems

likely that the Torrijos regime survived because its policies were either acceptable or tolerable to a broad array of Panamanian interests. For the rural peasants, there was a land reform program and new crop marketing mechanisms, which at least held out the promise of better times. For urban popular constituencies, a new labor code and new canal treaties could lead to an expanded urban employment base. As for the traditional rural and urban elite interests, most of the above-mentioned programs had no serious direct impact. The availability of state land underwrote land reform. Growth of the service sector compensated a wide spectrum of urban commercial-industrial interests for industrial stagnation.

The ability of General Torrijos and the National Guard to reconcile these various interests and to adjust the mix of policies over time, given existing economic realities, is not something that should be taken for granted. It is difficult to divorce the question of legitimacy and survivability from that of leadership. General Torrijos's personal style was conciliatory and forgiving. This is not to say that he never used strong-arm tactics. But he was not a tyrant. Political foes were treated quite leniently with co-optation as the ultimate goal. Nowhere was this more obvious than in his treatment of dissidents within the National Guard.

Obviously, it is important to consider the leadership skills that Torrijos possessed as they related to regime stability and legitimacy. However, it would be wrong to ignore the role of the military as an institution. The National Police/National Guard had only three commanders during the forty-one year span between 1940 and 1981. Founding father of the reinvigorated National Police was José Antonio Remón, a cavalry officer trained at the Mexican Military Academy. He was followed in the mid-1950s by Bolívar Vallarino (trained in Peru) and finally by Omar Torrijos himself. It is not entirely clear why National Police and Guard officers were so highly cohesive and supportive of their commander during this forty year period, but it is the general consensus that such support did in fact exist and gave the commander a powerful voice in politics. If one looks at the career paths of most officers during the 1950s and early 1960s, one might suspect that the commander was held in considerable esteem, being one of the few officers with formal academy training. Also, the tenuous institutional position of the Police/Guard in relation to governing politicians may have played some role in maintaining unity at the highest levels. If these arguments have any merit, one would expect to find somewhat less unity at both the level of the General Staff and within the officer corps as a whole as academy-trained officers become the rule and as the political/institutional position of the Guard is further consolidated.

The unity within the Guard who was maintained under Torrijos also demonstrates his considerable leadership skills. In 1974, a National School for Political Capacitation (ESCANAP) was established under the direction of Lieutenant Colonel Roberto Díaz Herrera. This school served the purpose of politically educating both officers and enlisted men through frequent seminars held with cabinet officers, labor leaders, and politicians. Such political education was important for several reasons. First, key officers within the Guard who supported Torrijos's left-of-center policies during the early 1970s were not in step with the rather conservative General Staff. Second, Torrijos changed policy directions so frequently that an institutionalized means of keeping his military comrades up to date was necessary.

In sum, Omar Torrijos demonstrated considerable leadership skills during his tenure, and that ability may partially explain regime survival. These skills allowed him to control the military and, through their continued support, impose his policies on society. While his policies were not always supported, they were usually grudgingly accepted by a sufficient number of people to prevent his ouster. Although the National Guard frequently harassed the opposition, particularly during the early 1970s, this harassment was selective and relatively mild. It has been said of Somoza that it was the implementation of a vigorous human rights program by President Jimmy Carter that was his undoing. However, given Torrijos's success in avoiding the human rights stigma, one must wonder whether the real problem in Nicaragua was one of tyrannical leadership rather than U.S. policy.

External Influences on Crisis and Adaptation

As noted earlier, Panama's major historical crises have often derived from the intended and unintended effects of foreign penetration. This continues to be the case. During the 1970s, activities of global multinational corporations led to the strengthening of the Panamanian service sector. The country became an international banking, transportation, and warehousing center supporting corporate activities in Latin America and elsewhere. Within the international corporate division of labor, Panama's role was not primarily to produce goods (although some were assembled there for export) but rather to provide services.

The rapid growth of the service economy has created both economic and, potentially, political problems. Economically, the rural population has become even more marginal in relation to the dynamism in Panama City. The industrial sector has reached a plateau from which there is likely to be little forward movement except as a result of overseas-oriented assembly activities. Conditions for potential political crises derive directly from these economic developments. While serious unrest in the countryside seems unlikely, urban organized labor may become increasingly frustrated. Emphasis on the service sector coupled with the "relative exhaustion" of the industrial phase may lead the regime to further de-emphasize organized labor as a base of support. It may fear that a strong labor sector would antagonize the multinational corporations upon which the regime increasingly depends. Finally, there is the question of whether an essentially populist civil-military regime remains compatible with the classes and interests represented within the increasingly sophisticated service sector.

The paradox of the current situation is that the same foreign interests that are largely responsible for creating Panama's crisis conditions are best positioned to provide solutions. The global multinational corporations and the governments of the major capitalist world powers have the resources to ease the economic and political transition that Panama must make. But while many foreign interests play a role, it is U.S. companies and the U.S. government that must serve as the "lead" institutions, given their historical role on the Isthmus. What resources can and will they provide?

If history is any guide, the U.S. government will continue to provide Panama with relatively large amounts of development aid. U.S. aid to Latin America has generally been concentrated in the poorer countries, with Panama remaining a major exception to the rule. If Panama were a normal Latin American country, it would be expected to have received $59 per capita in U.S. aid between 1946 and 1975. It actually received six times that amount.

The U.S. government has also distributed additional resources to Panama through revision of canal treaties. The original 1903 Treaty was not very financially beneficial to Panama, but improvements were made in 1936, 1955, and 1978. The 1978 Treaty negotiated during the presidency of Jimmy Carter was particularly lucrative. Panama receives $10 million annually in the form of a fixed annuity and another $10 million to provide basic services to the Canal Commission. Most importantly, the government receives $0.30 for every ton of cargo transiting the canal. Income from this source until the year 2000 is estimated at between $50 and $60 million annually.

The reasons why the U.S. government has proven willing to grant considerable amounts of foreign aid to Panama are not hard to divine. Dating back to 1846 and the signing with Colombia of the Bidlack-Mallarino Treaty, the United States has considered itself protector of the Isthmian transit route. After construction of the canal, Panama came to be considered even more vital from both an economic and a security point of view. The continued presence of U.S. troops in the Canal Area is further evidence that the United States government still perceives the Isthmus to be of considerable importance.

As for the multinational corporations, their pattern of economic activity also attests to the significance they attach to the Isthmus. While discussions of U.S. investments in Central America tend to emphasize countries such as Guatemala, where there has been an obvious political impact, it is clear that Panama emerged after 1950 as a location for U.S. multinational investments that dwarfs the rest of the region. By 1978, total direct investment had reached approximately $2.4 billion. This was equal to U.S. investment in all the rest of Central America and Peru combined. Panama led all Latin American nations with over $1,300 invested per person. This level was eight times that of U.S. per capita direct investment in Venezuela and twenty times that of per capita investment levels in countries such as Brazil and Mexico.[23]

U.S. banks play a particularly critical role in support of Panamanian governments. In exchange for favorable operating conditions during the 1970s, they were willing to underwrite a large number of projects by the central government and autonomous agencies. By 1978, over 56 percent of Panama's government debt was owed to private banks. The continued willingness of these institutions to support the current regime will undoubtedly play a critical role in relation to survival and/or adaptation.

Conclusions

In the preceding analysis, an attempt has been made to determine how crisis conditions in Panama are similar to and different from those existing elsewhere in Central America. Panamanian society is subject to many of the strains that have afflicted neighboring countries. Specifically, serious problems exist regarding income distribution, inflation, unemployment and mass rural-to-urban migration. On the positive side, Panama has not experienced intense land pressure given the small size of its population and relatively low rates of growth, and the widespread availability of state land. Additionally, the economy is not wedded as closely as in most Central American countries to the production of agricultural crops for export. Income from a large service sector associated with the canal and with activities of the multinational corporations buffers the economy from unstable commodity prices.

With the death of Omar Torrijos, the current regime is experiencing a leadership crisis; and a power struggle is taking place both within the National Guard and within the broader popular coalition that Torrijos assembled. Although the principle of leadership based on seniority is strong within the Guard, it remains to be seen whether this tradition will continue to be followed. A new generation of officers that received professional military training in Latin American academies has emerged in recent years. At some future date, it may seek to challenge directly the semiprofessional officer cadre associated with Torrijos that continues to direct the Guard.

Even if the issue of leadership within the Guard is successfully resolved, it remains to be seen whether the broader popular coalition that supported the Torrijos regime will remain intact. When Torrijos moved to establish an official personalist party in 1978, some of the popular groups that had supported him in earlier years were forced to the sidelines. Within the PRD, the private sector was increasingly well represented and the Party gave every indication of shifting even further to the right in its bid to successfully contest the 1984 presidential elections. The regime coalition has become so broad in ideological terms that it will take strong and imaginative political leadership to hold it together.

This crisis of regime leadership and internal cohesion may be compounded by a crisis of regime function.[24] It can be argued that the populist Torrijos regime successfully performed the function of integrating the organized labor movement produced by import substitution industrial development into the political system. This regime may have also functioned to facilitate the transition from this initial period of industrialization (now exhausted) to a new period characterized by the complete dominance of a powerful service sector tied to the multinational corporations.[25]

The question then is whether such a populist regime relying heavily on guidance from the National Guard is compatible with the emergence of this new and relatively sophisticated sector and the classes associated with it. This is a difficult question to answer given that we have little previous experience suggesting the regime types and personalities that relate best functionally to nonmarginal service sectors in developing countries. The characterization of such a postpopulist and perhaps *sui generis* regime type is likely to be a difficult theoretical task.

Whether these crises of leadership and structural change can be successfully bridged short of revolution will depend to a considerable degree on the activities of the U.S. government and the multinational corporations. External powers have historically been responsible for both the creation of Panama's major regime crises and for their resolution. The continued geostrategic importance of the canal and the growing economic importance of the associated service activities will probably ensure that Panama's future crises will not be treated lightly by global interests.

Notes

1. Ralph Lee Woodward Jr., *Central America: A Nation Divided* (New York: Oxford University Press, 1976), p. 146.
2. Inter-American Development Bank, *Economic and Social Prog-*

ress in Latin America: 1980–81 Report (Washington, D.C.: Inter-American Development Bank, 1981), p. 395.

3. Ibid., p. 325.

4. The best account is Omar Jaén Suárez, *La población del Istmo de Panamá del Siglo XVI al Siglo XX* (Panamá: Impresora de la Nación, 1978).

5. Ibid.

6. J. Conte Porras, *Arnulfo Arias Madrid* (Panamá: Litho-Impresora Panamá, S.A., 1980), p. 62.

7. The percentage of foreign born residents of Colón Province dropped from 24.0 in 1940 to 6.6 in 1970. In Panama Province, it dropped from 13.7 to 5.2. Dirección de Estadística y Censo, Contraloría de la República, *Censos nacionales de 1970, compendio general–población*, Vol. 3, pp. 16–17.

8. Inter-American Development Bank, *Economic and Social Progress in Latin America: 1980–81 Report*, pp. 80–81 and p. 395.

9. Dirección de Estadística y Censo, Contraloría de la República, *Situación económica: año agrícola, 1978–79*, pp. 11, 15, and 26.

10. Dirección de Estadística y Censo, Contraloría de la República, *Press Release Bulletin*, No. 9, 1980.

11. Raúl Alberto Leis, *La ciudad y los pobres: las clases sociales en la ciudad transitista* (Panamá: Centro de Estudios y Acción Social en Panamá, 1979), pp. 127–28.

12. Guillermo Castro Herrera, "Panama, 1977," *Tareas*, No. 41 (January-March 1978), pp. 10–11.

13. Richard Nyrop, ed., *Panama: A Country Study* (Washington, D.C.: U.S. Government Printing Office, 1981), p. 220.

14. Marco A. Gandásegui, Alejandro Saavedra, Andrés Achong, and Iván Quintero, *Las luchas obreras en Panamá: 1850–1978* (Panamá: Centro de Estudios Latinoamericanos "Justo Arosemena," 1980), p. 103.

15. Guillermo Castro Herrera, "Nacionalismo y política nacional," *Revista Mexicana de Sociología*, 42, No. 2 (April-June 1980).

16. Guillermo O'Donnell, *Modernization and Bureaucratic Authoritarianism: Studies in South American Politics* (Berkeley: Institute of International Studies, University of California, Politics of Modernization Series No. 9, 1973).

17. See for example James MacGregor Burns, *Leadership* (New York: Harper and Row, 1978); and Glenn D. Paige, *The Scientific Study of Political Leadership* (New York: The Free Press, 1977).

18. Paige, ibid., pp. 38–39.

19. Paige identifies eighteen dimensions of political leadership behavior of which only a few are examined in this chapter. They are violent coercion, nonviolent influence, control, responsiveness, con-

flict, compromise, consensus, positive affect, negative affect, distribution, association, space, time, communication, technicity, activeness, creativity, and morality. Ibid., p. 139.

20. One major exception was the situation which developed in the fall of 1978. Some members of the General Staff and civilian politicians allied with them felt that Torrijos's domestic and foreign policies had drifted too far to the left. Torrijos retired several key officers and moved many remaining personnel to new assignments.

21. Omar Torrijos, letter to Senator Edward M. Kennedy, reprinted in *Todo por la Patria,* July 1970.

22. Omar Torrijos, *La batalla de Panamá* (Buenos Aires: Editorial Universitaria de Buenos Aires, 1973), p. 88.

23. Inter-American Development Bank, *Economic and Social Progress in Latin America: 1978 Report* (Washington, D.C.: Inter-American Development Bank, 1979), p. 415; U.S. Department of Commerce, *Survey of Current Business* (August 1979), p. 27.

24. One major theory of regime change holds that transformation may result from functional "success" in performing certain tasks at a given level of economic development. Adam Przeworski, "Some Problems in the Study of the Transition to Democracy," *Working Paper* (The Wilson Center Latin American Program, 1980).

25. Steve C. Ropp, *Panamanian Politics: From Guarded Nation to National Guard* (New York: Praeger, 1982).

8

Conclusions

Having looked in some detail at the nature of the crisis in the various countries of Central America through the eyes of our contributors, we can now turn to the more general question of similarities and differences within the region. We will begin by summarizing the major points made by each author with regard to the nature of the crisis in his or her specific country and the factors that seem to be associated with regime adaptation or lack of it. This will be followed by a discussion of the types of crises that appear to be occurring in the region. We will suggest that there are certain common features associated with countries that have demonstrated an ability to adapt. Finally, we will discuss the implications of our findings for thinking about the role of the United States in Central America.

Stephen Gorman's analysis of the Nicaraguan case stresses certain unique historical features that should not be overlooked, given the common legacy of underdevelopment and dependent capitalist structures that Nicaragua shares with its Central American neighbors. In contrast with other Isthmian countries except Panama, population centers were in lowland areas where a natural pass brought Nicaraguans into early contact with British and U.S. interests. This geographically determined contact led to the early emergence of a virulent antiimperialist nationalism in Nicaragua, which was exacerbated by the twentieth century U.S. occupation.

The Somoza dynasty's failure to adapt can be attributed to a number of specific regime features. As Nicaraguan society became increasingly modern and complex after World War II, the political apparatus remained essentially unchanged. The National Guard, which had been molded by Anastasio Somoza in his own image, retained its fundamental allegiance to the dynasty, and opposition political parties were not permitted to operate freely. Yet in spite of the anachronistic nature of these institutions, government scope expanded during the 1960s and 1970s, imposing an outmoded structure and vision on broader segments of society.

Gorman blames the last Somoza (Tachito) for much of this failure to adapt political institutions to the changing times. Anastasio Somoza managed to sell himself to the Nicaraguan people as a progressive dictator interested in national development. His son Luis continued in this vein and also moved slowly in the direction of modernizing political structures. Tachito resorted to a "more open dictatorial style of rule." Not only was he unable to deal creatively with the demands and aspirations of the new agrarian and industrial middle class, but he further strengthened the regime's antinationalist and proimperialist image. The result of this combination of organizational and personal shortcomings was a revolution that overthrew the dynasty.

Tommie Sue Montgomery's discussion of the Salvadoran case emphasizes the long-term historical nature of the crisis—reaching back to the initial establishment in colonial times of a monocrop economy. While the main crops changed from cacao to indigo and later to coffee, their sequential introduction led to the increasing concentration of landholdings and the progressive marginalization of the peasantry. With the establishment of the coffee economy, a set of repressive mechanisms and institutions were introduced to keep this marginalized peasantry in line.

Montgomery describes the cyclic nature of crisis development and response in El Salvador since the early 1930s, when the oligarchy relinquished political control to the armed forces. Consolidation of a new military regime would be followed by increasing repression, which in turn would spark a reaction by the public and among the more progressive officers. This disenchantment would culminate in a series of coups by progressive officers who would promulgate new reforms, but they, too, eventually would be challenged from within the armed forces by conservative officers fearful of the reforms' consequences.

The inability to break out of this cyclic pattern is attributed to a number of reinforcing factors. First, the extreme laissez-faire ideology of the oligarchy set limits on the extent to which the government could be used as an instrument of reform. Second, the military's commitment since the 1930s to its political role and to the economic benefits to be gained through such a role made the transition to any civilian government (whether reformist or not) difficult to achieve. Finally, increasing U.S. intervention in Salvadoran affairs during recent decades tended to reinforce the intransigency of both the oligarchy and the armed forces. Montgomery maintains that the growing power and influence of reformist institutions, such as the Catholic church and revolutionary organizations, would have already led to the collapse of the existing government were it not for U.S. economic and military aid.

Julio Castellanos's examination of the contemporary crisis in Guatemala also emphasizes roots reaching back as far as the Spanish Conquest. He views the Conquest as the "fundamental act of violence" that created a system of racial stratification that has been perpetuated to this day. Class stratification resulted from racial stratification, and both were reinforced by the introduction of coffee during the mid-nineteenth century. Coffee cultivation is seen as a critical determinant of the current crisis because it extended the system of racial domination to all areas of the country, expanded the network of dependent capitalism, attracted a new class of foreign landowners and investors, and forced the Indians off their communal lands. This period also resulted in the militarization of rural society and the formation of military institutions whose paramount loyalty was to the coffee oligarchy.

From this perspective, the failure of all Guatemalan governments to adapt to pressures for change can be traced to the historically rooted racism of the governing elite and of potential ladino counterelites. Unlike Nicaragua, where the counterelite (the Sandinistas) embraced the Indian cause, the Guatemalan reforms of the 1940s were aborted when the urban middle class began to fear that they might go too far. The constraints placed on regime adaptation by a large Indian mass with no real stake in the political system are as great as the constraints placed on the current South African regime.

Castellanos also notes that adaptation is complicated by foreign landowners and the armed forces. The alliance forged during the mid-nineteenth century between the Germans and the local Hispanic elites reinforced the intransigence of the latter. As for the armed forces, their leaders directly participated in the coffee economy for a century and were not distinguishable in terms of their economic interests from the planter class itself. Given this fact, the armed forces could not play a mediating role between races and classes.

John Booth suggests that the political crisis in Costa Rica is somewhat narrower in scope than that in each of the three previously discussed countries. It is essentially the product of economic difficulties that may at some point threaten the legitimacy of existing political arrangements. Economic problems included the decline of export revenues (derived primarily from coffee) and rising import bills for oil, consumer goods, and foodstuffs. Stagflation, unemployment, and the dramatic growth of the nation's debt have made it increasingly difficult to support Costa Rica's large public sector. These economic difficulties have spilled over into the political arena, leading to public employee unrest, and a decision-making stalemate between the legislative and executive branches. Splits within the governing PLN coalition and a decline in the broader political consensus have been aggravated by pressures from the regional crisis.

In spite of these growing difficulties, Booth suggests a number of features of Costa Rican society that may favor adaptation. The low degree of social stratification relative to other Central American countries facilitates interclass dialogue. Most social groups feel that they have access through the democratic process to government decision-making and resource allocation. This gives them a stake in the system and reinforces the legitimacy of government institutions. Elite flexibility leads to imaginative responses to a crisis. Finally, the absence of a large army with a traditional political role has freed resources for the solution of economic problems.

James Morris views the Honduran crisis as a complex and multilevel phenomenon. On the one hand, Honduras faces a series of old and new economic problems with potentially serious economic consequences. The country remains the least developed in the region and is at the mercy of world commodity price fluctuations because of its monocultural export economy.

At the same time, it is experiencing stagflation and pressures on the national budget due to recent public sector expansion. Political leaders are struggling to adapt to new political expectations arising from lower class mobilization. The traditional parties have remained intact but have been increasingly rent by internal factionalism. Conflict has also increased between these traditional political parties and newer interest groups. The result has been a long-term crisis of political legitimacy that is compounded by the issue of military participation in politics.

However, as in Costa Rica, adaptation is promoted by a relatively low degree of social stratification. While the ideologies of the traditional parties to some extent impede the search for solutions to national problems, their multiclass nature and remaining legitimacy give the country well-developed institutional mechanisms for adjusting disputes between groups and classes. The recent origins of the military and its lack of ties to a traditional oligarchy give the country a second institution capable of managing disputes. Morris also notes that Honduras can avail itself of a number of sources of external economic support (the United States, Mexico, and Venezuela) in attempting to address its current problems.

Steve Ropp's analysis of Panama suggests that economic problems similar to those experienced by other countries in the region (stagflation, public sector costs, debt, and so forth) are aggravating several political crises that are of relatively recent origin. At one level, there is a crisis of "fit" between government and economy occurring as Panama moves beyond the import substitution phase and toward participation in the multinational service economy. At a second level, a crisis of individual leadership exists as top officers in the National Guard and civilian leaders try to fill the vacuum created with the death of Omar Torrijos in 1981.

Ropp notes that some of Panama's adaptive characteristics seem to be unique within the region. The country's economy is not tied to coffee (nor to any "basket" of export crops) but rather to services supplied to the U.S. government and multinational corporations operating within the canal area. These services have a much more stable market, which places a so-called floor under the Panamanian economy. In addition, Panama appears to have unique access to the coffers of both the U.S. government and multinationals. The U.S. government, concerned with the political stability of a country surrounding one of its strategic arteries, has been willing to grant sizable loans. Multinational banks, concerned with Panama's stability for economic rather than geostrategic reasons, have been equally generous. Finally, Panama can rely on both traditional political parties and the National Guard to supply relatively flexible leadership for resolving political crises.

When we look at the full range of descriptions given by our chapter authors of crisis conditions in their individual countries, we find that the crises they describe fall into two distinct categories. First, there are those countries where the crisis appears to be limited to the level of the *regime*. In these countries, what is problematical is the continued survival of the particular system of relations between the main political institutions and actors (the executive, the legislature, the political parties, the military, and so forth). John Booth asks whether the economic crisis in Costa Rica will undermine the legitimacy of the set of regime relationships generally characterized as democratic that have survived there since World War II. James Morris suggests that the Honduran crisis centers around the question of whether it is possible to construct a viable new regime relationship around the traditional political parties, the armed forces, and newer socioeconomic groups. Panama also seems to be a country in which regime relationships are exceedingly fluid and reaching crisis proportions due to economic pressures.

While these regime crises (both manifest and latent) are no doubt serious, they differ in both scope and kind from a second type of crisis that is described by the authors of our chapters on El Salvador and Guatemala. Here, the crises appear to be crises of the *state* in that the entire structure of dominant-subordinate socioeconomic relationships has been called into question.[1] In El Salvador, the erosion of a system of economic domination based on export agriculture lies at the root of the crisis of the state. Tommie Sue Montgomery forecasts inevitable revolution as the structure of dominant-subordinate relationships unravels there. According to Julio Castellanos, the primary axis of conflict in Guatemala is racial rather than economic, but the crisis is akin to that in El Salvador in terms of magnitude.[2] What is being challenged is not merely the nature of regime relations but the very structure of the state.

Using this dichotomous framework of regime and state crises, the Nicaraguan case is the most difficult to classify. Gorman describes a growing crisis of legitimacy experienced by a Nicaraguan regime grounded in a well-established system of dependent capitalism. And yet his analysis suggests that the unique historical development of Nicaragua did not foster the development of as rigid a pattern of class relationships as was the case in El Salvador and Guatemala. The collapse of the Somoza dynasty was due in large part to its maintenance of a rigid political apparatus in a context of rapid modernization. Maintenance of this apparatus was determined as much by the political ineptness and personal rigidity of the last Somoza as by deep class or racial divisions. From such a perspective, Nicaragua can be viewed as having experienced a regime crisis which led to the accession to power of revolutionary leaders seeking to impose revolutionary programs on the general populace.

Since a crisis of the state takes place at the most comprehensive level, it will necessarily be accompanied by a regime crisis. This is clear in the case of both El Salvador and Guatemala, where the rapidly changing regime structures that rely heavily on the military for support are experiencing serious problems of legitimacy and consolidation. However, it is not equally true that a regime crisis will necessarily be accompanied by a crisis at the level of the state. While latent crises of socioeconomic relations may exist in Costa Rica, Honduras, and Panama, they do not appear to be of sufficient intensity to threaten revolution.

What factors help explain why two Central American countries (El Salvador and Guatemala) are experiencing crises of the state while the others are experiencing regime crises? For a partial explanation, we can return to our historical observation that no single avenue was pursued for the achievement of wealth in all countries. In Panama and Nicaragua, commercial interests were important during the colonial period because of natural transit routes existing there. Stockraising and subsistence agriculture became the primary economic activities in Costa Rica and Honduras. In Guatemala and El Salvador, agricultural commodity exports of cacao, indigo, cochineal, and later, coffee allowed for the early development and self-capitalization of a strong indigenous agrarian elite. In the Guatemalan case, the elite's status and cohesion was reinforced by the country's historical importance as a colonial administrative center and by fear of the Indian masses.

It was not the introduction of coffee per se that led to the creation of inflexible elites in El Salvador and Guatemala. Rather, coffee reinforced rigid systems of dominance where they had developed earlier. In Costa Rica and Honduras, the introduction of coffee came well after more egalitarian patterns of class relations had been established. In Panama and Nicaragua, the existence of influential commercial elites prevented the consolidation of rural oligarchies sufficiently powerful to dominate the country.

These historical distinctions are critical to an understanding of the different responses of various Central American regimes to more recent catalytic, crisis-reinforcing events. All of our chapter authors have noted the importance of a constellation of economic difficulties associated with the global economic crisis of the past decade. More important than these conditions themselves is the different impact they had on various countries. In Panama, Honduras, and Costa Rica, existing regimes were challenged. In El Salvador and Guatemala, the entire structure of the state was further threatened.

Not only do the crises in various Central American countries appear to be of two distinct kinds, but these countries differ in how they deal with them (see Table 8.1). Our chapter authors suggest that certain features are rather consistently associated with the ability to adapt.

One important indicator of a society's ability to adapt is the degree of social stratification. Social stratification has been recognized since the time of the Greeks as an important factor affecting political stability and adaptability. As nations modernize, strains are created when emerging classes experience a sense of relative deprivation.[3] At the same time, traditionally influential classes experience a sense of status reversal and downward mobility that creates resentment toward both upwardly mobile and stationary social groups.[4] The greater the preexisting degree of social stratification within a given society, the less likely that adaptation will occur in a peaceful and evolutionary fashion.

Both the Honduran and Costa Rican case studies suggest that

Table 8.1. Factors associated with national adaptation and inability to adapt

	Associated with Adaptation		Associated with Inability to Adapt
Costa Rica	openness and pluralism of political system elite political skills and flexibility low degree of social stratification	Nicaragua	closed and centralized political system no autonomous military rapidly expanding regime scope lack of individual leadership skills regime association with external power
Honduras	institutionalized traditional multiclass parties autonomous military low degree of social stratification economic resources and support available from external sources	El Salvador	elite laissez-faire ideology military commitment to military rule regime association with and support from external power
Panama	individual leadership skills economic resources and support available from external sources	Guatemala	racism of elites and counterelites alliance between local elites and foreign entrepreneurs closed and centralized political system

a lower degree of social stratification has promoted compromise and evolutionary change through its impact on political culture, institutions, and elites. In highly stratified El Salvador and Guatemala, adaptation is less likely to occur. Although violent conflict will continue in these two countries because they are unable to adapt, it will take different forms because of differences in the nature of their systems of social stratification. In countries like El Salvador, where this system is based primary in class, dissident groups tend to emphasize economic goals such as income redistribution through welfare policies, taxation, and land reform. In countries like Guatemala, where stratification is based primarily on race, the struggle centers around redefinition of the symbols and sociocultural character of the nation-state.[5]

A second feature, which appears to be associated with adaptability, is a higher degree of differentiation within the political system. Differentiation refers to the process by which roles and institutional spheres within a given society become increasingly separate and specialized. It was once assumed that the more "modern" a society became, the more differentiated its political and administrative structures would become. This, in turn, was believed to imply greater governmental capacity to coordinate and conciliate relations among various social groups and classes. The view that differentiated political structures necessarily contributed to increased social coordination and cooperation has more recently been recognized as overly simple and as too heavily influenced by biological analogies. Among other problems, highly differentiated political structures in developing countries often suffer from feuding and bureaucratic immobility. While these tendencies can indeed contribute to a crisis at the regime level, bureaucratic and general political differentiation increases the likelihood that crises at the level of the state will be ameliorated. Groups on the periphery are more likely to develop access to the center through new channels of participation. Nonelite groups and classes may find allies of convenience among the competing bureaucrats at the top, winning concessions in exchange for their political allegiance.[6] Such appears to have been the case, for example, in Honduras during the mid-1970s when the armed forces supported peasant demands for land reform.

In the cases of Nicaragua, El Salvador, and Guatemala, our

authors suggest that the regimes were relatively undifferentiated.[7] For example, in Nicaragua neither the political parties nor the National Guard functioned independent of central authority. By way of contrast, both Costa Rica and Honduras contain viable, established political parties that represent alternative policies and class interests. In both Honduras and Panama, military institutions have developed an autonomous identity that has allowed them to mediate interclass disputes. What seems to be important in relation to adaptation is not so much the existence of civilian or military forms of government but rather the existence of a range of institutions (whether civil or military) that are not totally responsive to some dominant socioeconomic group.[8]

Our authors' analysis also suggests that individual leadership skills play an important role in adaptation. Nicaragua and Panama offer two starkly contrasting examples of such leadership ability. In the case of the former, a brutal and callous dictator made a difficult situation worse by recentralizing power and extending the scope of government activity at a time when precisely the opposite was called for. In the latter, a more politically skilled authoritarian leader fashioned a variety of supple coalitions that allowed Panama to traverse a difficult decade of change in the composition of the regime. Further evidence of the importance of such skills can be seen in the Costa Rican and Honduran cases where elite politicians have proven flexible and imaginative. On the other hand, the Salvadoran case suggests that the vacillation and naiveté of key junior officers and civilian reformists contributed to the inability to carry through with regime transformation in 1979. The reformists were outmaneuvered by more conservative individuals such as Colonels Jaime Abdúl Gutiérrez and José Guillermo García.

One final feature of these societies highlighted by our case studies stands in confusing relationship to regime adaptability. Most of these regimes rely heavily on economic and military aid, particularly from the United States, but our authors disagree concerning its impact. Gorman argues that external aid reinforced the intransigency of the Somoza dictatorship, and Montgomery suggests that it plays a critical role in perpetuating the inflexible regime in El Salvador. However, regime adaptation appears to have been enhanced in Honduras and Panama. How can we reconcile these different points of view? One approach is to consider external aid as a secondary feature of crisis dynamics in these countries, either reinforcing the intransigency of rigid regimes or facilitating the process of adaptation in more flexible ones. What is critical is the nature of the recipient government. On the other hand, external aid may promote short-term rigidity and long-term adaptability (or vice versa). A case in point is El Salvador, where it can be argued that U.S. aid props up the current conservative regime in the short run while undermining it in the long run through encouragement of increased military autonomy. Given such complexities, we need to look at the impact of external aid on a case-by-case basis.

What are the implications of these findings for our thinking concerning the course that the United States should pursue in Central America? We have suggested that regional crises are of different types and that we need to adjust our thinking about them accordingly. With regard to regime crises, we must ask whether the perpetuation of existing regimes is compatible with U.S. interests and national values. In at least one case, the answer to this question appears to be an unqualified "yes." Given the democratic nature of the present Costa Rican regime and its ability to accommodate a wide range of socioeconomic interests, continued support for that regime would appear to be desirable.

In the cases of Panama and Honduras, the answer is somewhat less clear. Our analysis suggests that both countries are dominated by civil-military regimes rather than by civilian ones, and yet it is precisely the existence of strong, independent military institutions that allowed these regimes to move during the 1970s toward reform and away from complete domination by traditionally powerful vested interests. Assuming that our primary goal is encouraging further reform and secondarily encouraging movement toward democracy, we should pursue a course of action that attempts to calibrate carefully the existing civil-military relationship. In both Panama and Honduras, civil-military coalitions are tilted in the direction of military dominance. By encouraging the further development of a democratic opening in these countries, we can bring civilian and military institutions into closer balance.

For countries where the entire system is in crisis (crises of the state), there is the question of whether perpetuation of the existing configurations of power is in our long-term national interest. Given the nature of dominant-subordinate relationships in Guatemala and El Salvador, particularly their high level of social stratification, it is doubtful whether such is the case. This presents at least the alternative of reducing ties with the military government in Guatemala and of reversing U.S. policy toward El Salvador. The real tragedy of U.S. policy in El Salvador is that it was one of the few countries in Central America where the United States' role has not been dictated by long-term political or economic involvement. There, the existence of a strong indigenous elite precluded significant or sustained U.S. influence prior to the 1960s.

As for Nicaragua, we have seen that the collapse of the Somoza regime stemmed largely from the effort to maintain a rigid and undifferentiated set of institutional structures during a period of rapid modernization. If similarly rigid structures developed by the Sandinistas merely replace those imposed by the somocistas, then a new regime crisis can be expected at some future date. Assuming that Nicaragua is continuing to experience a regime crisis rather than a crisis of the state, U.S. policy should seek to encourage the development of strong, autonomous institutions that contribute to economic and social change.

As a general rule, it would seem reasonable that the United States attempt to reinforce those features within all Central American countries that are associated with adaptation. First, we should support economic and social policies aimed at decreasing social stratification—even at the risk of encouraging further social unrest. This can be done through a variety of programs that would redistribute income and open the political process to excluded segments of society. We have seen that adaptation is associated with the existence of autonomous institutions such as political parties and the armed forces. As paradoxical as it may seem, U.S. efforts to bolster Central American military institutions in an effort to impede change may actually facilitate it in the long run. Strong independent military institutions can serve as a "bridge" between intransigent oligarchies and the forces of change. However, we must recognize that any policy designed to encourage regime adaptability by increasing the strength of the armed forces runs the risk of militarizing society, which would clearly conflict with our national values.

To avoid this outcome, the United States should simultaneously strengthen civilian institutions such as political parties and national interest groups. Finally, we should seek to promote adaptation by encouraging flexible elites and individual political leaders.

No magic formula exists for accomplishing these goals. Forming a sound national policy toward Central America requires that we recognize that the crises in different countries vary in character and in intensity. At the same time, we must recognize that the area is experiencing a "crisis of crises" where the whole is greater than the sum of its parts.[9] Policy makers rarely have the luxury (as did the National Bipartisan Commission on Central America) of "disaggregating" the regional crises that face them, minutely examining the constituent elements, and designing policies that are carefully tailored to the unique necessities of each individual country involved. The central question in this regard would seem to be whether the regional "crisis of crises" poses such a serious security threat to the United States that it calls for a uniform regional response that ignores the country differences that we have discussed. For example, in the name of regional security, such a uniform policy response might aim at stabilizing all regimes supportive of the United States, regardless of their character and prospects for long-term survival.

Surely, the worst possible regional response would be one involving the direct and long-term application of U.S. military force. John Booth has noted the devastating impact that the introduction of U.S. troops into the region would have on the Costa Rican regime. We have only to go back to the early twentieth century to find a case in which such an imposed military solution created some of the very problems that the United States faces today. When Marines were dispatched to Nicaragua, the regime there was much like the one in Honduras. Political parties vied with an incipient army for control of the government. But U.S. policies centralized power in the hands of a new National Guard, encouraging the growth of a personal dictatorship. Centralized institutions controlled by the right virtually ensured the subsequent emergence of centralized institutions controlled by the left. Such lessons of history should not be ignored in the current context, and we can only hope that the dispatch of U.S.

troops to Grenada in October 1983 did not signal a return to militarily imposed solutions to political problems.

In our opinion, any successful U.S. policy must be guided by recognition that these Central American crises have their origins both in domestic history and in patterns of external involvement. In El Salvador and Guatemala, where crises of the state are manifest, U.S. support for existing regimes could delay but not prevent their collapse. It would be folly for the United States to pursue a course of action that runs against the strong historical currents at work there in a misplaced effort to protect legitimate national security interests. Elsewhere in the region, we should encourage the process of adaptation by using the tactics mentioned above. Such a country-specific approach may be more difficult to explain to the U.S. public, but it stands a better chance of long-term success.

Notes

1. Fernando Henrique Cardoso, "On the Characterization of Authoritarian Regimes in Latin America," in *The New Authoritarianism in Latin America*, ed. David Collier (Princeton, N.J.: Princeton University Press, 1979), p. 38.

2. The term "axis" as used here has a quite specific meaning. Sociologist Daniel Bell describes the use of axial principles and structures as the effort "to specify not causation . . . but centrality. Looking for the answer to the question of how a society hangs together, it seeks to specify . . . the organizing frame around which other institutions are draped." In Guatemala, this primary axis has been race, while in El Salvador it has been class and the system of property relations. Daniel Bell, *The Coming Post-Industrial Society: A Venture in Social Forecasting* (New York: Basic Books, 1973), pp. 10–11.

3. "Relative deprivation" has been defined by Ted Gurr as the "actors' perceptions of discrepancy between their value expectations (the goods and conditions of the life they believe they are justifiably entitled to) and their value capabilities (the amount of those goods and conditions that they think they are able to get and keep)." See his "Causal Models of Civil Strife: A Comparative Analysis Using New Indices," *American Political Science Review* 62, no. 4 (December 1968), p. 1104.

4. On this point, see Joseph Greenblum and Leonard Pearlin, "Vertical Mobility and Prejudice: A Socio-Psychological Analysis," in *Class, Status, and Power: A Reader in Social Stratification*, ed. Reinhard

Bendix and Seymour M. Lipset (Glencoe, Ill.: Free Press, 1953), pp. 480–91.

5. Myron Weiner, "Political Participation: Crisis of the Political Process," in Leonard Binder, et al., *Crises and Sequences of Political Development* (Princeton, N.J.: Princeton University Press, 1971), p. 168.

6. James Coleman, "The Development Syndrome: Differentiation–Equality–Capacity," in Binder, et al., *Crises and Sequences*, pp. 75–93.

7. The crises in Nicaragua, Guatemala, and El Salvador are all crises associated with highly centralized political structures, However, it does not follow that these structures are the same or are centralized for the same reasons. In Nicaragua, centralization was the product of specific events associated with U.S. intervention (i.e., formation of the National Guard). In Guatemala, it was the product of historical conditions which created a military closely aligned with the coffee elite. The contemporary centralized political structure of Guatemala differs from that of El Salvador in terms of the relationship between the armed forces and political parties. After 1963, the Guatemalan military ruled politically through a number of conservative parties. In El Salvador, only one party has been allowed to represent the dominant faction within the military since World War II.

8. One might speculate as to whether the increased independence since 1980 of the Salvadoran armed forces from the oligarchy, which is noted by Montgomery, will increase the likelihood of regime adaptation. It would be supremely ironic if U.S. military and economic aid aimed at bolstering a relatively conservative regime resulted in sufficient military autonomy to allow the institution to redefine its relationship to the Salvadoran masses.

9. The concept of "crisis of crises" is drawn from John Platt, "What We Must Do," in *Search for Alternatives: Public Policy and the Study of the Future*, ed. Franklin Tugwell (Cambridge, Mass.: Winthrop Publishers, 1973), pp. 4–7.

Notes on Bibliography

During the past several years, writings and reflections on Central American affairs have increased at a phenomenal rate. For a region once subject to the benign neglect of scholars, journalists, and politicians, the recent rise in attention has been almost too much to bear. The small but steady output of a handful of scholars has been overwhelmed by a wave of instant punditry purporting to explain contemporary events. In spite of this trend, scholars who have studied the area for years, along with a number of talented newcomers, are rapidly producing a new literature on the Central American crisis that is rich in insights. The purpose of these notes is to introduce the beginning student of Central American affairs to the diversity of viewpoints existing within this literature.

There are a number of major areas of disagreement reflected in the literature on the Central American crisis. Lack of agreement stems in large part from the existence of a wide variety of ideological and analytical perspectives that focus various observers' attention in different ways on different aspects of the crisis. The wide range of perspectives has led to disagreement concerning the fundamental nature of the crisis. Is it primarily political, economic, or demographic? There is also disagreement as to the major participants in the crisis and the relative weight one should give to the activities of these participants. Are the major participants domestic groups and interests? Are they external actors and, if so, which ones? Finally, there is a lack of agreement as to the time frame within which the crisis is most appropriately analyzed. Is it best analyzed as the product of long-term historical forces and structures, or is it of medium or even short-term origins and duration?

One explanation widely used in the literature on the regional crisis is that it results from a fixed set of economic and social conditions. Many popular accounts start with the assumption that conditions such as mass poverty and unequal patterns of land distribution are sufficient in and of themselves to explain the growing violence of the oppressed classes. More common among U.S. policy makers is the view that this fixed set of economic conditions has operated in conjunction with a more dynamic cluster of recent economic developments (escalating oil costs, declining export prices, inflation, and unemployment) to produce an explosive situation. Oddly enough, general agreement existed in both the Carter and Reagan administrations as to the primacy of these static and dynamic economic factors in explaining the crisis. Disagreements centered around the precise mix of such factors and the extent to which the situation had been exacerbated by outside forces.

The statements and writings of U.S. policy makers reflect belief in the existence of major indigenous problems, but they tend to assume that these problems are the product of the region's autonomous historical development. While there may be recognition that some of the factors affecting regional stability are linked to global developments (for example, the post-1973 energy crisis), policy makers do not consistently attribute regional problems to the external environment. On the other hand, the writings of many Latin Americans and some U.S. scholars reflect the view that the Central American crisis results primarily from conditions created by regional ties to the global capitalist system. Particularly from the perspective of Marxist scholarship, the historical subordination of the lower classes, unequal patterns of land distribution, and monocultural economies are viewed as the product of a global system of domination and exploitation.

The Latin American left's analysis of the crisis sometimes stresses the regressive and stagnating impact that Central America's dependent relationship to the world capitalist system has had on regional conditions such as land and income distribution. However, more common on the left is the view that this dependency relationship has had a dynamic and tremendously destabilizing effect on the region, particularly since World War II.

Central America is viewed as having experienced a period of "delayed dependent development," when area economies dominated by export agriculture were replaced by ones in which industry and the public sector played a more important role. Growth of the Central American Common Market (viewed as a product of the logic of a higher stage of global capitalist development) created new entrepreneurial classes. The creation of these new classes led, in turn, to a breakdown in elite consensus and to intra-elite feuding. This process of delayed dependent development has been used by some scholars to explain the Nicaraguan Revolution.

Although left-wing scholars and U.S. policy makers differ radically with regard to the perspectives they use to analyze the Central American crisis, some agreement is reflected in the literature with regard to the political effects of recent economic developments. Both recognize that old elites associated with export agriculture are losing their ability to govern by themselves, and are engaged in an increasingly desperate effort to retain control. There is also widespread agreement that the breakdown of this old elite consensus has resulted in the emergence of the military as a key institution attempting to mediate disputes between old and new interests through the use of force. Reference is made to praetorianism, Bonapartism, and the "new military." Different ideological perspectives color the view taken of military participation in politics, but this new reality is recognized by all.

The erosion of political control by landed elites and the fluid mix of groups, institutions, and classes currently vying for control of Central American governments has raised age-old political questions that are extensively discussed in this literature. Does the crisis fundamentally result from the fact that area regimes have lost their legitimacy? Are they no longer able to perform in accordance with the expectations of developmentally oriented masses and middle sectors in a developmentally oriented world? Was the collapse of the Somoza dynasty due in the final analysis to the inability of the last Somoza to convince a sufficient number of Nicaraguans that his government was legitimate and governed in their interests?

Some writings focus on the timeless issue of political participation. Historically, most Central American political systems were dominated by landed elites that sometimes allowed a degree of contest among elite factions but did not extend participation to include emerging middle sectors or the masses. Many observers of the regional scene suggest that it is the struggle for more inclusive modes of political organization and representation which lies at the heart of the Central American crisis.

In addition to political and economic explanations, some writers have noted the role that demographic and environmental factors have played in the crisis. Developments such as rapid population growth, urbanization, the changing relationship of peasants to land as a result of the commercialization of agriculture, and environmental degradation have been discussed. It is widely believed that the so-called soccer war between El Salvador and Honduras in 1969 was partially the result of population pressures in El Salvador that forced many peasants to emigrate to Honduras. However, those who recognize the impact of such factors tend to view them as of secondary importance. The structure of political and economic systems are seen as ultimately determining such matters as land availability and environmental degradation.

Regarding the issue of participants in the crisis, the existing literature reflects considerably more agreement concerning the role of foreign participants. Most observers agree that Central American political systems are subject to extensive outside influence, but strong ideological differences separate these observers when they come to assess its sources and purposes. Those on the far right of the political spectrum emphasize the role of international communism to the virtual exclusion of other considerations. More moderate U.S. observers, while attributing an important role to Soviet and Cuban influence in exacerbating the regional crisis, nonetheless place greater emphasis on the domestic conditions that created such opportunities for outside involvement. From a left-wing perspective, the primary external participants in Central American events are believed to be the United States and the global multinational corporations. The Central American crisis is viewed as largely the product of a capitalist world-system dynamic that has produced and helped to perpetuate internal economic and political structures incapable of solving problems of development. However, not all of the literature dealing with external sources of influence is so heavily colored by ideology. Much of it simply attempts to come to grips with the reality that the small countries of Central America are very much swayed by actors and forces operating within the international system.

Many writings reflect the view that transnational actors have played a critical role in the crisis, with the Catholic church being perceived as one of the most important. Prior to the Second Vatican Council convened under Pope John XXIII in 1962, the church was only marginally concerned with social issues. Vatican II and the Latin American Bishops Conference held in Medellín, Colombia in 1968 focused attention on poverty and social injustice. The church began to change its outlook as priests moved into the countryside to organize peasants into grass-roots communities for both social and religious purposes. A new "theology of liberation" was embraced by large segments of the Central American priesthood.

It is widely noted in the literature that the Catholic church played a quite different role in the Nicaraguan Revolution than it had played in Cuba's revolution two decades earlier. The growth of a new social consciousness among Nicaraguan priests coincided with the growing repressiveness of the Somoza regime, particularly after the 1972 earthquake. The church became radicalized, first attempting to mediate between Somoza and the Sandinistas and later siding openly with the guerrillas. After the revolution, a number of priests assumed high government positions. Today, the Catholic church and certain Protestant groups are socially active throughout Central America, bringing the external power of religious principle and organization to bear on the continuing crisis in the region.

Some writings stress the role of political parties as transnational actors. The Communist Party is frequently cited by the right as a major source of influence through the Cuban and Soviet connection, and many observers view the Social Democratic and Christian Democratic parties as also playing an important role. The Social Democrats are organized through the Socialist International, which brought together national party leaders such as Felipe Gonzales of Spain, Olaf Palme of Sweden, and Willy Brandt of West Germany. Links to the Caribbean and Central America were made with regional parties including Venezuela's Acción Democrática, Costa Rica's Liberación Nacional, and Panama's

Partido Revolucionario Democrático. The Christian Democrats were internationally organized in much the same fashion and had the ability through their international network to influence Central American events.

One of the primary reasons that international political parties are able to influence events in Central America is that they are associated with another important transnational actor, the nation-state. Some, such as the Communist Party, are associated with a superpower. Others, such as the Social Democrat or the Christian Democrat parties, tend to be associated with "middle powers." Although writings of both the right and left frequently depict the global power equation as one dominated by the United States and the Soviet Union, events since World War II have led to the emergence of a number of other nation-states capable of exercising considerable independent influence. The influence of the Social and Christian Democratic parties in Central American events derives indirectly from the strength of West Germany as a major industrial power and the strength of Mexico and Venezuela as oil producers.

Much of the crisis literature tends to suggest that there is a single set of explanatory factors applicable in all six countries. However, not all observers have accepted this initial premise—that the crisis is truly regional in the sense that a common set of factors can be used to explain each individual case of violence and instability. For example, some have argued that the Nicaraguan Revolution was a unique case, serving as a catalyst but not necessarily as a model for the broader regional crisis. The fall of the regime is viewed as the idiosyncratic result of the tyrannical leadership exercised by Somoza and the National Guard.

The lack of consensus with regard to the time frame within which the crisis is most appropriately analyzed adds another dimension of disagreement to the existing literature. Such differences cut across ideological perspectives and relate primarily to the background and academic training of the observer. For the historian the crisis tends to be viewed as the long-term culmination of historical dynamics such as the unraveling of the system of the dependent capitalism or the collapse of the nineteenth-century Liberal model of development (stressing economic progress achieved through a strong central government and the growth of export agriculture). Mid-term explanations emphasize changes in a variety of social, economic, and demographic factors during the past three decades. These factors lie within the general "field of vision" of social scientists, so it is not surprising that this professional group stresses their importance. Extremely short-term explanations of the crisis are usually associated with poor journalism or considerable ideological bias.

From this survey of trends in the existing literature on the Central American crisis, it is apparent that a number of areas of general agreement and disagreement are attributable to differences in ideological and analytical perspective. General agreement across perspectives can be seen in recognition of the fact that 1) old regimes based on landed oligarchies have collapsed and have been replaced by unstable coalitions mediated by the armed forces, and 2) Central American nation states are highly susceptible to outside influence. Areas of disagreement are more extensive and relate not only to the crisis activities observed but to the causal dynamics of the crisis and the motives imputed to various participants. Both the left and the right attribute a high degree of influence to outside participants, but ideological differences lead them to focus on different ones. Major differences also exist with regard to the time frame deemed relevant by observers to analyze the crisis. For historians and some social scientists, the crisis appears to be the product of long-term forces. Those less inclined to see in the past "the baby figure of the giant mass of things to come" stress more recent developments and changes.

Selected Bibliography on Central America

Adams, Richard N. "Cultural Components of Central America." *American Anthropologist* 58, no. 5 (1956), 881–907.
———. *Cultural Surveys of Panama-Nicaragua-Guatemala-El Salvador-Honduras.* Scientific Publications, no. 33. Washington, D.C.: Pan American Sanitary Bureau, 1957.
———. *Crucifixion by Power: Essays on Guatemalan National Power Structure, 1944–1966.* Austin: University of Texas Press, 1970.
———. "The Sandinistas and the Indians." *Caribbean Review* 10, no. 1 (Winter 1981), 22–25, 55–56.
Aguilera P., Gabriel. "El estado, la lucha de clases y la violencia." *Revista Mexicana de sociología* 42, no. 2 (April-June 1980), pp. 21–44.
Alegria, Claribel, and D. J. Flakoll. *Nicaragua, La revolución sandinista: una cronica politica, 1855–1979.* Mexico: Ediciones Dra, 1982.
Allman, T. D. "Rising to Rebellion." *Harper's Magazine* 262, no. 1570 (March 1981), 31–50.
———. "Reagan's Manifest Destiny." *Harper's Magazine* 267, no. 1600 (September 1983), 30–39.
Ameringer, Charles D. *Democracy in Costa Rica.* New York: Praeger, 1982.
———. *Don Pepe: A Political Biography of José Figueres.* Albuquerque: University of New Mexico Press, 1978.
Anderson, Charles W. "Politics and Development Policy in Central America." *Midwest Journal of Political Science* 5, no. 4 (1961), 332–50.
———. "Nicaragua: The Somoza Dynasty." In *Political Systems of Latin America*, edited by Martin C. Needler, 108–31. New York: Litton Educational Publishing, 1978.

Anderson, Thomas P. *Matanza: El Salvador's Communist Revolt of 1932*. Lincoln: University of Nebraska Press, 1971.

———. *Politics in Central America: Guatemala, El Salvador, Honduras, and Nicaragua*. New York: Praeger, 1982.

Armstrong, Robert, and Janet Shenk. *El Salvador: The Face of Revolution*. Boston: South End Press, 1982.

Arnson, Cynthia. *El Salvador: A Revolution Confronts the United States* Washington, D.C.: Institute for Policy Studies, 1982.

Baloyra, Enrique. *El Salvador in Transition*. Chapel Hill: University of North Carolina Press, 1982.

Bardini, Roberto. *Conexión en Tegucigalpa: El somocismo en Honduras*. México D.F.: Universidad Autónoma de Puebla, 1982.

Bell, John Patrick. *Crisis in Costa Rica: The Revolution of 1948*. Austin: University of Texas Press, 1971.

Bialer, Sewerlyn, and Alfred Stepan. "Cuba, the U.S., and the Central American Mess." *New York Review of Books* 29 (May 27, 1982), 17–18, 20, 22.

Black, George. "Garrison Guatemala." *NACLA Report on the Americas* 17, no. 1 (January-February 1983), 2–26.

Black, Jan. "The Canal and the Caribbean." In *The Restless Caribbean: Changing Patterns of International Relations*, edited by Richard Millett and W. Marvin Will, 90–102. New York: Praeger, 1979.

Blasier, Cole. *The Hovering Giant: U.S. Responses to Revolutionary Change in Latin America*. Pittsburgh: University of Pittsburgh Press, 1976.

Blutstein, Howard I., et al. *Area Handbook for El Salvador*. Washington, D.C.: American University, 1970.

———. *Area Handbook for Honduras*. Washington, D.C.: American University, 1971.

Bodenheimer, Susan, et al. *La inversión extranjera en Centroamerica*. 2d ed. San José: Editorial Universitaria Centroamericana (EDUCA), 1975.

Booth, John A. "A Guatemalan Nightmare: Levels of Political Violence, 1966–72." *Journal of InterAmerican Studies and World Affairs* 22, no. 2 (May 1980), 195–225.

———. "Celebrating the Demise of Somocismo: Fifty Recent Spanish Sources on the Nicaraguan Revolution." *Latin American Research Review* 17, no. 1 (1982), 173–89.

———. *The End and the Beginning: The Nicaraguan Revolution*. Boulder, Colo.: Westview Press, 1982.

Bossert, Thomas John. "Can We Return to the Regime for Comparative Analysis? Or the State and Health Policy in Central America." *Comparative Politics* 15, no. 4 (July 1983), 419–41.

Bowdler, George A., and Patrick Cotter. *Voter Participation in Central America, 1954–1981: An Exploration.* Washington, D.C.: University Press of America, 1982.

Brown, Gene, ed. *Central America and the Caribbean.* New York: Arno Press, 1980.

Browning, David. *El Salvador: Landscape and Society.* Oxford: Clarendon Press, 1971.

Burbach, Roger, and Patricia Flynn, eds. *The Politics of Intervention: The United States in Central America.* New York: Monthly Review Press, 1983.

Cardoso, Ciro F. S. "Historia económica del café en Centroamerica (Siglo XIX): estudio comparativo." *Estudios sociales centroamericanos* 4, no. 10 (January-April 1975), 9–56.

———, and Héctor Pérez Brignoli. *Centroamerica y la economía occidental (1520–1930).* San José: Editorial de la Universidad de Costa Rica, 1977.

Carías, Marco Virgilio, and Daniel Slutzky. *La guerra inútil; análisis socioeconómico del conflicto entre Honduras y El Salvador.* San José: Editorial Universitaria Centroamericana (EDUCA), 1978.

Carvajal Herrera, Mario. *Actitudes políticas del costarricense.* San José: Editorial Universitaria Centroamericana (EDUCA), 1978.

Caspi, Dan, and Mitchell A. Seligson. "Toward an Empirical Theory of Tolerance: Radical Groups in Israel and Costa Rica." *Comparative Political Studies* 15, no. 4 (January 1983), 385–404.

Castro Herrera, Guillermo. "Panamá ante la década del 1980," *Centroamerica en crisis.* México D.F.: Colegio de México, 1980.

"Central America: A Season of Martyrs." *Christianity and Crisis* 40 (May 12, 1980), entire issue.

"Central America and the Caribbean: New Political Earthquake Zone?" *Great Decisions* (1981), 43–52.

"Central America: The Process of Revolution," *Latin American Perspectives,* vol. 10, no. 1 (Winter 1983), entire issue.

Central America Information Office. *El Salvador, Background to the Crisis.* Cambridge, Mass.: Central American Information Office, 1982.

Centro de Estudios Internacionales. *Centroamerica en crisis.* México D.F.: Colegio de México, 1980.

CEPAL. *Tenencia de la tierra y desarrollo rural en Centroamerica.* San José: Editorial Universitaria Centroamericana (EDUCA), 1973.

Chacón Leon, Edwin. *El sindicalismo en Costa Rica.* San José: Comentarios Centroamericanos del Centro de Estudios Laborales, 1980.

Clegern, Wayne. "Change and Development in Central America." *Caribbean Studies* 5, (1966), 28–34.

Colvin, Gerard. *The Lands and Peoples of Central America: Guatemala, El Salvador, Costa Rica, Honduras, Nicaragua, Panama, British Honduras.* New York: Macmillan, 1961.

Crain, David A. "Guatemalan Revolutionaries and Havana's Ideological Offensive of 1966–1968," *Journal of InterAmerican Studies and World Affairs* 17, no. 2 (May 1975), 175–205.

Crawley, Eduardo. *Dictators Never Die: A Portrait of Nicaragua and the Somoza Dynasty.* New York: St. Martin's Press, 1979.

Cruz, Arturo J. "Nicaragua's Imperiled Revolution," *Foreign Affairs*, vol. 61, no. 5 (Summer 1983), 1031–47.

Devine, Frank J. *El Salvador: Embassy under Attack.* New York: Vantage Press, 1981.

Diederich, Bernard. "Did Human Rights Kill Anastasio Somoza?" *Caribbean Review* 10, no. 4 (Fall 1981), 4–7, 41–43.

———. *Somoza and the Legacy of U.S. Involvement in Central America.* New York: E. P. Dutton, 1981.

Di Giovani, Cleto, Jr., and Mose L. Harvey. *Crisis in Central America: Facts, Arguments, Importance, Dangers, Ramifications.* Washington, D.C.: Advanced International Studies Institute, 1982.

Dixon, Marlene, and Susanne Jonas, eds. *Revolution and Intervention in Central America.* Synthesis Publications, 1981.

Dombrowski, John, et al. *Area Handbook for Guatemala.* Washington, D.C.: American University, 1970.

Domínguez, Jorge I. *U.S. Interests and Policies in the Caribbean and Central America.* Washington, D.C.: American Enterprise Institute for Public Policy Research, 1982.

Doran, Charles F. "U.S. Foreign Aid and the Unstable Polity: A Regional Case Study." *Orbis* 22, no. 2 (Summer 1978), 435–52.

Dow, Leslie, Jr. "Ethnic Policy and Indigenismo in Guatemala." *Ethnic and Racial Studies* 2 (April 1982), 140–55.

Duner, Bertil. "Proxy Intervention in Civil Wars." *Journal of Peace Research* 18, no. 4 (1981), 353–61.

Durham, William. *Scarcity and Survival: The Ecological Origins of the Soccer War.* Stanford, Calif.: Stanford University Press, 1979.

Ebel, Roland H. "The Coming of the Post-Agricultural Society: An Exercise in Economic and Political Futurism." *Inter-American Economic Affairs* 35, no. 4 (Spring 1982), 77–96.

———. "Political Instability in Central America." *Current History* 81, no. 472 (February 1982), 56–59, 86.

Elam, Robert Varney. "Appeal to Arms: The Army and Politics in El Salvador 1931–1964." Ph.D. diss., University of New Mexico, 1968.

Ellis, Frank. "La valoración de exportaciones y las transferencias entre companias dedicadas a la industria de exportación en Centroamerica." *Estudios sociales centroamericanos* 8, no. 22 (January-April 1979), 227–47.
Enders, Thomas O. "A Comprehensive Strategy for the Caribbean Basin: The U.S. and Her Neighbors." *Caribbean Review* 11, no. 2 (Spring 1982), 10–13.
Erisman, H. Michael, and John D. Martz, eds. *Colossus Challenged: The Struggle for Caribbean Influence.* Boulder, Colo.: Westview Press, 1982.
Etchison, Don L. *The United States and Militarism in Central America.* New York: Praeger, 1975.
Fagen, Richard. "Dateline Nicaragua: The End of the Affair." *Foreign Policy* 36 (Fall 1979), 178–91.
Fagen, Richard, and Olga Pellicer, eds. *The Future of Central America: Policy Choices for the U.S. and Mexico.* Stanford: Stanford University Press, 1983.
Fajardo, Jose, ed. *Centroamerica hoy: todos los rostros del conflicto.* Bogotá: Editorial La Oveja Negra, 1980.
Feinberg, Richard E. "Central America: No Easy Answers." *Foreign Affairs,* 59, no. 5 (Summer 1981), 1121–46.
———, ed. *Central America: International Dimensions of the Crisis.* New York: Holmes and Meier, 1982.
Fried, Jonathan L., et al., eds. *Guatemala in Rebellion: Unfinished History.* New York: Grove Press, 1983.
Gil, Federico G., Enrique Baloyra, and Lars Schoultz. *Report on Central America.* Washington, D.C.: U.S. Department of State, 1980.
Gilly, Adolfo. "The Guerrilla Movement in Guatemala." *Monthly Review* 17, nos. 1 and 2 (May and June 1965), 9–40, 7–41.
Gleijeses, Piero. "The Case for Power Sharing in El Salvador." *Foreign Affairs* 61, no. 5 (Summer 1983), 1048–63.
———. "The Elusive Center in Central America: . . . ." *Working Papers of a New Society* 8, no. 3 (November-December 1981), 30–37.
———. *Tilting At Windmills: Reagan in Central America.* Occasional Papers in International Affairs. Washington, D.C.: SAIS, Johns Hopkins Foreign Policy Institute, April 1982.
Gómez, Leonel, and Bruce Cameron. "El Salvador: The Current Danger." *Foreign Policy* 43 (Summer 1981), 71–78.
González-Solien, Nancy L. *Black Carib Household Structure: A Study of Migration and Modernization.* Seattle: University of Washington Press, 1969.
Gorman, Stephen M. "Power and Consolidation in the Nicaraguan

Revolution." *Journal of Latin American Studies* 13, part 1 (May 1981), 133–49.
Grabendorff, Wolf, Heinrich-W. Krumwiede, and Joerg Todt, eds. *Political Change in Central America*. Boulder, Colo.: Westview Press, 1983.
Grieb, Kenneth J. *Guatemalan Caudillo: The Regime of Jorge Ubico*. Athens, Ohio: Ohio University Press, 1979.
Griffith, William J. "The Historiography of Central America Since 1830." *Hispanic American Historical Review* 40, no. 4 (November 1960), 548–69.
Grubb, Kenneth G. *Religion in Central America*. New York: World Dominion Press, 1937.
"Guatemala: drama y conflicto social." *Estudios Centroamericanos* 33. Special edition (June-July 1978), 32–50.
Harvey, Robert. "Central America: A Potential Vietnam?" *World Today* 38, nos. 7–8 (July-August 1982), 282–87.
Hayes, Margaret Daly. "The Stakes in Central America and U.S. Policy Responses." *AEI Foreign Policy and Defense Review* 4, no. 2 (May 1982).
Helms, Mary W. *Middle America: A Cultural History of Heartland and Frontier*. Englewood Cliffs, N.J.: Prentice-Hall, 1975.
Herrera Zúñiga, René. "Nicaragua: el desarrollo capitalista dependiente y la crisis de la dominación burguesa, 1950–1980." In *Centroamerica en crisis*. México D.F.: Colegio de México, 1980.
Hildebrand, John R. "Farm Size and Agrarian Reform in Guatemala." *Inter-American Economic Affairs* 16, no. 2 (Autumn 1962), 51–58.
Hinshaw, Robert E. *Panajachel: A Guatemalan Town in Thirty-Year Perspective*. Pittsburgh: University of Pittsburgh Press, 1975.
Immerman, Richard H. "Guatemala as Cold War History." *Political Science Quarterly* 95, no. 4 (Winter 1980–1981), 629–53.
———. *The CIA in Guatemala: The Foreign Policy of Intervention*. Austin: University of Texas Press, 1982.
Jamail, Milton H. "Guatemala 1944–1972: The Politics of Aborted Revolution." Ph.D. diss., University of Arizona, 1972.
Jenkins, Brian, and Caesar Sereseres. "U.S. Military Assistance and the Guatemalan Armed Forces." *Armed Forces and Society* 3, no. 4 (1977), 575–95.
Jiménez Veiga, Danile. *El sindicalismo en Centroamerica y la intervención del estado en la década de 1980*. México, D.F.: Secretaría del Trabajo y Previsión Social, 1981.
Johnson, Kenneth F. "On the Guatemalan Political Violence." *Politics and Society* 4, no. 1 (Fall 1973), 55–82.

Jonas, Susanne. "CONDECA: Military Maneuvers." *NACLA Report on the Americas* 11, no. 3 (March 1977), 38–39.

———, and David Tobis, eds. *Guatemala*. Berkeley: North American Congress on Latin America (NACLA), 1974.

Jones, Chester L. *Guatemala: Past and Present*. Minneapolis: University of Minnesota Press, 1940.

Jordan, David C. "U.S. Options—and Illusions—in Central America." *Strategic Review* 10, no. 2 (Spring 1982), 53–62.

Kalijarvi, Thorsten N. V. *Central America: Land of Lords and Lizards*. Princeton, N.J.: Van Nostrand, 1962.

Kantor, Harry. "El Salvador: The Military as Reformists." In *Patterns of Politics and Political Systems in Latin America*, 107–29. Chicago: Rand McNally, 1969.

Karnes, Thomas L. *The Failure of Union: Central America, 1824–1975*. Rev. ed. Tempe, Ariz.: Center for Latin American Studies, Arizona State University, 1976.

Kearns, K. C. "A Transisthmian Sea-Level Canal for Central America: Proposals and Prospects." *Journal of Geography* 60, no. 4 (1971), 19–53.

Kelsey, Vera, and Lilly de Jongh Osborne. *Four Keys to Guatemala*. Rev. ed. New York: Funk and Wagnalls, 1961.

Kiracofe, Clifford A. "The Soviet Network in Central America." *Midstream* 27, no. 5 (May 1981), 3–6.

Kirkpatrick, Jeane. "U.S. Security and Latin America." *Commentary* 72 (January 1981), 29–40.

Kramer, Michael. "A Quagmire Close to Home." *New York Magazine* 15, no. 1 (May 31, 1982), 20–23, 25–26.

LaFeber, Walter. *The Panama Canal: The Crisis in Historical Perspective*. New York: Oxford University Press, 1978.

———. "Inevitable Revolutions." *The Atlantic Monthly* 249, no. 6 (June 1982), 74–83.

Lainez, Vilma, and Víctor Meza. "El enclave bananero en la historia de Honduras." *Estudios sociales centroamericanos* 2, no. 5 (May-August 1973), 115–56.

Lappe, Francis Moore, and Joseph Collins. "Now We Can Speak: A Journey through the New Nicaragua." San Francisco: Institute for Food and Development Policy, 1982.

Latin American Perspectives 7, nos. 2–3 (Spring-Summer 1980), entire issue.

Leo Grande, William. "The Revolution in Nicaragua: Another Cuba?" *Foreign Affairs* 58, no. 1 (Fall 1979), 28–50.

———. "The Not So Secret War in Central America." Special Report. Washington, D.C.: Democratic Policy Committee, April 25, 1983.

———, and Carla Robbins. "Oligarchs and Officers: The Crisis in El Salvador." *Foreign Affairs* 58, no. 5 (Summer 1980), 1084–1103.
Leiva Vivas, Rafael. *Un país en Honduras.* Tegucigalpa, D.C.: Imprenta Calderón, 1969.
Levine, Barry B., ed. *The New Cuban Presence in the Caribbean.* Boulder, Colo.: Westview Press, 1983.
Lowenthal, Abraham F., and Samuel F. Wells, Jr., eds. *The Central American Crisis: Policy Perspectives.* Working Paper no. 119. Washington, D.C.: Wilson Center, 1982.
MacCameron, Robert. *Bananas, Labor and Politics in Honduras, 1954–1963.* Foreign and Comparative Studies/Latin American Studies, No. 5. Maxwell School of Citizenship and Public Affairs, Syracuse University, 1983.
Macaulay, Neill. *The Sandino Affair.* Chicago: Quadrangle Books, 1967.
McDonald, Ronald H. "El Salvador: The High Cost of Growth." In *Latin American Politics and Development*, edited by Howard J. Wiarda and Harvey F. Kline, 388–98. Boston: Houghton Mifflin, 1979.
MacLeod, Murdo J. *Spanish Central America: A Socioeconomic History 1520–1720.* Berkeley: University of California Press, 1973.
Martínez de la Vega, Zoilio. *Central América: alarma mundial.* México D.F.: Compania General de Ediciones, 1981.
Martz, John D. *Central America: The Crisis and the Challenge.* Chapel Hill: University of North Carolina Press, 1959.
Matloff, Judith. "Elections in Central America." *NACLA Report on the Americas* 16 (March-April 1982), 35–44.
May, Jacques Meyer, and Donna L. McLellan. *The Ecology of Malnutrition in Mexico and Central America.* 1st ed. New York: Hafner Publication Co., 1972.
McCamant, John F. *Development Assistance in Central America.* New York: Praeger, 1968.
McCreery, David J. "Coffee and Class: The Structure of Development in Liberal Guatemala." *Hispanic American Historical Review* 56, no. 3 (August 1976), 438–60.
McCullough, David. *The Path between the Seas: The Creation of the Panama Canal, 1870–1914.* New York: Simon and Schuster, 1977.
McIntosh, Jane. "Radio and Revolution: The Importance of Broadcasting in Central America." *Index on Censorship* 11 (October 1982), 11–13.
McIntosh, Terry L. "Local Government in Guatemala and Its Relation within the Central Government." *Planning and Administration* 5, no. 2 (Autumn 1978), 15–27.
Meléndez, Carlos. *Historia de Costa Rica.* San José: Editorial Universidad Estatal a Distancia, 1979.

Melville, Thomas and Marjorie. *Guatemala: The Politics of Land Ownership.* New York: Free Press, 1971.

Menges, Constantine. "Central America and Its Enemies." *Commentary* 72 (August 1981), 32–38.

Menjívar, Rafael. *La inversión extranjera en Centroamerica.* San José: Editorial Universitaria Centroamericana (EDUCA), 1975.

Millett, Richard. *Guardians of the Dynasty.* New York: Orbis Books, 1977.

Molina Chocano, Guillermo. "La crisis política centroamericana y el nuevo cuadro internacional en la cuenca del caribe." *Revista mexicana de sociología* 42, no. 2 (April-June 1980), 711–30.

———. "Crisis capitalista, inflación, y papel económico del estado." *Estudios Sociales Centroamericanos* 10, no. 28 (January-April 1981), 9–41.

Monteforte Toledo, Mario. *Centroamerica, subdesarrollo y dependencia.* Vols. 1 and 2. México D.F.: Instituto de Investigaciones Sociales and UNAM, 1972.

———. "Mecanismos ideológicos del poder en los paises dominados: el caso de Centroamerica." *Cuadernos Americanos* 213, no. 4 (July-August 1977), 14–16.

Montgomery, Tommie S. "El Salvador: The Descent Into Violence." International Policy Report. Washington, D.C.: Center for International Policy, 1982.

———. *Revolution in El Salvador: Origins and Evolution.* Boulder, Colo.: Westview Press, 1982.

Moore, Richard E. *Historical Dictionary of Guatemala.* New York: Scarecrow Press, 1967.

Morris, James A. *The Honduran Plan Político de Unidad Nacional, 1971–1972: Its Origins and Demise.* Occasional Paper, Center for Inter-American Studies, University of Texas at El Paso, 1975.

———. "Honduras: An Oasis of Peace?" *Caribbean Review* 10, no. 1 (Winter 1981), 38–41.

———. *Honduras: Caudillo Politics and Military Rulers.* Boulder, Colo.: Westview Press, 1984.

———, and Marta Sánchez. "Factores de poder en la evolución política del campesinado hondureño." *Estudios sociales centroamericanos* 6, no. 16 (January-April 1977), 85–106.

———, and Steve C. Ropp. "Corporatism and Dependent Development: A Honduran Case Study." *Latin American Research Review* 12, no. 2 (Summer 1977), 27–63.

Munro, Dana G. *The Five Republics of Central America: Their Political and Economic Development and Their Relations with the United*

States. Edited by David Kinley. New York: Oxford University Press, 1918.
Murga Frassinetti, Antonio. *Enclave y sociedad en Honduras.* Tegucigalpa, D.C.: UNAH, 1978.
Newfarmer, Richard, ed. *From Gunboats to Diplomacy: New Policies for Latin America.* Papers prepared for the Senate Democratic Policy Committee. Washington, D.C., June 1982.
North Liisa. *Bitter Grounds: Roots of Revolution in El Salvador.* London: ZED Press, 1982.
Nyrop, Richard, ed. *Panama: A Country Study.* Washington, D.C.: U.S. Government Printing Office, 1981.
Palmer, David Scott. "Military Governments and U.S. Policy: General Concerns and Central American Cases." *AEI Foreign Policy and Defense Review* 4, no. 2 (May 1982), 24–29.
Parker, Franklin D. *The Central American Republics.* New York: Oxford University Press, 1964.
Pastor, Robert. "Our Real Interests in Central America." *The Atlantic Monthly* 250, no. 1 (July 1982), 27–39.
Payeras, Mario. "Days of the Jungle: The Testimony of a Guatemalan Guerrillero, 1972–1976." *Monthly Review* 35, no. 3 (July-August 1983), 19–94.
Pearson, Neale J. "Guatemala: The Peasant Union Movement, 1944–1954." In *Latin American Peasant Movements,* edited by Henry A. Landsberger, 323–79. Ithaca: Cornell University Press, 1969.
———. "Nicaragua in Crisis." *Current History* 84, no. 96 (February 1979), 78–80, 84, 96.
———. "Peasant Pressure Groups and Agrarian Reform in Honduras, 1962–1977." In *Rural Change and Public Policy: Eastern Europe, Latin America, and Australia,* edited by William P. Avery, et al., 297–320. New York: Pergamon Press, 1980.
Philip, George. "The Crisis in Central America." *Contemporary Review* 241, no. 1398 (July 1982), 1–5.
Pierson, William Whatley, Jr. "The Political Influences of an Inter-Oceanic Canal, 1826–1926." *Hispanic American Historical Review* 6, no. 4 (November 1926), 205–31.
Pike, Frederick B. "The Catholic Church in Central America." *The Review of Politics* 21, no. 1 (January 1959), 83–113.
Pippin, Larry La Rae. *The Remon Era.* Stanford, Calif.: Institute of Hispanic American and Luso-Brazilian Studies, 1964.
Poitevin, Rene. *El proceso de industrialización en Guatemala.* San José: Editorial Universitaria Centroamericana (EDUCA), 1977.
Posas, Mario. "Honduras at the Crossroads." *Latin American Perspectives* 7, nos. 2 and 3 (Spring-Summer 1980), 45–56.

———. *Luchas del movimiento obrero hondureño.* San José: Editorial Universitaria Centroamericana (EDUCA), 1981.

———, and Rafael del Cid. *La construcción del sector público y del estado nacional en Honduras, 1876–1979.* San José: Editorial Universitaria Centroamericana (EDUCA), 1981.

Premo, Daniel L. "Political Assassination in Guatemala: A Case of Institutionalized Terror." *Journal of InterAmerican Studies and World Affairs* 23, no. 4 (November 1981), 429–56.

Rabkin, Rhoda Pearl. "U.S.–Soviet Rivalry in Central America and the Caribbean." *Journal of International Affairs* 34, no. 2 (Fall-Winter 1980/81), 329–51.

Rangel, Carlos. "Mexico and Other Dominoes." *Commentary* 71, no. 2 (June 1981), 27–33.

Real, Blas, and Mario Lungo. "La problematica regional en centroamerica." *Estudios sociales centroamericanos* 8, no. 23 (May-August 1979), 9–33.

Reed, Roger. *Nicaraguan Military Operations and Covert Activities in Latin America.* Washington, D.C.: Washington Council for Inter-American Security, 1982.

Riding, Alan. "The Central American Quagmire." *Foreign Affairs* 61, no. 3 (1983), 641–59.

Rivas, José M. "Elecciones presidenciales en Guatemala: 1966–1978: ilegitimidad progresiva del gobierno." *Estudios Centroamericanos* 33, no. 2, 429–36.

Rodríguez, Mario. *Central America.* Englewood Cliffs, N.J.: Prentice-Hall, 1965.

———, and Vincent C. Peloso. *A Guide for the Study of Culture in Central America: Humanities and Social Sciences.* Washington, D.C.: Pan American Union, 1968.

Rodríguez Vega, Eugenio. *Apuntes para una sociología costarricense.* San José: Editorial Universidad Estatal a Distancia, 1977.

Ropp, Steve C. "Military Reformism in Panama: New Directions or Old Inclinations." *Caribbean Studies* 12 (October 1972), 45–63.

———. "The Honduran Army in the Sociopolitical Evolution of the Honduran State." *The Americas* 30, no. 4 (April 1974), 504–28.

———. *Panamanian Politics: From Guarded Nation to National Guard.* New York: Praeger, 1982.

Rosenberg, Mark B. "Honduran Scorecard: Military and Democrats in Central America." *Caribbean Review* 12, no. 1 (Winter 1983), 12–15, 40–42.

Rudolph, James D., ed. *Honduras, A Country Study.* Washington, D.C.: American University, 1984.

———, ed. *Nicaragua: A Country Study.* Washington, D.C.: American University, 1982.

Ruhl, J. Mark. "Agrarian Structure and Political Stability in Honduras." *Journal of InterAmerican Studies and World Affairs* 26, no. 1 (February 1984).

Ryan, John Morris, et al. *Area Handbook for Nicaragua.* Washington, D.C.: American University, 1970.

Salamón, Leticia. *Militarismo y reformiso en Honduras.* Tegucigalpa, D.C.: Editorial Guaymuras, 1982.

Sanders, Thomas G. "Mexican Policy in Central America." *USFI Reports, 1982,* no. 27, North America. Hanover, N.H.: Universities Field Staff International, 1982.

Saxe-Fernández, John. "El Consejo de Defensa Centroamericano y la Pax Americana." *Cuadernos Americanos* 150, no. 3 (May-June 1967), 39–57.

Schall, James V. "Central America and Politicized Religion." *World Affairs* 144, no. 2 (Fall 1981), 126–49.

Schlesinger, Stephen, and Stephen Kinzer. *Bitter Fruit: The Untold Story of the American Coup in Guatemala.* Garden City, N.Y.: Doubleday, 1982.

Schmidt, Steffen Walter. *El Salvador: The Inevitable Crisis.* Salisbury, N.C.: Documentary Publications, November 1983.

Schneider, Ronald M. *Communism in Guatemala: 1944–1954.* New York: Praeger, 1959.

Schori, Pierre. "El dilemma Centroamericana." *Nueva sociedad* 52 (January-February 1981), 7–22.

Seligson, Mitchell A. *Peasants of Costa Rica and the Development of Agrarian Capitalism.* Madison: University of Wisconsin Press, 1980.

SIECA. *VII Compendio Estadístico Centroamericano.* Guatemala: SIECA, 1981.

Simons, Marlise. "Guatemala: The Coming Danger." *Foreign Policy* 43 (Summer 1981), 93–103.

Sloan, John W. "Electoral Frauds and Social Change: The Guatemalan Example." *Science and Society* 34, no. 1 (Spring 1970), 78–91.

Smith, Laun C., Jr. "Central American Defense Council: Some Problems and Achievements." *Air University Review* (March-April 1969), 67–75.

Snarr D. N. and E. L. Brown. "Ph.D. Dissertations Concerning Social Change and Development in Central America and Panama (1960–1974): An Annotated Bibliography." *Rural Sociology* 40, no. 3 (Fall 1975), 284–318.

———. "An Analysis of Dissertations on Central America: 1960–1974," *Latin American Research Review* 12, no. 2 (1977), 187–202.

Solnick, Bruce B. *The West Indies and Central America 1898.* New York: Knopf, 1970.
Solórzano Martínez, Mario. "Guatemala: 'Democracia' con fraude y repressión." *Nueva Sociedad* 42 (May-June 1979), 103–18.
Squier, Ephraim G. *Notes on Central America, Particularly the States of Honduras and San Salvador: Their Topography, Climate, Population, Resources, Production, etc., and the Proposed Honduras Inter-Oceanic Railway.* New York: Harper and Bros., 1855.
Stanford Central America Action Network, ed. *Revolution in Central America.* Boulder, Colo.: Westview Press, 1982.
Stanger, Francis M. "National Origins in Central America." *Hispanic American Historical Review* 12, no. 1 (February 1932), 18–45.
Stansifer, Charles L. "José Santos Zelaya: A New Look at Nicaragua's 'Liberal' Dictator." *Revista Interamericana* 7, no. 3 (Fall 1977), 468–85.
St. John, Jeffrey, "The Guns of Costa Rica." *Policy Review* 20 (Spring 1982), 51–56.
Stokes, William S. *Honduras: An Area Study in Government.* Madison: University of Wisconsin Press, 1950.
Stoltz Chinchilla, Norma. "Class Struggle in Central America: Background and Overview." *Latin American Perspectives* 7, nos. 2 and 3 (Spring and Summer 1980), 2–23.
Stone, Samuel. "Costa Rica's Political Turmoil." *Caribbean Review* 10, no. 1 (Winter 1981), 42–46.
Struckmeyer, Horst J. "Coffee Prices and Central America." *Finance and Development* 14, no. 3 (September 1977), 28–31, 40.
Taylor, Philip B. "The Guatemalan Affair: A Critique of United States Foreign Policy." *American Political Science Review* 50, no. 3 (September 1956), 787–806.
Torres Abrego, José E. "Panamá: efectos del régimen de Torrijos en la estructura económica." *Comercio Exterior* (México, D.F.) 32, no. 1 (January 1982), 56–69.
Torres Rivas, Edelberto. *Centro América Hoy.* 2d ed. México, D.F.: Siglo XXI, 1975.
———. "Vida y muerte en Guatemala: reflexiones sobre la crisis y la violencia política." *Foro internacional* 20, no. 4 (April-June 1980), 549–74.
———. "La formación del estado y el sector público en Centroamerica y Panamá." *Revista mexicana de sociología* 42, no. 2 (April-June 1980), 561–90.
———. "The Central American Model of Growth: Crisis for Whom?" *Latin American Perspectives* 7, nos. 2 and 3 (Spring and Summer 1980), 24–56.

———. *Crisis del poder en Centroamerica.* San José: Editorial Universitaria Centroamericana (EDUCA), 1981.

———. *Interpretación del desarrollo social Centroamericano.* 7th ed. San José: Editorial Universitaria Centroamericana (EDUCA), 1981.

———, and Vinicio González. "Naturaleza y crisis del poder en centroamerica." *Estudios sociales centroamericanos* 1, no. 3 (September-December 1973), 37–81.

U.S. Congress, House of Representatives, Committee on Foreign Affairs. *Central America, 1981.* Committee Print, 97th Congress, 1st session. Washington, D.C.: U.S. Government Printing Office, 1981.

———. *Observance of Honduran National Elections: Report of a Congressional Study Mission, 28–30 November 1981.* Committee Print, 97th Congress, 2d session. Washington, D.C.: U.S. Government Printing Office, 1982.

———, House of Representatives, Permanent Select Committee on Intelligence, Subcommittee on Oversight and Evaluation. *U.S. Intelligence Performance on Central America: Achievements and Selected Instances of Concern.* Committee Print, 97th Congress, 2d session. Washington, D.C.: U.S. Government Printing Office, 1982.

———, Senate, Committee on Foreign Relations. *The Situation in Honduras.* Committee Print, 97th Congress, 2d session. Washington, D.C.: U.S. Government Printing Office, 1983.

Valenta, Jiri. "The USSR, Cuba, and the Crisis in Central America." *Orbis* 25, no. 3 (Fall 1981), 715–46.

Valle, Rafael Heliodoro. *Historia de las ideas contemporáneas en Centroamerica.* México D.F.: Fondo de Cultura Económica, 1960.

Vega, José Luis. *Poder política y democracia en Costa Rica.* San José: Editorial Porvenir, 1982.

Walker, Thomas W. *Nicaragua: The Land of Sandino.* Boulder, Colo.: Westview Press, 1981.

———, ed. *Nicaragua in Revolution.* New York: Praeger, 1982.

Wesson, Robert, ed. *Communism in Central America and the Caribbean.* Stanford, Calif.: Hoover Institution Press, 1982.

West, Robert C., and John P. Augelli. *Middle America: Its Lands and Peoples.* Englewood Cliffs, N.J.: Prentice-Hall, 1976.

Wheelock, Jaime. *Imperialismo y dictadura: crisis de una formación social.* Mexico: Siglo XXI, 1980.

Whelan, James R. *Through the American Looking Glass: Central America's Crisis.* Washington, D.C.: Council for Inter-American Security, 1980.

White, Alastair. *El Salvador.* Boulder, Colo.: Westview Press, 1973.

White, Robert Anthony. "Structural Factors in Rural Development: The

Church and Peasant in Honduras." Ph.D. diss., Cornell University, 1977.

White, Robert E. "Central America: The Problem that Won't Go Away." *New York Times Magazine*, July 18, 1982, 21–25, 28, 32, 43.

Wiarda, Howard J., et al., eds. "The Crisis in Central America." *AEI Foreign Policy and Defense Review* 4, no. 2 (May 1982), 2–7.

Woodward, Ralph Lee. *Central America: A Nation Divided.* New York: Oxford University Press, 1976.

―――. "The Twilight of Liberalism in Central America: The Present Crisis in Historical Perspective." *RMCLAS Proceedings*, edited by John J. Brasch and Susan R. Rouch. Rocky Mountain Council on Latin American Studies, 29th Meeting, Las Cruces, N.M., February 12–14, 1981.

Worcester, Donald E. "Central America Since Independence." In *The Caribbean: The Central American Area*, edited by A. Curtis Wilgus, 85–93. Gainesville: University of Florida Press, 1961.

Wortman, Miles L. *Government and Society in Central America: 1680–1840.* New York: Columbia University Press, 1982.

Wynia, Gary W. *Politics and Planners: Economic Development Policy in Central America.* Madison: University of Wisconsin Press, 1972.

Note on Editors and Contributors

Steve C. Ropp

Professor Ropp is author of *Panamanian Politics: From Guarded Nation to National Guard* (Praeger/Hoover, 1982) and has published articles in professional journals on various aspects of Panamanian, Honduran, and Nicaraguan politics. He teaches political science at New Mexico State University.

James A. Morris

Dr. Morris has taught political science at a number of southwestern universities and has been a visiting scholar at the University of New Mexico. He is an authority on Honduran politics and has published articles on the subject in journals such as the *Latin American Research Review*, *Caribbean Review*, and *Estudios Sociales Centroamericanos*. He is author of a chapter on Honduras in a major textbook on Latin American politics and of *Honduras: Caudillo Politics and Military Rulers* (Westview, 1984).

Stephen M. Gorman

Professor Gorman wrote articles on Latin American politics which appeared in the Journal of *InterAmerican Studies and World Affairs*, *Inter-American Economic Affairs*, and the *Journal of Latin American Studies*. He edited *Post-Revolutionary Peru: The Politics of Transformation* (Westview, 1981) and contributed to a volume on the Nicaraguan Revolution. Until his untimely death in 1983, he taught political science at North Texas State University.

Tommie Sue Montgomery

Dr. Montgomery teaches politics at Ithaca College and has been affiliated as a Senior Research Associate with the Centro de Investigación y Asesoría Socio-Económica (CINASE) in Managua, Nicaragua. She is editor of *Mexico Today* (Institute for the Study of Human Issues, 1982) and author of *Revolution in El Salvador: Origins and Evolution* (Westview, 1982). She has also published widely on the subject of churches and social change in Central America.

Julio Castellanos Cambranes

Dr. Cambranes is a Guatemalan scholar who is currently affiliated with the Instituto de Estudios Latinoamericanos in Stockholm, Sweden. He received his doctorate in history from the University of Leipzig. While in Sweden, he plans to complete a lengthy study on the impact of coffee production in Guatemala (1845–1980) that will be published by the University of San Carlos.

John A. Booth

Professor Booth is an expert on Central America who has published widely on Costa Rica, Guatemala, and Nicaragua. He is coeditor with Mitchell Seligson of a two volume work entitled *Political Participation in Latin America* (Holmes and Meier, 1978) and author of *The End and the Beginning: The Nicaraguan Revolution* (Westview, 1982). Booth teaches political science at the University of Texas at San Antonio.

Index

ACOGE. *See* Costa Rican Management Association
African slaves, 12, 36, 71
agriculture, 6–7, 11, 12, 20–21, 25
Aguán River, 4
Alas, Father José, 87, 88, 90, 92
Alliance for Progress, 44, 50, 83
Almond, Gabriel, 48
Alta Verapaz (Guatemala), 129
Alvarado, Pedro de, 9
Álvarez Córdova, Enrique, 99
Álvarez Martínez, Col. Gustavo, 203–4
Amatitlán (lake), 4
ANDE. *See* National Educators Association
Andino, Mario, 96–97, 99
ANEP. *See* National Public Employees Association
ANFE. *See* National Association for the Promotion of Enterprise
Antillean Negroes, 192, 235
Aparicio, Bishop Pedro, 86
APSE. *See* National Secondary Teachers Association
Aquino, Anastacio, 73
Arabic immigrants, 192

Araujo, Arturo, 75–76
Arbenz Guzmán, Jacobo, 138–41, 142
ARENA. *See* Nationalist Republican Alliance
Arévalo, Juan José, 134–35
Arias, Arnulfo, 234, 235, 236, 240
Arias, Harmodio, 234
Arias Gómez, Jorge, 76
Armed Forces of Liberation (FAL), 92
armies, national, 28
Association of Nicaraguan Women, 62
Association of Rural Workers (ATC), 62
Atitlán (lake), 4
Autonomous National University of Nicaragua, 47
AyA. *See* Water and Sewer Service
Azuero Peninsula, 229

banana industry, and black population, 8, 161; and Chinese population, 161; and Communism, 163, 167; decline of importance of, 193,

238; foreign control of, 18–19; important source of income, 18, 21, 169; labor organization in, 19, 167, 193, 198; and political dynamics, 196–97; price fluctuations in, 177–78
Barbados, 233
Barrios, Justo Rufino, 130, 132, 133
Bay Islands of Honduras, 15–16
beans, 230
beef, 12, 21, 126, 193, 236
Belize, 15–16, 192
Bernouilli, Gustav, 132
Bidlack-Mallarino Treaty, 250
Bienen, Henry, 55
black population, 7–8, 164, 192, 231, 233–35
Bocas del Toro (Panama), 5, 6
Bonilla, Policarpo, 197
Booth, John, 54
Bourbons, 10–11
Bourgois, Philippe, 36
BPR. *See* Popular Revolutionary Bloc
Broad Opposition Front (FAO), 59
Browning, David, 84

cacao, 12, 70–71
Calderón Guardia, Rafael Ángel, 163
capitalism, 16, 24, 134, 170
Captaincy General of Guatemala, 9
Carazo Odio, Rodrigo, 172, 177
Cardoza y Aragón, Luís, 135
Carías Andino, Tiburcio, 20, 197–98, 205
Caribbean coast, 5–6, 7, 15
Carranza, Col. Nicolás, 97, 99
Carrer, Rafael, 126
Caratasca lagoon, 221

Carter, Jimmy, 104, 105, 249, 250
Castillo, Fabio, 86
Castillo Armas, Col. Carlos, 141–42, 143
Castro Herrera, Guillermo, 240
Catholic church, and colonial government, 10; and defense of the poor, 86, 145; dominance of, 7; in El Salvador, 86–90; persecution of, 88; poverty of in Honduras, 192; role in politics, 29, 69, 161
Catto, Henry, 104
caudillo politics, 14, 39, 196
Cayetano Carpio, Salvador, 90
Cayman Islands, 192
CCTD. *See* Costa Rican Democratic Workers Confederation
CELAM II. *See* Second Conference of Latin American Bishops
Central America, ability to adapt to crisis, 264–69; capitalist influence, 16; climate of, 5; constitutional alteration in, 20; development of, 21–25; economy of, 11–13, 16–19, 20–30; geography of, 1–8; history of, 8–30; population of, 5–6, 7–8; and social change, 27–30; and Spanish exploration, 8–9
Central American Common Market, 22–23, 27, 84, 85, 199
Central American Defense Council (CONDECA), 28
Central American Democratic Community, 181–82, 183
Central American University, 47, 89
Central Bank, 169

INDEX

Central Intelligence Agency (CIA), 109–10, 141–42
Cerna, Vicente, 129, 130
CGT. See General Confederation of Workers
Chagres River, 231
Chamorro, Pedro Joaquín, xvii, 48, 59
Chavez y González, Archbishop Luís, 86
Cheek, James, 105–6
Chibchan, 7
Chiriquí (Panama), 230
Choluteca (Honduras), 191, 193
Choluteca (river), 4
Christian Base Communities (CEB), 86–87
Christian Democratic Federation (CTC), 174
Christian Democratic Party (PDC), 83, 99, 100
Christian Democrats (PDCH), 29, 203
CIA. See Central Intelligence Agency
Cinchoneros, 210
civil wars, 13–15
Clayton-Bulwer Treaty, 16
CNUS. See National Committee of Syndical Unity
cochineal, 12, 126, 127
Coclé (Panama), 230
Coco River, 4
coffee industry, 16, 264; in Costa Rica, 159, 169, 177–78; in El Salvador, 15, 18, 21, 71, 73, 74; in Guatemala, 21, 127–29, 132; in Honduras, 193; in Nicaragua, 18, 38, 41–42; in Panama, 18, 230
Colombia, 233–36, 250
Colón, 191, 192, 230–31, 243
Columbus, Christopher, 8

Comayagua (valley), 4
Committee of Peasant Unity (CUC), 145
Communism, in Central America, 19; in Costa Rica, 161, 163, 167; in El Salvador, 75, 76–77; in Guatemala, 138, 141; in Nicaragua, 43
Communist Party of El Salvador, 76–77, 90
Confederación de Trabajadores de Nicaragua, 43
Confederation of Workers of Costa Rica, 163
CONIP. See National Conference of the Popular Church
Conservative Party, 13, 16, 37; in Guatemala, 125, 126, 130; in Nicaragua, 38–39, 51–52, 53
Constituent Assembly (Honduras), 203
Contadora Group, 181
Copán, 192
Córdoba, Hernández de, 9
corn, 230, 236–37
Cortés, Hernán, 8–9
Costa Rica, banana industry in, 5–6, 161, 169, 177, 178; civil disturbances in, 163–64, 167–68; coffee industry in, 15, 159, 169, 177, 178, 264; colonial, 158–59; Communist unions in, 167; democracy in, 38–39, 153, 155, 158–59, 161, 163–65, 166–67, 179; economic philosophy, 170; economic problems, 169, 175, 176, 177–79, 185, 260; economic reforms, 161; European influence, 8; fear of U.S. intervention in Central America, 183, 184, 185; foreign policy of, 181, 182;

future of, 185–86; geography of, 158; government stability, 155–56, 157–58, 176; isolation of, 14; labor organizations, 163, 174, 180; land distribution, 158, 159, 167; literacy in, 159, 161; military in, 159, 161, 168; and oil imports, 177, 178; political system of, 172–73, 179–84, 267; pressure groups in, 173–76; and problems of neighboring countries, 181–82, 184–85; quality of life, 170, 176, 179; regime crisis in, 262; Revolution of 1948, 28; and Socialist bloc, 182; and social stratification, 264–66; terrorism in, 168, 180; U.S. aid to, 268
Costa Rican Democratic Workers Confederaton (CCTD), 174
Costa Rican Electrical Institute (ICE), 169, 179
Costa Rican Management Association (ACOGE), 175
Costa Rican Petroleum Refinery (RECOPE), 169
Costa Rican Social Security System (INSS), 169
cotton, 21, 43–44, 46
Creoles, 124–45
crises, ability to adapt, 264–69
crises, types, 262–64, 265
Cruz, Ramón Ernesto, 201
Cruz, Serapio, 130
CTC. See Christian Democratic Federation
Cuba, 57, 182
Cuban Revolution, 30, 143
CUC. See Committee of Peasant Unity

CUT. See Unitary Confederation of Workers
Cuyamel Fruit Company, 197
Cuzcatlán (El Salvador), 70

Dada Hirezi, Héctor, 99, 100
Dalton, Roque, 92
Darién (Panama), 6
Darwin, Charles, 243
D'Aubuisson, Roberto, 100, 111
Declaration of Independence (Guatemala), 124–25
Democratic Front against Repression (FDCR), 145
Democratic Revolutionary Front (FDR), 90, 94, 99, 110
dependent capitalism, 40, 42, 43–45, 63
Devine, Frank, 105
Díaz Herrera, Lt. Col. Roberto, 249
Dieseldorff, Erwin Paul, 132
DNC. See Sandinista National Directorate
DRU. See United Revolutionary Directorate
Duarte, José Napoleón, 83–84, 101, 106
Dueñas, Francisco, 74
Durham, William, 82
dyewoods, 15

Eastern Coast of Central America Commercial and Agricultural Company, 125–26
Eckstein, Harry, 56
"Edgar Ibarra" guerrilla force, 145
EGP. See Guerrilla Army of the Poor
Eisenstadt, S. N., 57
El Salvador, agrarian elite, 263–64; agrarian reform, 101–2; and cacao, 70–71; Catholic church

in, 69, 86–90, 259; coffee industry, 15, 258, 264; crisis in, 258–59, 262; economic dependence on U.S., 103, 112; economy, 70–72; 82, 84–86; guerrillas, 69, 87, 92; human rights, 95, 97, 104; independence from Spain, 73; and indigo, 71; labor movement, 20, 75, 80; land distribution, 70–72, 84–85; literacy in, 74; *mestizos* in, 67; military coup in, 67, 77–86, 95, 259, 263; October coup, 95–103; oligarchy of, 67, 70–77, 95, 98, 106; and pact of Chinandega, 14; political system, 266–67; revolutionary organizations in, 90, 92–94; social stratification in, 266; U.S. intervention, 259, 267–69; war with Honduras, 22–23, 85
encomienda, 121–23
Enders, Thomas, 110
English language, 8, 15
ERP. *See* Revolutionary Army of the People
Escalón, Pedro José, 74
ESCANAP. *See* National School for Political Capacitation
Estrada Cabrera, Manuel, 134
Estudios Centroamericanos, 101
Euro-African cultures, 7
Euro-Indian cultures, 7
European population, 8

FAL. *See* Armed Forces of Liberation
Falkland Islands, xix
FAO. *See* Broad Opposition Front
FAPU. *See* United Popular Action Front
Farabundo Martí Front for National Liberation (FMLN), 90, 108, 110
FDR. *See* Democratic Revolutionary Front
February 28 Popular Leagues (LP-28), 93
Federación Nacionalista de Sindicatos Democráticos (FNDS), 43
Fernando V, 119
fertility of soil, 1, 4, 6, 7
Figueres Ferrer, José, 163, 164, 170, 172
Figueroa, Fernando, 74
FMLN. *See* Farabundo Martí Front for National Liberation
Forché, Carolyn, 79–80
Forum for Peace and Democracy, 221
FPL. *See* Popular Forces of Liberation
FPN. *See* National Patriotic Front
France, 8, 77, 108, 232
FRP. *See* Popular Revolutionary Forces
Freud, Sigmund, 243
FSLN. *See* Sandinista Front of National Liberation
FUSEP. *See* Public Security Forces

Gaceta de Guatemala, 124
Gálvez, Juan Manuel, 198
García, Col. José Guillermo, 96–100, 267
Gatun Lake, 231
General Confederation of Guatemalan Workers, 141
General Confederation of Workers (CGT), 174
geography of Central America, 1–8

German influence, in El Salvador, 69, 103–4; in Guatemala, 131, 132, 134, 260
Golfito (Costa Rica), 4
Gómez, Leonel, 79–80
González Flores, Alfred, 161
González Vízquez, Cleto, 161
Government of National Reconstruction (JGRN), 61–62
Gracias a Dios (Honduras), 5, 191
Granada, 9
Grande, Father Rutilio, 88
Great Britain, 15–16, 69, 191
Grenada, 270
Guatemala, agrarian elite, 127, 130, 132, 134, 139–40, 142–43, 145–46, 263–64; agrarian reform, 131–32, 139; Catholic church, 145; *caudillo* government of, 20, 39; coffee industry, 127–29, 259, 264; colonial period, 119, 121–24; economic influence, 12, 13; economy, 124, 125, 147–48; European immigration, 125–26; government stability, 15; guerrilla movement, 126, 129, 144–45; Indians in, 8, 119, 121; labor exploitation, 125–26, 129, 131–32, 135, 138; labor organizations, 138; land distribution, 119, 121–24; military, 131, 145–46, 263; political system, 266–67; racism, 124; 259–60, 262; reforms, 134–35, 138–42; social stratification, 259, 266; social unrest, 142–49; Spanish conquest, 259; U.S. aid, 269
Guatemala City, 4, 134
Guatemalan Labor Party, 138

Guerra y Guerra, Lt. Col. René, 96
Guerrilla Army of the Poor (EGP), 145
Gulf of Fonseca, 1, 4
Gurr, Ted Robert, 55, 56
Gutiérrez, Col. Jaime Abdúl, 96, 97, 98, 267
Gutiérrez, Victor Manuel, 141

Haiti, 233
Hapsburgs, 9–10
Hay-Bunau-Varilla Treaty, 231
Heredia (Costa Rica), 6
Hernández Martínez, Gen. Maximiliano, 20, 76
Herrera (Panama), 230
Hinton, Deane R., 108, 110
Hobbes, Thomas, 74
Honduras, agrarian reform, 199; agriculture, 203, 208; banana industry, 193, 194, 196–97, 198; coffee industry, 195, 264; crises of the 1980's, 204–5; economy, 192, 193, 194–95, 198, 207–9, 220, 260–61; and foreign investors, 193, 197; geography, 191; government instability, 196; health care, 207; human rights, 219; land use patterns, 194, 208; Liberal reforms, 196, 199; literacy in, 207; Mexican-Venezuelan oil agreement, 219–20; military in, 198, 199–203, 205, 206, 213, 216; national defense, 221; Pact of Chinandega, 14; petroleum costs, 209; political history, 195–204; political problems, 205–7, 213–17, 262, 266, 267; population, 191, 192; and problems of neighboring countries, 209–12, 220–22;

social stratification, 193, 213, 264–66; Spanish settlers in, 189, 191; terrorism, 210; U.S. aid, 211–12, 217–19, 267, 268; war with El Salvador, 22–23, 85, 201, 216
Hoover administration, 103
Housing and Urbanization Institute (INVU), 169
Huntington, Samuel, 51, 53–54, 57
Hurricane Fifi, 209

ICE. *See* Costa Rican Electrical Institute
IFAM. *See* Institute of Municipal Development
Indians, 7, 8, 10; in Costa Rica, 158; in Guatemala, 119, 121, 131, 148; in Nicaragua, 7; in Panama, 231
indigo, 12, 71
Innovation Party (PINU), 203
INSS. *See* Costa Rican Social Security System
Institute of Land and Colonization (ITCO), 167, 169
Institute of Municipal Development, 169
Insurreccionales. See Terceristas
Inter-American Commission on Human Rights, 85
Inter-American Development Bank, 103
International Coffee Agreement, 147
International Monetary Fund, 220
International Red Cross, 109
Intibuca (Honduras), 192
INVU. *See* Housing and Urbanization Institute
Islas de la Bahia (Honduras), 191

Italy, 103–4
ITCO. *See* Institute of Land and Colonization

Jamaica, 192, 233
JGRN. *See* Government of National Reconstruction
Jiménez Oreamuno, Ricardo, 19, 161
John Paul II, Pope, 89
Johnson, Chalmers, 55
Juárez, Benito, 130
July 19th Sandinista Youth, 62

Kennedy, John F., 83
Kissinger, Henry, xx

labor, exploitation of, 40, 42, 125–26, 129, 131–32, 135, 138
labor, organization of, 19–20, 25, 28; in Costa Rica, 161, 163, 174, 180; in El Salvador, 75, 80, 107; in Guatemala, 138; in Nicaragua, 42–43, 45, 49, 62; in Panama, 238, 253
La Ceiba (Honduras), 191
Lake Managua, 4
Lake Nicaragua, 4
Lake Yojoa, 4
land distribution, 25–26; in Costa Rica, 158, 159; in El Salvador, 72, 74, 84–85; in Guatemala, 119, 121, 123–24; 128–29, 132–33, 135, 139, 142; in Honduras, 194; in Panama, 238
La Paz (Honduras), 192
Lempa (river), 4
Lempira (Honduras), 192
Lemus, José María, 81
Lenca Indians, 70, 189, 192
León (Nicaragua), 9
Liberal Party, 13, 16–17, 18, 20;

in Costa Rica, 161; in Guatemala, 125, 130, 131, 133, 134; in Honduras, 194, 197, 198, 199, 205, 214–15; in Nicaragua, 37–38, 39, 41–42, 43, 51
Liberal Party of Honduras, 197
Liberal Reformism, 16–19
Limón (Costa Rica), 6
Linz, Juan, 157
Locke, John, 74
López Arellano, Col. Oswaldo, 199–201
Lorenzo Zelaya Brigade, 210
Los Santos (Panama), 230
Lozano Díaz, Julio, 199
LP-28. *See* February 28th Popular Leagues
Lucas García, Romeo, 138
lumber, 15

Majano, Col. Arnaldo Adolfo, 96, 97, 98, 100, 101, 106
Malloy, James, 56, 57
Managua (Nicaragua), 36, 47, 48, 50, 53
Mancha Brava (Honduras), 206
Marroquín, Bishop Francisco, 121
Marroquín Rojas, Clemente, 145
Martí, Augustín Farabundo, 76–77
Martínez, Maximiliano Hernández, xix
Marx, Karl, 243
Marxism, 57, 60
Masferrer, Alberto, 74–75
Mayan civilization, 7, 189
Mayorga Quiroz, Román, 96
Medellín, Colombia, 86
Mejía Flores, Gen. Oscar Humberto, 149
Meléndez, Francisco, 74

Melgar Castro, Col. Juan, 201
Mesoamerican influence, 7
mestizos, 7; in El Salvador, 67; in Guatemala, 123–24, 131, 133, 134, 143; in Honduras, 192; in Nicaragua, 36; in Panama, 231, 234, 236
Mexico, 13, 108
minerals, 193
Miskitu Indians, 36, 210
MLP. *See* Popular Liberation Movement
MNR. *See* National Revolutionary Movement
Molina, Arturo, 104
Monge Álvarez, Luis Alberto, 172; government of, 177–79, 180, 182, 183–84, 185
Morales Erlich, José Antonio, 99, 101
Mosquitía (Honduras), 191, 221
Mosquito Coast, 5
Motagua River Valley, 4
Mount Tajumulco, 1
Movement of National Liberation, 146
MPSC. *See* Popular Movement of Social Christians
MPU. *See* United People's Movement
Munro, Dana, 15

Nájera Saravia, Antonio, 147
National Association for the Promotion of Enterprise (ANFE), 175
National Bipartisan Commission on Central America, xx
National Committee of Syndical Unity (CNUS), 145
National Conciliation Party, 83–84
National Conference on the

Popular Church (CONIP), 89–90
National Democratic Union (UDN), 83–84, 93
National Educators Association (ANDE), 175
Nationalist Republican Alliance, 111
National Guard, in El Salvador, 78, 88; in Nicaragua, 50, 52, 53, 58, 60, 62; in Panama, 235, 240–41, 245, 247–49, 252
National Liberal Party (Nicaragua), 50, 51
National Liberation Party (Costa Rica), 163, 164, 167, 170, 172, 180–81
National Party (Honduras), 197, 198, 199–200, 201, 205, 214–15, 216
National Patriotic Front (FPN), 60, 62
National Public Employees Association (ANEP), 174
National Resistance (RN), 92, 94
National Revolutionary Movement, 83–84, 99
National School for Political Capacitation, 249
National Secondary Teachers Association (APSE), 175
National Unity Plan, 201
Navarro, Alfonso, 88
Nazi ideology, 143
New York–Honduras Rosario Mining Company, 197
Nicaragua, border incidents with Costa Rica, 181; commercial elite, 264; and dependent capitalism, 257; economic growth, 44, 46; education in, 47–48; geography, 35, 36; government stability, 33; health services, 33, 61; labor organizations, 62; literacy, 33, 61; Pact of Chinandega, 14; political system, 38–39, 60, 61–62, 263, 266–67; revolution in, 33, 35, 55–63; social complexity, 257–58; urbanization of, 46–49; and U.S. aid, 269
North American consortia, 134
Núñez de Balboa, Vasco, 8
Nutting, Lt. Gen. Wallace H., 110–11

Obrerismo Organizado de Nicaragua (OON), 43
O'Donnell, Guillermo, 241–42
Oduber, Daniel, 180–81
Olancho (Honduras), 5, 191, 192, 195
Organization of American States, 21–22
Ortega Saavedra, Humberto, 45
Osorio, Oscar, 80

Pact of Chinandega, 14
Paige, Glenn, 243
Panama, agriculture, 230, 236–37; armed forces in, 235–36, 240, 245; banana industry, 230, 238; canal treaties, 248, 250; class structure, 232–33; coffee industry, 230; coup, 239–49; commercial elite, 240; economy of, 238, 239, 242–43, 250, 261; foreign interests in, 250–52; geography, 229–30; government agencies, 239; and industry, 237–38; 250; labor organization, 238, 248, 250, 253; land distribution, 238; leadership, 261, 267; literacy, 231; National Guard, 235,

240–41, 245, 247–49, 252; political parties in, 241; political system, 267; population, 231, 232, 236, 237; and problems of neighboring countries, 227, 229; racial problems, 234–36; trade with Canal Zone, 238–39, 242–43; transportation network, 230, 231, 263; U.S. aid, 234, 267
Panama Canal, 8, 250
Panama City, 8, 230, 232, 233, 237
Panama Railway, 18
Pancasán, battle of, 57–58
PAR. See Renovating Action Party
Patuca River, 4
Paz García, Policarpo, 201, 203
PCN. See National Conciliation Party
PCS. See Communist Party of El Salvador
PDC. See Christian Democratic Party
PDCH. See Christian Democrats
PDCR. See Democratic Front against Repression
People's Revolutionary Party, 172–73
Petén (Guatemala), 5
Petras, James, 59
Pinto, Julio César, 121
PINU. See Innovation Party
Pipil Indians, 70
pirates, 15
PLH. See Liberal Party of Honduras
PLN. See National Liberation Party
PNH. See National Party of Honduras

Popular Forces of Liberation, 90, 94
Popular Liberation Movement, 93, 210
Popular Movement of Social Christians (MPSC), 100
Popular Revolutionary Bloc (BPR), 92
Popular Revolutionary Forces, 210
Popular Sandinista Army, 62
Popular Vanguard Party, 167, 172–73
populism, 40–41
positivism, Comtean, 16
Powell, Bingham, 48
PPU. See United People's Party
PRD. See Revolutonary Democratic Party
Proclamation of the Armed Forces, 97
Productive Alliance, 103
Proletarian Tendency (TP), 58–59
Prolonged Popular War (GPP), 58–59
PRTC. See Revolutionary Party of Central American Workers
Puerto Castilla (Honduras), 221
Puerto Cortés (Honduras), 191
Puerto Lempira (Honduras), 221
Punta Arenas, 4

Reagan, Ronald, xx, 107, 109; administration, 108, 111, 211–12
Recinos, Adrián, 135
RECOPE. See Costa Rican Petroleum Refinery
Reformist Party, 163
Regalado, Tomás, 74
regime crises, 262–63
regimes, types of, 241–42

Reina, Dr. Jorge Arturo, 206
Remón, José Antonio, 235, 241, 248
Renovating Action Party (PAR), 86
revolution, causes of, 55–57
Revolutionary Army of the People (ERA), 90, 92, 93
Revolutionary Democratic Party, 246
Revolutionary Party of Central American Workers (PRTC), 92
rice, 230
Río Grande de Matagalpa, 4
Río Hato, 245
Río Reventazón, 6
Ríos Montt, Gen. Efraín, 148–49
Rivera, Col. Julio Adalberto, 83
Rivera y Damas, Arturo, 89
RN. *See* National Resistance
Rodríguez, Father Nicolás, 88
Roman Catholic Church. *See* Catholic church
Romero, Gen. Carlos Humberto, xviii, 95, 104–5
Romero, Archbishop Oscar Arnulfo, xix, 87–88, 96, 111
Romero Bosque, Don Pío, 75
Roosevelt, Franklin D., 103
Rosario Mining Company, 17

Sacasa, Juan, xviii
Salvatierra, Sofonías, 43
Sánchez Hernández, Fidel, 85
Sandinista Defense Committees, 62
Sandinista Front of National Liberation, activities of, 58; border incidents, 181; goals of, 57; growth of, 58; Marxist leadership, 60; military defeat of, 58; popular support of, 40–41, 59–60
Sandinista National Directorate (DNC), 61–62
Sandinistas, 33, 63, 95, 181
Sandinista Workers Confederation, 62
Sandino, Augusto César, 38, 43, 57
Sandoval Alarcón, Mario, 146
San Pedro Sula (Honduras), 191, 192, 193, 210
Santa Barbara (Honduras), 192
Santiago de Guatemala, 9
Schick, René, 52
Second Conference of Latin American Bishops (CELAM II), 86
Second Vatican Council, 86
Segovia (Nicaragua), 35
Sisniega Otero, Leonel, 146
Smith, Adam, 74
"soccer war," 85
Social Christian Party, 163
social democratic movement, 163
socialism, 19
Socialist Party, 172–73
social mobilization, 47–48
social stratification, 264–66
Somoza, Luis, 45, 50, 52–53, 54, 258
Somoza, Tachito, xviii, 258
Somoza, Debayle, Anastasio, 52, 53, 54, 59
Somoza García, Anastasio "Tacho," as *caudillo*, 20; economic interests of family, 54; effects of corruption, 51; image, 258; and National Guard, 258; rise to power, xviii; and U.S. interests, 42, 45
Somoza regime, activity in

Honduras, 210; and complexity of society, 40; control of labor movement, 43; failure to adapt, 257–58; family members taken hostage, 58; and human rights, 249; and Nicaraguan entrepreneurs, 49; overthrow of, xix, 57; power of, 50–54; responsibility for rise of Sandinistas, 63; rigidity of, 263; role of U.S. aid, 39, 267; stability of, 33
Soto, Marco Aurelio, 17
Soviet Union, 109, 182
Spanish influence, 7, 8–9, 10, 11, 13; in Costa Rica, 158, 159; in El Salvador, 70, 73, 77, 78; in Guatemala, 119, 121–24; in Honduras, 189–91; in Nicaragua, 36, 37
Standard Fruit and Steamship Company, 193
Standard Fruit Company, 197
Suazo Córdova, Dr. Roberto, 203, 206, 220, 221
sugar cane, 21, 126, 230, 236

Tegucigalpa (Honduras), 4, 191, 192, 193
Tela Railroad Company, 193
Terceristas, 58–59
Tinoco brothers, 161–62
tobacco, 12, 21
Torres-Rivas, Edelberto, 146
Torrijos, Omar, analysis of, 242–43; control of political parties, 241, 245; death of, xv, 252; image of, 247–48; leadership skills of, 240, 245–46, 249; and National Guard, 248
Treasury Police, 78

Turcios Lima, Luis Augusto, 143–44, 145

Ubico, Jorge, 20
UDN. *See* National Democratic Union
Ulate, Otilio, 164
Ulúa River, 4
Ungo, Guillermo Manuel, 83–84, 96, 98–99
Unified Revolutionary Directorate (DRU), 94
Unitary Confederation of Workers (CUT), 174
United Brands, 230
United Fruit Company, 134, 139, 141–42, 197
United Nations, 21–22
United People's Movement (MPU), 60, 62
United People's Party, 167, 172–73
United Popular Action Front (FAPU), 92, 93
United Provinces of Central America, 37, 195
United States influence in Central America, and changing conditions, 30; and Central American national security, 28; economic activity after World War I, 19; foreign policy recommendations, 268–71; impact of aid, 267–71; Point Four program, 21; public opinion, 111; threat of military intervention, 181, 183
United States influence on El Salvador, 103–112; alliance with oligarchy, 83; intervention in crisis, 259; military aid, 69; support for junta, 99, 100, 101

INDEX

United States influence on Guatemala, 134, 135, 141–42, 143, 148
United States influence on Honduras, 211, 217–19
United States influence on Nicaragua, xvii, 38, 39, 42
United States influence on Panama, aid to, 250–52; control of fiscal system, 234; economic ties to, 239, 261–62; and multinational investments, 251–52; and transit systems, 227, 232, 251; and urban elite, 234
Unity Party, 172
Unity government (Honduras), 201

Vallarino, Bolívar, 248
Vance, Cyrus, 104
Vatican, 89
Vatican II. *See* Second Vatican Council
Veraguas (Panama), 230
Vides Casanova, Carlos Eugenio, 98
Villeda Morales, Dr. Ramón, 199, 205
volcanic mountains, 1, 7, 158

volcanic soil, 1, 4, 6, 7, 11, 71, 230
Volio, Jorge, 163

Walker, Lt. Col. Gerald, 105
Walker, Thomas, 43
Washington Post, 109
Water and Sewer Service (AyA), 169
Webre, Stephen, 83, 84
Wheelock, Jaime, 49
White, Alastair, 81
White, Robert, 79, 100, 106, 107
Williams, Murat, 83, 104
women, 164
wood, 193
Woodward, Ralph Lee, 42
World War I, 19, 161

Ydígoras Fuentes, Gen. Miguel, 143, 146
Yon Sosa, Marco Aurelio, 143–44
Yoro (Honduras), 192
Yojoa (lake), 4

Zelaya, José Santos, 38, 41
Zelaya (Nicaragua), 5, 15
Zúñiga, Ricardo, 199–200, 201, 206, 214

**IUPUI
UNIVERSITY LIBRARIES**
COLUMBUS CENTER
COLUMBUS, IN 47201